STUDIES IN

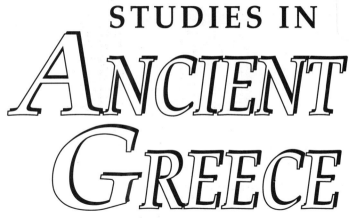

ANCIENT GREECE

EDITED BY
DIANNE HENNESSY

Contributors
Kate Cameron, Bruce Dennett, Jane Dennett,
Dianne Hennessy, Gary Kenworthy, Larissa Treskin

NELSON

First published in Australia in 1991
Reprinted 1992

THOMAS NELSON AUSTRALIA
102 Dodds Street
South Melbourne Vic 3205

Front cover reproduction:
Greek, by the Achilles Painter
Attic White-Ground Lekythos c. 460–450 BC (detail)
Earthenware
H. 35.5 cm
Felton Bequest 1971
Reproduced by permission of the National Gallery of Victoria, Melbourne

National Library of Australia
Cataloguing-in-Publication data

Studies in Ancient Greece.

Bibliography.
Includes index.
ISBN 0 17 007541 9.

1. Greece — History — To 146 B.C. I. Hennessy, Dianne 1952–
II. Cameron, K. E.

938

Designed by Sarn Potter
Cover design by Diana Murray
Illustrated by Vicki-Lee Trufitt
Maps by Diana Murray
Typeset in Bembo by Post Typesetters, Brisbane
Printed in Hong Kong

ii

CONTENTS

PREFACE

Studies in Ancient Greece is aimed at senior secondary students of ancient history. Prepared by experienced, practising teachers, it focuses on the history of Greece beginning with the elaborate civilisations of Crete (Minoan) and Mycenae dating from 1600–1100 BC until the death of Alexander the Great in 323 BC. The major events of the period are covered, including Greek colonisation, tyranny, the creation of a distinctive Spartan society, and the Persian and Peloponnesian Wars. A chapter each is devoted to an in-depth study of three major figures: Pericles, Philip of Macedonia and Alexander. There is also a chapter detailing the system of religious belief that pervaded every part of Greek life.

Each chapter includes a range of primary source material which will enhance students' understanding of the issues and encourage further exploration of the topic. Archaeological evidence is integrated into the text or used as illustrative material. The material provided has been deliberately chosen to be a mixture of standard sources and some that are more obscure, with the aim of providing a different perspective on the individual histories and stimulating students to delve deeper into topics for which different interpretations may be valid. A series of tasks has been provided to promote critical thinking about the major issues, based on the available evidence.

Studies in Ancient Greece is the second in a series of senior ancient history books. The other books in the series are *Studies in Ancient Rome* and *Studies in the Ancient Near East*.

NOTES TO REFERENCES

The notations to all quoted material list the author and title (sometimes abbreviated), details of which are provided in full in the list of references at the end of each chapter. In addition, each entry includes either a page number (in the case of secondary sources) or line or paragraph reference (in the case of ancient sources).

Wherever possible, the traditional referencing systems for the ancient sources have been used. Note that while quotations from ancient sources have been taken from a particular edition, the notations refer to the traditional division of books and paragraphs. I have adopted this system so that students undertaking further research will be able to find the appropriate book, chapter and paragraph in an ancient source should they use a different translation from that used in this book.

Dianne Hennessy

CHAPTER ONE

MINOANS AND MYCENAEANS

JANE AND BRUCE DENNETT

INTRODUCTION

It has only been during the last hundred years that the elaborate civilisations of Crete (Minoan) and Mycenae have been uncovered. Until then our knowledge of the history of the Aegean region began around 776 BC — everything before this date was regarded as part of myth and legend. Two men, Heinrich Schliemann and Arthur Evans, were responsible for unearthing the remains of civilisations dating beyond 2000 BC, and revealed

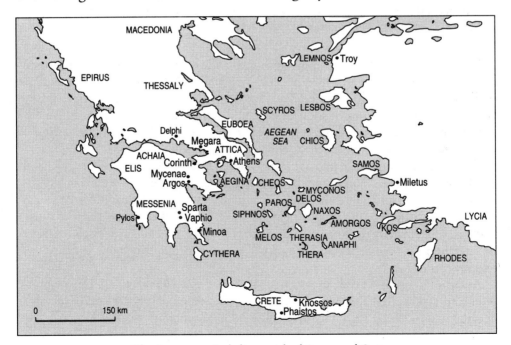

The Aegean area including mainland Greece and Crete

important aspects of the world of the second millennium (2000–1000 BC), part of the Bronze Age, when bronze became the main metal for weapons and the more valuable domestic utensils.

In the 1870s Schliemann discovered the site of ancient Troy by following the claims of the legendary Greek poet Homer. This led him to a civilisation on mainland Greece dating from 1600–1100 BC although Homer had referred to these people as Achaeans, Danaans and Argives, Schliemann called the newly uncovered civilisation Mycenaean after the site of his find at Mycenae.

In 1900 Evans excavated an even earlier civilisation at Knossos on the island of Crete, dating from as early as 3000 BC, but reaching a peak between 2000 and 1400 BC, which he labelled Minoan after a supposed King Minos mentioned in ancient literature.

These archaeological finds were not the end of the puzzle: Schliemann and Evans opened new areas of study and controversy that continue into the 1990s.

FOCUS QUESTIONS

↘ **How do historians use different sources — archaeological, documentary and scientific — to help them discover the past?**

↘ **What were the Minoans and Mycenaeans really like? How did they live?**

↘ **Why did two such rich and relatively sophisticated civilisations disappear?**

Many questions about both the Minoans and the Mycenaeans remain open to speculation, for example whether the earlier Minoan civilisation controlled or culturally dominated Mycenaean Greece in the sixteenth century BC. Arthur Evans thought so, as did J.D.S. Pendlebury writing in the 1930s. Pendlebury described Crete as a 'World Power', with an empire called a *thalassocracy*, based on control of the seas.

Other archaeologists, such as Alan Wace, Carl Blegen and recently Colin Renfrew, disagree. Wace and Blegen suggest that even though the Mycenaeans traded with and borrowed culturally from Crete, Mycenaean society was not a Minoan puppet and was in fact far more than a mere transplant from Crete. Renfrew describes a thalassocracy as a fifth century BC Athenian concept and regards claims of a Minoan empire as exaggerated.

Another controversial question is whether the Mycenaeans later occupied and controlled the Minoan centre of Knossos after that civilisation's decline around 1400 BC. The idea of Mycenaean occupation of Knossos has been generally accepted by many scholars, including Alan Wace and Sinclair Hood, for some time. Their conclusions are based upon the presence of Mycenaean-style writing (Linear B Script), pottery, frescoes (wall paintings) and burial methods, as well as the 'throne room' in the palace at Knossos which was said to be typically Mycenaean.

In 1976, however, J.T. Hooker in his book *Mycenaean Greece* disagreed, claiming that although a Mycenaean cultural presence was apparent after the Minoan decline, it was due to trading contacts and social influence. He maintains that there is insufficient archaeological evidence to claim Mycenaean political control and occupation.

The mystery of why Minoan civilisation disappeared still remains also. Evans suggested internal strife following a series of disastrous earthquakes. Others like Professor Matz in the *Cambridge Ancient History* argue for an invasion by the more warlike Mycenaeans. Greek archaeologist Spyridon Marinatos claims that massive volcanic eruption on the island of Thera, just north of Crete, might have destroyed not only Thera but also Minoan civilisation as a whole. Other theories include an invasion by the Dorian Greeks, the possibility of civil war, and the American archaeologist Rhys Carpenter has suggested there may have been a prolonged drought due to long-term climatic changes starting around 1200 BC.

Two of the more controversial theories about the Bronze Age Aegean are that Crete was the lost Atlantis and that Knossos was built for burial of the dead.

All of these questions will be examined while reviewing what the evidence tells us about the lives of the ancient citizens of Crete and Mycenae.

HISTORICAL METHOD AND EVIDENCE

When Heinrich Schliemann published his findings on Troy in 1873 and proved that Homer's stories in *The Iliad* and *The Odyssey* about the Trojan Wars and the adventures of Odysseus were not all fairy tales, many academics who had subscribed to what we now call the 'Burnarbashi heresy' were left red faced. The embarrassment arose from their absolute declaration that the stories of ancient lore, known as the 'Epic Cycle', were fiction. These historians were guilty of having closed minds; they had rendered a final judgement without conclusive proof. By contrast the great historian George Grote, writing in 1846, almost thirty years before Schliemann's first discoveries, had left room for doubt, asserting that if there was insufficient evidence to draw a conclusion, that should be admitted, rather than absolute judgements being made.

Our quest to find out about the Bronze Age civilisations of the Minoans and Mycenaeans involves using a variety of skills and evidence from a range of sources:

- the archaeological study of physical remains such as buildings, monuments, pottery, weapons etc.

- linguistic studies, the study of documents (on clay tablets) and inscriptions, and the examination of accounts about the Minoans and Mycenaeans by contemporaries, such as the Egyptians and Hittites.
- the legends of Homer and the Epic Cycle.
- later Greek histories by ancient writers such as Herodotus (fifth century BC), Thucydides (fifth century BC), Aristotle (fourth century BC) and Pausanias (second century AD)
- the study of geology and volcanology
- long-range studies of climate and botany.

Neither the Minoans nor the Mycenaeans left written histories of their world. The earliest written source from Crete was a kind of hieroglyphics. This was followed around 1750 BC by what Evans described as Linear script, which is now classified as Linear A. It was in turn replaced by Linear B script about 1450 BC.

Modern scholars are currently unable to read the hieroglyphics, and without dramatic new clues from archaeological finds, it is unlikely they ever will. There are conflicting claims about Linear A. Cyrus Gordon believes it is a Semitic language, while S. Davis suggests that it is a form of Hittite. Neither claim has gained general acceptance. Meanwhile it was not

The Phaistos disc is an example of Linear A.

until the middle of this century that the key to Linear B script was found. In 1953 Michael Ventris and John Chadwick deciphered Linear B and declared that it was an early form of Greek. The script was found on thousands of clay tablets at a number of sites on Crete and mainland Greece, including Knossos, Pylos, Mycenae and Tiryns. Most of the tablets contain very brief messages followed by numbers, and appear to be business accounts and warehouse records. This discovery supports the conclusion that both the Minoans and Mycenaeans had extensive and well-organised trading and commercial interests, but these records provide only glimpses into the world of Knossos and Mycenae.

In 1976 John Chadwick published a book called *The Mycenaean World* in which he reviewed as much of the Linear B written evidence as was available. (However what Chadwick had to work with was only a random selection.) Linear B was recorded by scribes on small clay tablets. They were intended originally as temporary records, but by chance some of them were preserved. Fires, either deliberate — as part of a military assault — or accidental, baked the tablets, ensuring their survival.

In 1952, Michael Ventris announced the decipherment of Linear B script which he recognised as an archaic form of Greek. Carl Blegen confirmed his findings.

John Chadwick has endeavoured to supplement the archaeological remains by linking key words, names and titles from the tablets to conclusions drawn from physical remains. As he wrote in the introduction to his study, without some written evidence it would be impossible to gain a clear picture of, say, modern Christianity from its church buildings alone. Chadwick argued that the same was true for the world of the Minoans and Mycenaeans — scholars needed more than the palace and fortress buildings alone. Nevertheless Chadwick's work only adds to the archaeological evidence; it does not provide answers independently.

All of this means that the only other written sources we have at our disposal are the Epic Cycles, recorded legends, brief accounts from Egyptian and Hittite sources, and finally the histories of Herodotus, Thucydides, Aristotle and Pausanias, none of which is conclusive. They are all full of tantalising hints and clues, but no solid evidence. As a consequence, archaeology bears the real weight in our quest for the truth.

All the disciplines and various sources listed previously can provide some of the pieces to the puzzle of the Minoan and Mycenaean world, but we must also acknowledge that some of the puzzle pieces are missing. As historians, therefore, our task is:

- to put together the pieces of evidence we have,
- draw conclusions where we can,
- acknowledge doubt where the puzzle is incomplete.

THE MINOANS

The Bronze Age civilisation that flourished on the island of Crete between 2000 and 1400 BC was revealed to the world through the efforts of the British archaeologist Arthur Evans in 1900. Evans had originally been interested in small clay seals with hieroglyphic inscriptions that were common on the island. These seals were collected by local peasant women and worn in the belief that they ensured a good supply of mother's milk. At Knossos on the north coast of central Crete, however, Evans made a discovery far beyond his expectations. He unearthed what has been called a 'palace civilisation' of considerable size, complexity and sophistication, with architecture, engineering, artisanship and artistic skills of a very high order. The Minoans appear to have had a carefully ordered society centred on a series of palace complexes.

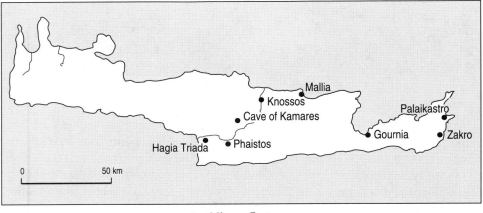

Minoan Crete

The image we now have of the Minoans is of a peaceful people: there are no defensive walls and the warlike trappings common to other civilisations are absent. Trade and the sea loom large in any review of the archaeological finds. The Minoans appear to have established either colonies as part of their thalassocracy (their maritime empire) or at least strong trading links with a number of islands in the Aegean — Cheos, Cythera, Melos, Rhodes and Thera — in addition to mainland Greece itself.

ORIGINS AND NATURE OF MINOAN CIVILISATION

Carbon 14 dating indicates that the ten Neolithic (New Stone Age) levels below the Bronze Age Knossos discoveries by Evans date from 6000 to 3000 BC. The earliest inhabitants of the site appear to have lived in wooden huts. This Neolithic civilisation provided a sound agricultural basis for the Bronze Age civilisation that followed. The archaeological evidence for dating these New Stone Age and Bronze Age societies on Crete is supplemented by Egyptian records. Egyptian inscriptions indicate contact with the Minoans and a clear record of Egyptian dynastic dates that can be verified.

There are two classifications used for dating the periods of Minoan civilisation. The earliest was developed by Evans, based upon changing styles of pottery, and is listed on the left; more recently Nicolas Platon revised the system and his classifications, based upon architectural and cultural changes in the palaces, are listed on the right.

Evans	Dates	Platon
Early Minoan	3000–2000 BC	Pre-palatial
Middle Minoan I & II	2000–1700 BC	First-palatial
Middle Minoan III,		
Late Minoan I & II	1700–1400 BC	Second-palatial
Late Minoan III	1400–1100 BC	Post-palatial

STOP AND THINK: LOOKING AT THE SOURCES

Look closely at the pottery samples pictured here. Write a description of each one, noting differences in style and design. These samples are typical of the different periods. What propositions, then, might be put forward about the Minoans?

Kamares style pottery.

This two-handled marine style jug was reconstructed from the shattered remains.

Palace style pottery jar

Attempts to explain the origins of Minoan culture provide a good example of two of the key theories for the rise of large organised and structured social groups. One of these is the *diffusionist* view. It maintains that external cultural influences trigger changes in an area which alter the nature of a society as it becomes organised. The diffusionists argue, therefore, that commercial and cultural contact between the people of Crete and those from Egypt and Western Asia before 2000 BC sparked the cultural changes that became the Minoan civilisation.

The *anti-diffusionists*, who include the British archaeologist Colin Renfrew, argue that internal factors can multiply and interact to produce major social and cultural change. In the case of Crete Renfrew points to the stable, almost self-sufficient agricultural base that led to the cultivation of a surplus. This surplus food production, according to Renfrew, freed individuals to become artisans, merchants, traders, sailors and so on. He cites one social advance leading to another, producing change by what Renfrew calls the 'multiplier effect'. Some scholars acknowledge the validity of both of these theories and suggest that Minoan civilisation may very well have been the consequence of a combination of foreign influence (diffusion) and internal change (multiplier effect).

STOP AND THINK: INVESTIGATING SOURCES

A legend well known in Athens referred to the Athenian hero Theseus visiting Crete and killing a monster, half-man and half-bull. The monster, called the Minotaur, lived in a labyrinth of passageways under the palace of Knossos.

King Minos of Crete had become ruler of Athens by force and once a year demanded as a tribute fourteen young men and women as sacrifices to the Minotaur. Theseus put an end to the practice by finding his way to the centre of the labyrinth and slaying the beast.

The legend of Theseus and the Minotaur c. second century BC

✻　✻　✻

Minos, according to tradition, was the first person to organize a navy. He controlled the greater part of what is now called the Hellenic Sea; he ruled over the Cyclades, in most of which he founded the first colonies, putting his sons in as governors after having driven out the Carians. And it is reasonable to suppose that he did his best to put down piracy in order to secure his own revenues.

Thucydides, *The Peloponnesian War*, 1, 4

✻　✻　✻

The island of Crete appears to be both very well placed and naturally suited to dominate the Hellenic world. It lies right across our sea, on whose coasts all around most of the Greeks are settled. At one end the Peloponnese is not far away, and at the Asiatic end the districts round Triopium and Rhodes are close at hand. This enabled Minos to build up his maritime empire too: he made some of the islands subject to himself, to others he sent settlers: in the end he attacked Sicily, where he met his death near Camicus.

Aristotle, *The Politics*, 2

Archaeologists and historians have reviewed these written and archaeological items and have come to the following, generally accepted conclusions:

- that aspects of Minoan society visible in archaeological evidence could have given rise to the Theseus and Minotaur legend.
- that Thucydides' and Aristotle's accounts of Minos were based upon that legend.

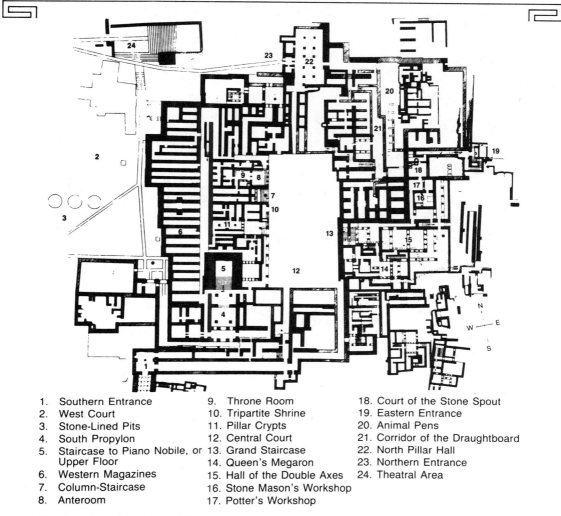

1. Southern Entrance
2. West Court
3. Stone-Lined Pits
4. South Propylon
5. Staircase to Piano Nobile, or Upper Floor
6. Western Magazines
7. Column-Staircase
8. Anteroom
9. Throne Room
10. Tripartite Shrine
11. Pillar Crypts
12. Central Court
13. Grand Staircase
14. Queen's Megaron
15. Hall of the Double Axes
16. Stone Mason's Workshop
17. Potter's Workshop
18. Court of the Stone Spout
19. Eastern Entrance
20. Animal Pens
21. Corridor of the Draughtboard
22. North Pillar Hall
23. Northern Entrance
24. Theatral Area

The floor plan of the palace of Knossos

Sacred horns at the palace of Knossos

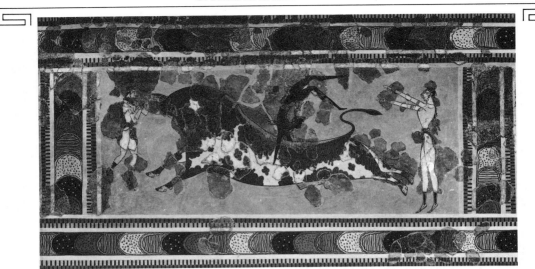

The bull-leaping fresco at Knossos

✎ **By reading a more detailed account of the legend of Theseus and the Minotaur and examining the visual evidence provided, try to ascertain the legend's origin. Complete the table below.**

SOURCE	CORRELATION WITH LEGEND
Thucydides	
Aristotle	
Floor plan of palace of Knossos	
Bull horns	
Bull leaping fresco	

✎ **As an extended writing exercise, account for the emergence of the legend of Theseus and the Minotaur.**

THE PALACE AT KNOSSOS

The palace at Knossos is where the first steps towards answering some of the questions about Minoan civilisation were taken and it remains a focal point for our study of the Minoans. The very location of the palace, for example, provides an important clue to their way of life. Unlike the Mycenaeans,

Palace of Knossos

who built mighty fortresses atop commanding hills, the Minoans selected a pleasant and agriculturally superior site for Knossos rather than the best defensive position. However, the site lent itself to a clear view out to sea and provided very limited access because the palace was actually built next to a river. Their geographic situation and outlook allowed the Minoans to be far less preoccupied with the threat of attack than the Mycenaeans. According to Professor R.F. Willets, Knossos and the other Minoan palaces were the central features of sizeable cities and each of the palaces was probably the administrative and religious centre of economic self-supporting regions of the island. The population of Knossos at its peak has been estimated as high as 50 000. The palace at Knossos dates from 2000 BC but around 1700 BC it appears to have been destroyed by an earthquake, only to be rebuilt on a grander scale.

The post-1700 BC palace covered about 22 000 square metres with three storeys on the western side and as many as four or five on the eastern side. There are 1500 separate rooms that Evans and later archaeologists identified as living quarters, reception rooms, workshops, offices and storage areas. The western wing of the palace seems to have been dedicated to religious cult ceremonies, which led to suggestions that Knossos was the centre of a theocratic administration. Evans in particular supported this idea of rule by religious leaders, the so-called 'priest-kings'. Archaeological evidence linked to this theory includes:

- the apparently sacred symbols of the double-headed axe
- the images of bulls and bulls' horns
- the bull leaping fresco

Beneath the west wing there are storage areas not unlike a labyrinth with large jars or *pithoi* used to keep olive oil and grain. Some archaeologists conclude that the storage magazines were needed for either taxes paid to the rulers or religious offerings or both.

One of the storage areas
Note the size of the *pithoi* in relation to the woman in the photograph.

The palace used water from wells and spring water piped from more than 10 kilometres away. There are extensive separate plumbing, sewerage and drainage networks. The Minoans were masters of hydraulics, dealing with sewerage, run-off from storms and providing fresh water for drinking, cooking and bathing. Both open drains and special terracotta pipes were used.

The palace of Knossos was serviced by terracotta pipes which were locked into each other to provide fast-flowing fresh water.

Minoan control of water was matched by their architecture and control of light. The Knossos palace is remarkable for its clever use of light shafts to brighten the lower levels of the complex.

Decorations and paintings or frescoes on the palace walls provide tantalising but imprecise clues to Minoan life.

A section of the intricate drainage system which was piped throughout the palace of Knossos.

STOP AND THINK: INVESTIGATING SOURCES

Examine the frescoes below.

✎ **For each fresco, describe in detail what you see.**

✎ **What suggestions might we propose about Minoan civilisation based upon the frescoes?**

✎ **Can you suggest any reasons why total reliance on frescoes would give an inaccurate view of Minoan society?**

✎ **Why is it difficult to draw conclusions about the Minoans from frescoes?**

The Dolphin fresco from the queen's megaron in the east wing of the palace

This fresco is called the 'Prince with the lilies' or 'Priest King'. A great deal of this has been lost; the reconstruction is of a male dressed very elaborately, but it may even be a woman.

'Ladies in blue' is another fresco which has had major parts restored; it is found in the east wing of the palace.

The Griffin fresco, found in the King's throne room, shows these mythical sacred animals on either side of the throne and the entrance.

RELIGION

Religion was apparently very important to both the Minoans and Mycenaeans, but archaeology is an imperfect tool in our bid to understand the nature of their Bronze Age religion. Artifacts of supposedly religious significance abound and many Minoan statues and frescoes of human figures have been called gods, goddesses or priests. The difficulty is that many of these conclusions remain speculative and even if the correct supposition is made, details of belief and religious practice remain vague. John Chadwick has attempted to supplement the archaeological evidence through his detailed study of the written evidence present in the Linear B tablets.

The Minoans' religion was dominated by nature; it was almost pantheistic (worship of nature). Frescoes depict sacrifices and women appear to play prominent roles in ceremonies. There are references to a 'mother-goddess' and a young god, perhaps her son, and there also appears to have been a goddess who may have been a kind of guardian spirit for Cretan households.

EVERYDAY LIFE — HOUSING, FOOD AND CLOTHING

The most significant sources about everyday Minoan life were discovered by Spyridon Marinatos in his extensive excavations of the Minoan settlement on Thera. Our knowledge of Minoan housing is based on these excavations at Thera and the principal sites on Crete, specifically at Gournia, in addition to painted tiles from Knossos depicting houses. The houses were typically two or three storeys high, with flat roofs, floors of beaten earth or stone slabs, and the walls were frequently plastered.

The Minoan diet appears to have been quite varied: meat, bread, milk, cheese, fruit, vegetables and seafood were available. Meat included pork, mutton, goat, deer, boar and hares, but despite the significance of bulls in Minoan art and architecture, beef does not appear to have been part of the diet. Duck, geese and partridges as well as fish and shellfish were available, while octopus seems to have been a delicacy.

Bread was made from wheat and barley, while milk, used also for cheese, came from sheep and goats. Fruit was plentiful with apples, pears, grapes, figs and dates apparently in good supply. Peas and lentils were the main vegetables.

Olive oil was also an important part of the diet as was honey, the latter probably being used for sweetening. Wine seems to have been the main drink, although there is evidence that the Minoans brewed a kind of tea from the herbs that grew on the island.

Evidence from Minoan houses — no fixed ovens or hearths — supports the idea that cooking was done on moveable braziers. The stirrup jar, a common find at a number of sites, seems to have been the most common household liquid container.

Our knowledge about the dress of Minoan women mostly comes from the frescoes. Long dresses with short sleeves and bare breasts are depicted, jewellery was lavish and hair dressing elaborate. (Note that this is unlikely to have been typical dress for all Minoan women or for everyday life.) The men are shown wearing a kilt-like skirt and high leather boots.

CONTROVERSIES
Did the Minoans rule the islands of the Aegean and part of mainland Greece?

Ancient Greek historians and the legends of the Epic Cycle support the idea of a Minoan empire; the archaeological evidence, however, is not conclusive. There is evidence of the work of Minoan artisans and Minoan-style art at Mycenae and there is extensive evidence of a range of Minoan goods and pottery spread across the islands of the Aegean. The closest links uncovered were between Crete and the island of Thera. All of this archaeological evidence indicates contact, influence and trade; it might also signify control but it does not amount to conclusive proof. Experts tend towards the view that, given the lack of military trappings on Crete and the fact that some military capacity would have been essential to supplement naval power to control an empire, then political and military control of the Aegean by Crete is unlikely.

STOP AND THINK: INVESTIGATING SOURCES
✎ **Consider the two swords on the opposite page.**
   The Minoan sword looks impressive but note the grip

and how likely it is to break. Compare it with the
Mycenaean sword.
What conclusions can you draw?

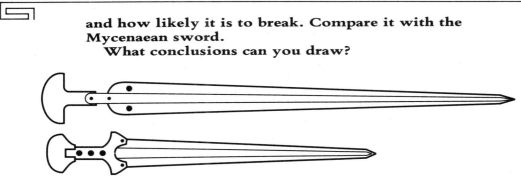

The larger Minoan sword and the shorter Mycenaean

The rejection of claims of a Minoan empire in ancient Greek history rests
on two hypotheses:

- that the Minoans, unlike the Mycenaeans, were not warlike and would
  therefore have found it difficult to enforce their rule.
- that strong social and cultural influence does not necessarily mean
  political control.

The first of these hypotheses has been tested in part above by looking at
weaponry. We will test the second in the exercise that follows.

STOP AND THINK: RESEARCH
**Walk through the centre of a major city or a local shopping
centre and identify and list examples of foreign cultural and
commercial influence, e.g. McDonalds, Kentucky Fried
Chicken, Coca-Cola (USA), BP (British), Shell (Dutch) etc.**

- **How many instances of foreign influence are there?**
- **Do these examples of foreign cultural influence
  automatically mean political control?**
- **Could the same situation have applied to the so-called
  Minoan thalassocracy?**

Why did the Minoan civilisation disappear?
Around 1450 BC the splendid Minoan civilisation went into a drastic
decline. The decline itself is well attested by the archaeological evidence;
what is not so clear are the reasons for the decline.

Three alternative hypotheses for the collapse of Minoan civilisation have
been suggested:

- natural decline or civil war   ] i.e. internal factors
- Mycenaean invasion
- destruction by the Thera volcano.   ] i.e. external factors

The main argument for the three hypotheses can be summarised as follows:

INTERNAL FACTORS	EXTERNAL FACTORS

NATURAL DECLINE — CIVIL WAR

- Colin Renfrew believes there is insufficient evidence for conclusions to be drawn about any calamity destroying Crete. He argues that Minoan society gradually went into decline, just as other great civilisations have flowered and withered through the ages, e.g. ancient Egypt, Greece, Rome or the British Empire of the nineteenth century AD.
- Renfrew argues for an exhaustion of resources as the population became too large for the island. He also refers to evidence of migration from Crete in the ancient Greek histories.
- Arthur Evans interpreted the archaeological evidence from Knossos as signifying a civil war. [NB: There is fire damage in the palace.]
- Evans felt that the civil war probably followed social unrest and shortages after a series of earthquakes.

STRENGTHS

- Renfrew's idea of gradual decline is compatible with what historians have seen occur elsewhere.
- There is physical evidence of earthquake damage at Knossos about this time to support Evans' argument.
- Perhaps the answer is a combination of these two ideas: the Minoans weakening to a degree that they were unable to recover from earthquakes as they had in 1700 BC.

WEAKNESSES

- Each of these theories ignores important items of archaeological evidence presented to support the other theories, e.g. evidence of Mycenaean influence at Knossos; geological and archaeological evidence of the possible impact of the Thera volcano.
- Renfrew's ideas in particular do not allow for the apparent suddenness of the Minoan decline.

MYCENAEAN INVASION

- Alan Wace favours this view, as does Matz. They believe that the more obviously warlike Mycenaeans invaded and occupied Crete and Knossos.
- Wace cites archaeological evidence of Mycenaean writing (Linear B script), burial methods, frescoes and pottery of Knossos. He also points to the addition of a Mycenaean-style throne room.
- The fire damage at Knossos and the other Minoan centres is used to support armed invasion and assault hypotheses.
- Invasion theorists accept that earthquake damage was present but that it was not the decisive factor. They acknowledge however that it may have weakened the Minoans and made invasion easier.

STRENGTHS

- The fact that Mycenae was obviously the dominant military and economic power in the region around 1450–1400 BC and more than capable of invading Crete.
- There is strong and widely accepted archaeological evidence for a Mycenaean presence at Knossos.

WEAKNESSES

- There is no way of being absolutely certain that the evidence of Mycenaean cultural influence was the result of conquest and occupation (see page 27).
- There is no way to prove what caused the fire damage.

THERA VOLCANO

- Spyridon Marinatos suggested a huge explosion on the island of Thera showered Crete with poisonous volcanic ash and generated huge tidal waves.
- The volcanic ash, found to be high in sulphate and chloride, would have been very harmful to soil and vegetation.
- The tidal waves (tsanamis) could have damaged the fleet and ports affecting Minoan trade.
- Marinatos pointed to the damage done by the Krakatoa eruption in 1883 AD: it was heard 3 500 km away; 36 380 people died. The Thera explosion was even larger.

STRENGTHS

- This hypothesis does explain the relatively sudden collapse of the Minoan civilisation.
- It is supported by strong geological evidence, especially for the poisonous volcanic ash; a study in 1965 indicated ash capable of destroying agriculture.

WEAKNESSES

- D.L. Page, while excavating Gournia on the north coast of Crete, directly in the path of tidal waves, claimed to find no evidence of flood damage (even though other archaeologists claim evidence of tidal wave damage at other cities, e.g. Zakro).
- Tidal waves are only dangerous to vessels in port, they offered no threat to the Minoan ships at sea.
- The Thera volcano did explode, but it is difficult to gauge its impact.

STOP AND THINK

✎ **Draw up a list on a chart, using the headings below, of the most significant points about the disappearance of Minoan civilisation.**

Fact   **Speculation**

From the list you have developed differentiating fact and opinion, write what you consider to be an acceptable theory for the disappearance of Minoan civilisation.

Was Crete the lost Atlantis?

The last of the major controversies surrounding Knossos and the Minoans indicates both the complexity of the evidence confronting us and the variety of possible interpretation. J.V. Luce *The End of Atlantis — New Light on an Old Legend* is the most recent in a long list of scholars who have linked Crete with the legend of Atlantis. The continent of Atlantis was meant to have been the home of a great civilisation that flourished in antiquity, only to disappear suddenly. The ancient writer and philosopher Plato records such a legend but places Atlantis far to the west of Crete and the Aegean. Nevertheless, the vagueness of the ancient sources has prompted theories that Plato's Atlantis might have been Crete.

Luce highlights a number of similarities between Minoan civilisation and the legendary Atlantis, for example:

- both Minoan civilisation and Atlantis were once part of an era of myth and legend.
- both were relatively rich and sophisticated societies.
- both were hailed as significant maritime powers.
- bull sports were a characteristic of both cultures.
- each was highly advanced in architecture, in particular the mastery of hydraulics, plumbing and drainage. Both were thought to have met sudden and violent ends.

Was the palace of Knossos a massive tomb?

Another of the more extreme views based upon research at Knossos comes from the German geologist H.G. Wunderlich. In his book *The Secret of Crete* he claimed that Knossos and the other Minoan palaces were cult structures, built for burial and veneration of the dead. Wunderlich charged that Arthur Evans and those who followed misinterpreted the archaeological evidence, pointing in particular to the use of gypsum as the main building material at

Knossos. As a geologist, Wunderlich was puzzled by this because, although attractive, gypsum is not a durable stone and was therefore unlikely to stand up to constant foot traffic and general wear. This led him to speculate about the purpose of the palace, claiming that it was meant for the dead rather than the living. Wunderlich argued that his hypothesis was more compatible with the use of gypsum since it is an easy material to work with, it looks like marble or alabaster and its poor wearing qualities would not have been a disadvantage in a tomb.

Below you will find key aspects of Wunderlich's argument, some of his evidence and conclusions:

- many of the so-called household items found at Knossos, like the Kamares ware cup shown below dating from around 2000 BC, are too fine and thin to be practical. Wunderlich claims that these bronze-coloured cups were meant to be replicas, compatible with ritual symbolism but not intended for day-to-day use.

Kamares eggshell ware from Knossos

- the bared breasts on the Snake Goddess, one of the best-known Minoan statuettes, link with finds in Egyptian tombs of women with breasts exposed as a sign of mourning. Wunderlich also draws the links between Knossos and Egypt acknowledged by other archaeologists.
- Wunderlich carries this link with Egypt still further, pointing to the significance of bulls in Minoan ritual life and adding that Egyptians sacrificed bulls to their dead.
- Wunderlich also points to what he regards as the problem of the Queen's bathroom and makes two points:
  (i)   if the room was simply a bathroom, why did water have to be carried in and out by hand? The Minoans were experts with plumbing — surely they could have arranged piped water and drainage?
  (ii)   the so-called Queen's bathtub was similar to coffins or sarcophagi found elsewhere in Crete.

STOP AND THINK: RESEARCH AND REVIEW
✎ **Take each point of Luce's and Wunderlich's arguments and assess them as either conclusive or highly speculative.**

Minoan Snake Goddess or 'Mother Goddess'

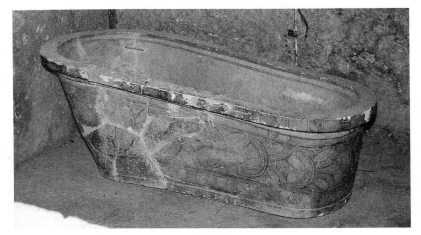

Queen's bathroom

✎ **Which aspects of their arguments do you find the most persuasive?**

✎ **List the questions that could be raised after reading through their arguments.**

✎ **Write up a review of the theories put forward by Luce and Wunderlich.**

THE MYCENAEANS

At around the time of the rise of Minoan civilisation the ancestors of those we now call the Mycenaeans moved into Greece and established themselves from Thessaly in the north to the Peloponnese. By 1600 BC they had become sailors and traders and had exhibited signs of Minoan cultural influence. The key centres of Mycenaean civilisation were Mycenae itself, Pylos and Sparta.

Our knowledge of this civilisation is due to the endeavours and vision of Heinrich Schliemann, who revolutionised our knowledge of the Bronze Age. His discovery of Homer's Troy encouraged him to search for the home of the victorious Greeks and he went on to uncover Mycenae and the fortress of Tiryns. Others followed in his wake, the most notable being Alan Wace and Carl Blegen.

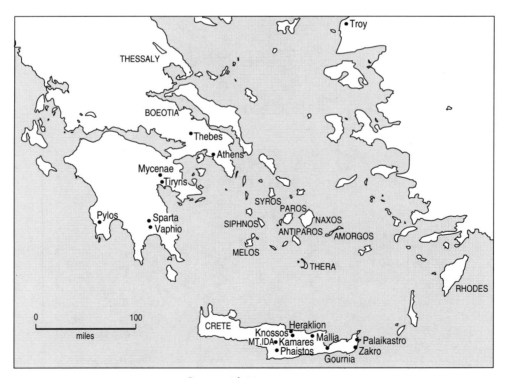

Greece with Mycenae centres

ORIGINS AND NATURE OF MYCENAEAN CIVILISATION

Archaeological investigations over the years have led to the conclusion that the Mycenaeans were the ancestors of the Greeks. This conclusion stems from a cultural continuity from Mycenaean to classical Greek times. Linguistic evidence also appears to support archaeological claims that the Mycenaeans were early Greeks.

Mycenaean settlements differed markedly from those on Crete: they were sited strategically, high atop commanding hills, with mighty walls. The stones in the walls of the Mycenaean fortress at Tiryns were so large that a legend grew that the walls had been built by a race of giants. The nature and location of these centres reflect the need to both defend against and deter attacks. This ever-present danger would have influenced the fabric of Mycenaean political and social life. Artifacts from Mycenaean sites reflect a greater preoccupation with war than do those on Crete and perhaps a more rigid central, political control.

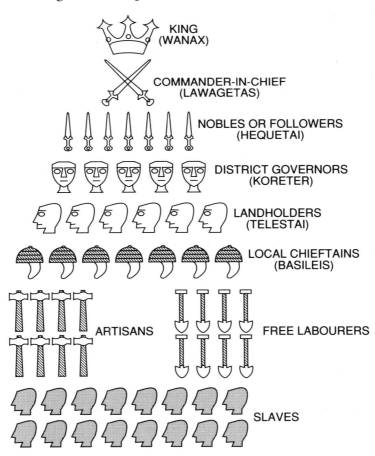

A simplified diagram of the Mycenaean social structure based on the evidence from Linear B tablets.

STOP AND THINK: RESEARCH

✎ **Using a variety of specialised texts which examine warfare, weaponry, art and architecture during the Mycenaean period, what evidence can you find to support the notion that Mycenae's civilisation was based on warfare?**

RELIGION

The eminent British archaeologist Lord William Taylour claims that, based on the archaeological evidence, it is possible to speak of a Minoan-Mycenaean religion. He suggests that Minoan and Mycenaean representations of their gods, goddesses and religious scenes are the same.

In contrast to later times Mycenaean gods were not afforded great temples; places for worship were the size of small shrines. Nevertheless there is strong evidence of a continuity of religion from Mycenaean into classical times. Inscriptions found at the Mycenaean centre of Pylos record the names of a number of later Greek deities such as Athena, Poseidon and Hera.

ARCHITECTURE

Excavations have revealed central palaces in the Mycenaean centres not unlike those on Crete in design and decoration. They are also reminiscent of the Minoan structures in that the palaces appear to be the consequence of a series of extensions and additions, one age expanding on the efforts of those who had gone before. There are differences, however, the most notable being the presence in Mycenaean palaces of a central throne room, called a megaron, a name derived from a term used by Homer for a great hall.

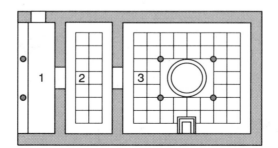

Plan of megaron at palace of Mycenae
Area 1 is an open *stoa* (porch) which leads into area 2, the vestibule. Area 3 is the main megaron with a central hearth surrounded by four columns.

These megarons are rectangular in shape, with a large fixed hearth or fireplace at the centre. The hearth highlights another difference between the Mycenaean palaces and those on Crete in that the Minoans did not use fixed hearths or fireplaces.

The palaces were surrounded by clusters of ordinary houses. Furniture in these included stone benches, footstools and stone tables, some of which have survived.

EVERYDAY LIFE

As for food, fashion, clothing and jewellery taste and design, all remind the observer of Crete. Archaeological finds of animal bones indicate that pigs, deer, hare, geese and duck were eaten, as on Crete, and sheep appear to have been more commonplace than cattle among the Mycenaeans and Minoans alike.

The Mycenaeans do, however, appear to have developed very distinct burial customs. The earliest Mycenaean graves were either a shallow pit or a small rectangular grave lined with stone slabs, called a cyst grave. A later development unearthed by Schliemann at Mycenae in what is called the 'grave circle' were shaft graves (see below). These were between 3 and 4

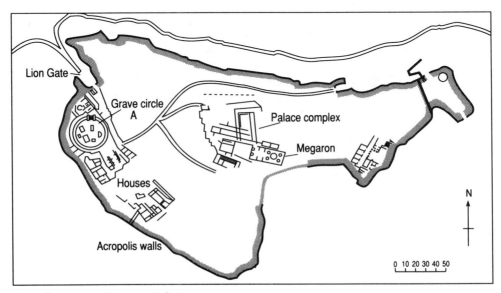

Plan of Mycenae with grave circle A
(Grave circle B is situated outside the walls of the citadel.)

metres long and were used for either single or multiple burials. This method appears to have been used until about 1400 BC. The third style of Mycenaean grave was the tholos tomb. Its origins are still the subject of speculation but it appears to have been used by the Mycenaeans between 1500 and 1250 BC. A tholos tomb was normally built into the side of a hill and was a large round and dome-shaped structure. The most impressive example of this type of tomb is the Treasury of Atreus at Mycenae.

CONTROVERSIES
Did the Mycenaeans finally occupy and rule Knossos?

The accepted view is that somewhere around 1450 BC the warlike Mycenaeans occupied and controlled the Minoan centre of Knossos. It is suggested that they remained in control until Knossos was ultimately

Treasury of Atreus or Tomb of Agamemnon

destroyed, either by local rebels or a rival power outside Crete. This view has been best expressed by Alan Wace and replaced the previously accepted view of Arthur Evans, who claimed that Knossos remained under Minoan control until the end.

Wace claimed that:

1   A great deal of Mycenaean-style pottery was found at Knossos. Mainland burial methods, such as the use of the tholos tombs, became common at Knossos.

2   The most recent frescoes on the walls of the palace at Knossos were Mycenaean in style, i.e. more concerned with depicting the human form and warlike scenes than earlier Minoan wall paintings.

3   A throne room, a megaron, of the Mycenaean type was found at Knossos and is thought to have been added to the palace at or near the date of Mycenaean occupation.

4   Many clay tablets with Mycenaean style Linear B writing were found at Knossos.

Hooker refuted each of these claims:

1. Hooker pointed out that Wace himself admitted that some of the pottery found at Knossos was an inferior imitation of mainland styles. Hooker felt that a true Mycenaean occupation would have corrected this either by using their own artisans or teaching the local people mastery of Mycenaean techniques.

2. Hooker disputed the date for the introduction of the tholos tombs, suggesting that they were present at Knossos earlier, during an undisputed period of Minoan rule.

3. Hooker indicated that the Minoan fresco uncovered by the Greek archaeologist Spyridon Marinatos on the island of Thera combined both the human form and nature, much like the paintings Wace believed were evidence of Mycenaean occupation.

4. Hooker believed that a throne was compatible with the function of Knossos as a special Minoan 'cult palace'. He also pointed to some important differences between the throne room at Knossos (which was smaller and had a different shape) and those on the mainland.

5. Hooker claimed that the Linear B tablets were the result of the extensive trading link between the Minoans and Mycenaeans.

Why did the Mycenaean civilisation fall?

There are two generally acknowledged theories about the fall of the Mycenaean civilisation.

Theory 1: A Dorian Invasion c. 1100–1050 BC

Pro-invasion theorists point to what they call cultural evidence of an invasion, e.g. a new type of dress pin (the fibula) came into use, as did a new type of sword.

In addition, around 1200 BC a special passage was built through the city wall at Mycenae, down to an extra source of water outside the walls. The suggestion is that they thought that this could be needed in the event of a long siege. (Athens and Tiryns took similar steps around the same time.)

A further sign that an invasion was feared was the construction of what the invasion theorists take to be a wall across the Isthmus of Corinth. Archaeologists have traced this wall for 3.5 kilometres from the Saronic Gulf. Its completion date is uncertain.

Theory 2: An Internal Revolution

Rhys Carpenter has claimed that there was a climatic change, which led to severe droughts, famines and therefore social revolution, and the pro-revolution theorists point to references in Homer to social discontent. These references can clearly be traced to the era of Mycenaean Greece.

After the collapse of the Mycenaean civilisation, the palace at Mycenae was not reinhabited by the people living in the area. The revolution theorists argue that this is unlikely in the event of an invasion. They suggest that the Dorian invaders would have used the best buildings as their centres of power.

The claim by the pro-invasion theorists that a wall was built across the Isthmus of Corinth can be countered by the claim that it was never a defensive wall, but simply a retaining wall to form the foundation for a road. However at least one small section of this wall could not possibly have been used as a road foundation.

CONCLUSION

Minoan and Mycenaean cultures existed — that is a fact. Certain aspects of the civilisations that developed and prospered on the island of Crete, mainland Greece and other centres in the Aegean and ancient Western Asia are also agreed upon by scholars. However, as students of history, what we recognise most clearly about this particular period is the danger of making claims based upon very limited material and written remains.

Our task is to examine the sources carefully, weigh up the evidence and theories and make suggestions that acknowledge the limitations of the data available to us.

STOP AND THINK: EXERCISE

✎ **Draw up a table that compares the Minoan and Mycenaean civilisations. You might consider including the following topic areas:**
  • **religion**
  • **food**
  • **clothing**
  • **housing**
  • **palaces**
  • **social/political organisation.**

LIST OF REFERENCES
ANCIENT SOURCES

Aristotle, *The Politics and Athenian Constitution*, ed. and tr. John
  Warrington, Dent, London, 1959
Thucydides, *The Peloponnesian War*, tr. Rex Warner, Penguin, 1954 repr.
  1980

SECONDARY SOURCES

Blegen, Carl, *Troy and the Trojans*, Thames & Hudson, London, 1963
Branigan, K. & Viders, M., *Hellas: The Civilisation of Ancient Greece*,
  McGraw-Hill, New York, 1980
Cambridge Ancient History, 3rd ed, Cambridge University Press, 1970

Carpenter, Rhys, *Discontinuity in Greek Civilisation*, Cambridge University Press, 1966

Chadwick, John, *The Mycenaean World*, Cambridge University Press, 1976

Cottrell, L., *The Bull of Minos*, Evans Brothers, London, 1971

Evans, Arthur (Sir), *The Palace of Minos at Knossos*, Vols. 1–4, London, 1921–35, repr. New York, 1963

Gordon, Cyrus, *Forgotten Scripts: The story of their decipherment*, rev. ed, Penguin, 1971

Higgins, R., *The Archaeology of Minoan Crete*, Bodley Head, London, 1973

Hood, Sinclair, *The Minoans: Crete in the Bronze Age*, Thames & Hudson, London, 1971

Hooker, J.T., *Mycenaean Greece*, Routledge & Kegan Paul, London, 1976

Luce, J.V., *The End of Atlantis — New Light on an Old Legend*, Thames & Hudson, London, 1969

Marinatos, Spyridon, *Crete and Mycenae*, Thames & Hudson, London, 1960

Pendlebury, J.D.S., *The Archaeology of Crete*, London, 1939, repr. New York, 1965

Renfrew, Colin, *The Emergence of Civilization*, Methuen, London, 1972

Schliemann, Heinrich, *Mycenae*, London, 1878

Stubbings, F.H., *Prehistoric Greece*, Rupert Hart-Davis, London, 1972

Taylour, William, *The Mycenaeans*, rev. ed, Thames & Hudson, London, 1983

Ventris, Michael & Chadwick, John, *Documents in Mycenaean Greek*, 2nd ed by John Chadwick, Cambridge University Press, 1973

Wace, Alan, *Mycenae: An Archaeological History and Guide*, Princeton, NJ, 1949

Willetts, R.F., *The Civilization of Ancient Crete*, Batsford, London, 1977

Wunderlich, H.G., *The Secret of Crete*, Souvenir Press, London, 1988

CHAPTER TWO

GREEK COLONISATION
BRUCE DENNETT

INTRODUCTION

From between 800 and 750 BC the Greeks began to travel, trade and settle beyond the shores of mainland Greece. This process was called the colonisation movement and continued for the next two hundred years. Colonisation began as Greece emerged from the period known as the Dark Ages following the disintegration of the Minoan and Mycenaean civilisations, and was the product of a broad range of social and economic factors, including an increase in population and growing commercial interests. In addition to these general elements, individual city-states often had specific or individual reasons for sending out colonists.

FOCUS QUESTIONS
╲ **What was Greek colonisation?**
╲ **Why did the Greeks establish colonies?**
╲ **What was the process of colonisation?**
╲ **What were the effects of colonisation in Greece?**

Information about this period in Greek history is based on both archaeological and written sources.

ARCHAEOLOGICAL SOURCES

The material remains take a number of forms.

POTTERY AND POTTERY FRAGMENTS (CALLED POTSHERD)

The ancient Greeks used fired clay pots with quite distinctive designs and styles. These pots were the all-purpose containers of the time; they fulfilled the role played today by bottles, jars, cardboard boxes, plastic bags, tins and tupperware.

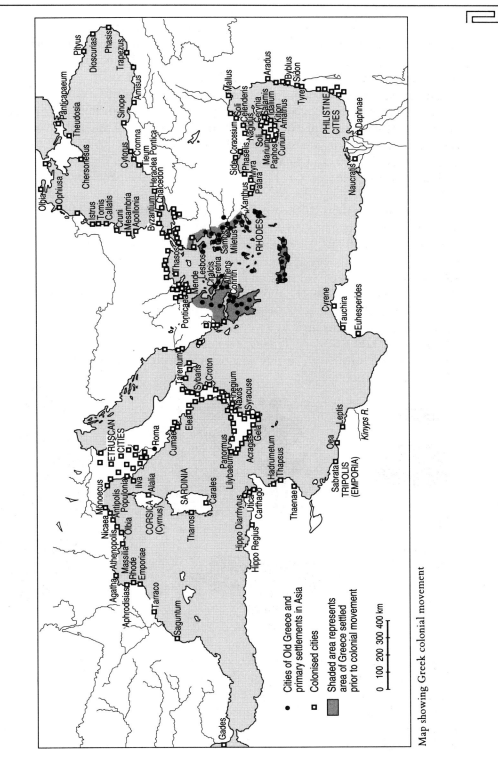

Map showing Greek colonial movement

Cities of Old Greece and
primary settlements in Asia

Colonised cities

Shaded area represents
area of Greece settled
prior to colonial movement

0 100 200 300 400 km

These pots and potsherds were extremely durable but once shattered were virtually worthless to all but the eager archaeologist. Therefore while other more valuable items might have been taken from a site and kept, or metal objects melted down and reused, the pots remained.

The presence of Greek pottery indicates the extent of Greek colonisation while changes in design and pattern provide clear guidelines for dating. Greek pottery was spread throughout the Aegean and Mediterranean region in Asia Minor, across North Africa and around the Black Sea, and in Sicily, Italy, France and Spain.

The development of Greek pottery passed through a series of clearly defined stages:

Protogeometric (c. 1050 BC)   This method of design saw simple, limited decoration with precise circles or semicircles.

Geometric (c. 850 BC)   During the ninth century BC a range of geometric patterns was applied to the whole vase or pot. From around 800 BC representation of animals and people were used.

Proto-Corinthian (c. 700 BC)   A form of design developed in Corinth apparently influenced by eastern techniques. A pattern known as 'black-figure' became common.

Corinthian (c. 600 BC)   This was a development of the proto-Corinthian style, but the figures were not as fine; the style of drawing became both bolder and simpler.

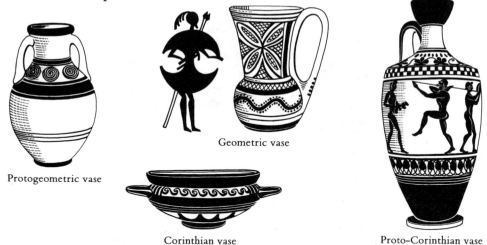

Protogeometric vase

Geometric vase

Corinthian vase

Proto-Corinthian vase

Athenian red-figure design (c. 530 BC)   This new technique replaced the black-figure style. In red-figure the background was painted in and the figure left to stand out in relief.

These changing styles have made approximate dating of sites possible in some instances. The nature of the pots themselves also provides useful archaeological clues to the nature of social life and commerce.

Red-figure drawing

COINAGE — WEIGHTS AND MEASURES

These should be examined as indications of colonisation but neither is as significant as pottery. It is difficult to draw conclusions from different standards of weight and measure, and coinage was not widespread until the end of the sixth century BC.

BUILDINGS AND COLONIAL SITES

These define for us location and aspects of lifestyle and wealth. The public buildings and temples of some colonial sites reflect a wealth and prosperity beyond the means of their founding '*mother city*'.

STOP AND THINK: INVESTIGATION

- Examine the images on a range of modern Australian coins and notes. What conclusions can you draw about our society from these? Why were these images chosen?

- The coins below are from Naxos, the Greek colony on Sicily. They show grapes and ears of wheat. Why do you think the Greeks of Naxos selected these images?

Coins of Naxos

INSCRIPTIONS AND GRAFFITI

An example of such an inscription was found on a stone at Cyrene in North Africa. It provides some useful details about why the people of Thera, a Greek island in the Aegean, chose to send out colonists. Thera apparently was unable to sustain its existing population.

Graffiti is not new: Greek mercenary soldiers left their mark on one of the great Egyptian statues at Abu Simbel. Even though the Egyptians limited Greek colonisation on their territory to a single trading colony at Naucratis, the graffiti and the presence of the soldiers reflect the Greek spirit of adventure, the extent of their travel and the potential for cultural exchange.

WRITTEN SOURCES

There are only fragments of written material for the early period of colonisation. The Epic Cycle, the legendary tales of Homer, provides one of the earliest clues. *The Odyssey* contains a reference to a people, the Phaeacians, being led by their king Nausithous to a new land because of repeated military clashes with a neighbouring state. It also includes a reference to 'a merchant crew' concerned about 'outward freight' and cargo.

Another hint about colonisation comes from the works of early Greek poets. Hesiod produced his most famous poem, *Works and Days*, in the eighth century BC. It includes references to the difficulties faced by Greek farmers, while his own family history reflects both the ability and willingness of the Greeks to migrate to improve their lot. Another useful poet is Sappho. She was born around 600 BC and her verse contains references to one of her brothers who was involved in trade with Egypt.

A controversial piece of ancient writing appears in the fragmentary remains of the work of one Hecataeus of Miletus. Hecataeus was apparently a traveller and writer from the sixth and fifth century BC, credited with two books, one dealing with his travels through Europe, the second through Asia. Although there is some doubt about the authenticity of the work, it is widely acknowledged that Hecataeus' efforts paved the way for one of the truly great figures of ancient history, Herodotus, who has been described as 'the Father of History'. Born at Halicarnassus, a Greek city in Asia Minor, Herodotus, writing in the middle of the fifth century BC produced *The Histories*. He seems to have attempted to provide a factual record of Greek history, free from the myth and legend of the Epic Cycle.

Herodotus makes references to colonisation and some of its causes and methods in the first four books of his *Histories*, highlighting overpopulation, trade, the processes of colonisation and the relationships between the 'mother city' and its colonies.

A much later source is the Athenian historian Thucydides, who produced his work *The Peloponnesian War* sometime after 430 BC. Thucydides deals with colonisation as part of his general introduction to Greek history. He refers to a general increase in sea travel and trade, noting also 'the poverty of soil' in parts of Greece and 'party strife' in nearly all the cities, factors he suggests as causes of colonisation.

THE GREEK *POLIS*

Before going any further into an investigation of colonisation it might be useful to consider the political structure of the Greek mainland. It is important to note that there was no such nation as 'Greece' in ancient times. We can speak of the Greek people, because there was a common bond of language and culture, but politically they were divided into states. Such a political unit was called a *polis* or *city-state*.

The polis emerged following the disintegration of the larger Minoan and Mycenaean civilisations. Homer referred to kings ruling large areas, but after the Dark Ages these extensive kingdoms were subdivided.

The smaller states that emerged might average 50 000 to 60 000 people although Athens and the surrounding area — which, when combined, was known as Attica — had as many as 350 000. The centre for any community during a time of danger was its stronghold, a good defensive position atop a commanding hill. In time this became the acropolis or 'high town', a natural focal point within the society. The term polis was initially applied to the acropolis but gradually the meaning of the word broadened to include a city and its surrounding territory (often called city-state), such as Athens and Attica. Polis could also mean the people, specifically the citizens of a city-state.

It was the city-states of Greece then who sent out their people to colonise and trade. The most prolific colonisers were Chalcis, Eretria, Corinth, Miletus and Megara.

REASONS FOR COLONISATION

The five main causes of Greek colonisation can be listed as follows:

- overpopulation and land hunger — a population grown too large to be sustained by the productivity of land in mainland Greece.
- trade — the financial gain to be achieved from the import and export of goods.
- political problems — tension arising from the shortage of good farmland and political differences within some city-states. The result was often either the forced departure of disruptive elements or discontented groups leaving voluntarily.
- spirit of adventure — the Greeks had always been a people ready to take to the seas in search of a better life.

- factors specific to individual city-states — although there were general factors encouraging colonisation, it was still a piecemeal process and different city-states frequently had unique or individual reasons for spawning colonies.

OVERPOPULATION AND LAND HUNGER

This is generally acknowledged as the prime cause of colonisation. J.B. Bury in his famous *History of Greece* supports the idea and claims that ancient writers such as Thucydides describe it as the main cause.

Following the Dark Ages, social conditions in Greece appeared to stabilise and the population grew, increasing demand for arable land. Mainland Greece was rugged and mountainous and the quantity of good farmland was already limited before the Dark Ages. Much of the better land had fallen under the control of aristocratic circles within the city-states, which further restricted the amount available to a rapidly growing population of peasant farmers.

Combined with a land shortage was the system of 'land tenure', namely the practice of deciding how the land could be distributed within a family. Aristocratic groups in some city-states practised primogeniture, which meant all the land went to the eldest son. Under this system younger sons were forced to look elsewhere for a livelihood. A few enterprising individuals became involved in trade; other younger sons became leading colonists venturing beyond the shores of mainland Greece in quest of land. However the opposite of primogeniture was far more common, especially among farming families. This meant the land was divided equally among all the sons. A number of ancient writers, including the poet Hesiod, alluded to this practice. Hesiod also provided a clue to the problems that ensued when he advised families to have only one son if they were going to retain their family wealth.

Giving an equal portion of land to each son meant that generation after generation the family land was divided and subdivided. The plots of farmland grew smaller as the numbers of people they had to feed grew larger.

Each of the city-states that became major sponsors of colonisation was influenced by overpopulation and land hunger to some degree. Chalcis and Eretria shared the island of Euboea; like other parts of Greece, it was not overendowed with fertile land. Shortage of land and trade saw them send out colonists and become rivals in the process. We know that they actually went to war with one another and this conflict appears to have been caused by their trading rivalry and disputes over land. In addition, Miletus, Megara, Corinth and the island of Thera to some degree appear to have owed their status as mother cities to population pressure.

TRADE

Commerce, the exchange of goods and often for the Greeks the pursuit of metals such as gold and iron in limited supply at home, prompted colonisation. The scholar W.G. Forrest in his book *The Emergence of Greek Democracy* and R.J. Littman in his work *The Greek Experiment* highlighted not only the importance of trade, but also its links with overpopulation and land hunger. Archaeological and written sources support the significance of trade. It appears that the earliest Greek colonies were in fact established as trading centres, for example Al Mina in Syria in the East and Pithecusae (now Ischia) in the Bay of Naples, in Italy.

Another Greek colony in Italy at Cumae followed shortly after. There is clear evidence that the fertile agricultural land around Cumae was ignored at this stage, establishing trade, in this case, as a significant independent cause for the establishment of some colonies. Cumae and Pithecusae were founded to provide access to the valuable metals of Etruria in northern Italy. Many of these early trading colonies such as those at modern Marseilles, Nice and Monaco in the west did, however, grow beyond their trading function to become important centres for large Greek populations.

POLITICAL PROBLEMS

As mentioned earlier, colonisation was in part the result of political problems and tension within some areas. There is also evidence to indicate a number of general causes of political unrest:

- grievances of peasant families over their inability to acquire sufficient land.
- the inequality created by control of most of the land in some city-states by small groups of wealthy aristocrats.
- political tension between different classes developing from the growth in wealth and influence of a merchant and trading class. This 'merchant class' at times challenged the authority of the old aristocratic groups. Thucydides refers to the political change and unrest that evolved with an expansion of trade and growing wealth in some parts.
- the younger sons of some aristocratic families, denied an inheritance of land and unable or unwilling to find an alternative role in life, occasionally became the focus of political agitation.

J.B. Bury refers to political problems operating in an age of major social and economic change as an inducement to colonisation. Discontented citizens could become colonists in search of a better life, and ruling elites in some city-states rid themselves of political malcontents by making them colonists.

In Corinth, Sparta and Mytilene there was pronounced political tension and even violence. Such a climate encouraged the use of colonisation as a remedy.

SPIRIT OF ADVENTURE

This is a very general cause, relating to a cultural state of mind among the Greek people. The Greeks appear to have displayed two characteristics that made colonisation likely and acceptable:

- *the willingness to move on*, to travel in search of something better when dissatisfied. This theme runs through Greek history and the surviving literature from Homer and the Epic Cycle to Hesiod and Herodotus.
- *an affinity with the sea.* No Greek ever lived more than 80 kilometres from the sea and since the Greek mainland was so rugged a journey by sea around the coast was often quicker and easier than travel by land. Among the ancient writers Plato compares the Greeks to frogs around a pond, while the famous story of Xenophon and his mercenaries rejoicing when they reached the sea in their retreat from Persia highlights the significance and familiarity with the sea and sea travel in the Greek mind.

INDIVIDUAL CAUSES

The Greek colonisation movement as a whole was not the result of any general co-ordinated or premeditated plan. Rather it reflected a series of individual responses by separate city-states and their citizens to specific problems. These specific, and at times unique, factors are labelled individual causes, and could be political, economic, social or geographic in nature.

The Ionian Greek polis of Miletus in Asia Minor had a growing population, but it was unable to expand eastward into the hinterland because of strong local opposition, unlike the Ionian Greek polis to its north which expanded west into Lydia. As a result the citizens, unable to expand inland, established colonies around the Black Sea to the far north. These colonies provided an outlet for a growing population, a source of grain to help feed those who stayed behind and an expanding area of trade.

The circumstances that led to Thera becoming a mother city are among the best documented in terms of written and archaeological evidence. Thera's volcanic soil was very fertile, but according to Herodotus the island was ravaged by a severe seven-year drought near the close of the seventh century BC. This drought ruined Thera's crops and the ability of the island to feed all its people. Thera addressed the drought emergency by sending part of its population to settle in Cyrene on the north African coast.

Sparta established a colony at Taras (now Tarentum) in response to a uniquely Spartan political problem. During the Messenian War many widowed Spartan women were encouraged to bear children to men who were not full citizens in an attempt to maintain the birth rate and population numbers. After the war, however, the citizens produced by these unions were denied full citizenships and were looked down upon. Political agitation followed and the solution was to use the revolutionaries as colonists in southern Italy.

A SUPPLEMENTARY FACTOR

Each of the five reasons reviewed above motivated the Greeks to colonise. However the colonisation process was assisted and defined by another supplementary factor that can be called the 'power vacuum'. In other words when the Greeks began to colonise around 750 BC, there was little competition from other powers for the land the Greeks settled. The Persians were preoccupied with affairs at home, Egyptian and Phoenician influence beyond their own shores had declined and the Greeks generally only had to contend with the local inhabitants of the regions they colonised.

The Greeks expanded relatively freely within the limits of this power vacuum. Nevertheless, the vacuum did have limits in the west where the Greeks began to clash with the emerging power of Carthage in North Africa, and their movements into northern Italy were restricted by the Etruscans. This supplementary factor is not in itself a cause; rather, given the existing causes, it made the process of colonisation easier.

STOP AND THINK
Draw up a table of causes and cities, using the headings shown below.

Cause	Cities that were colonised in response to cause

STOP AND THINK: DOCUMENT STUDY
Read the following passages and answer the questions about them.

Thus many years passed by and many difficulties were encountered before Hellas [Greece] could enjoy any peace or stability and before the period of shifting population ended. Then came the period of colonisation. Ionia and most of the islands were colonised by the Athenians. The Peloponnesians founded most of the colonies in Italy and Sicily, and some in other parts of Hellas. All of them were founded after the Trojan War...

The Corinthians are supposed to have been the first to adopt more or less modern methods in shipbuilding, and it is said that the first triremes ever built in Hellas were laid down in Corinth...

Corinth, planted on its isthmus, had been from time immemorial an important mercantile centre, though in ancient days traffic had been by land rather. than by sea. The communication between those who lived inside and those who lived outside the Peloponnese had to pass through Corinthian territory. So Corinth grew to power by her riches, as is shown by the adjective 'wealthy' which is given to her by the ancient poets. And when the Greeks began to take more to seafaring, the Corinthians acquired a fleet, put down piracy, and, being able to provide trading facilities on both the land and the sea routes, made their city powerful from the revenues which came to it by both these ways.

Later the Ionians were a great naval power. This was in the time of Cyrus, the first King of the Persians, and of his son Cambyses. Indeed, when they were fighting against Cyrus, they were for some time masters of all the sea in their region...

Then Polycratus, the tyrant of Samos, made himself powerful by means of his navy. He conquered a number of the islands, among which was Rhenea, which he dedicated to the Delian Apollo.

The Phocaeans, too, when they were founding Marseilles, defeated the Carthaginians in a naval engagement...

All the same these Hellenic navies, whether in the remote past or in the later periods, although they were as I have described them, were still a great source of strength to the various naval powers. They brought in revenue and they were the foundations of empire.

Thucydides, *The Peloponnesian War*, 1, 12–15

❋ ❋ ❋

> ✎ **Which Greeks established most of the colonies in Italy and Sicily?**
> ✎ **Which polis was the first to adopt modern methods of shipbuilding? How do you think this might have influenced colonisation?**
> ✎ **Why was Corinth so well placed for trade and colonisation?**
> ✎ **What clues does Thucydides provide about why Greek colonisation did not spread further east in huge numbers?**
> ✎ **What is Thucydides' view of the importance of Greek naval power?**

The Phocaeans were the first Greeks to make long sea voyages; it was they who showed the way to the Adriatic, Tyrrhenia, Iberia, and Tartessus. They used to sail not in deep, broad-beamed merchant vessels but in fifty-oared galleys...

The Phocaeans at once launched their galleys, put aboard their women and children and moveable property, including the statues and other sacred objects from their temples — everything, in fact, except paintings, and images made of bronze or marble — and sailed for Chios. So the Persians on their return took possession of an empty town.

The Phocaeans made an offer for the islands known as the Oenussae, but the Chians, who were afraid that they might be turned into a new centre of trade to the exclusion of their own island, refused to sell; so the Phocaeans prepared to sail to Corsica... Then they tried to secure unity for their expedition by laying fearful curses upon any man who should fail to accompany it. They also dropped a lump of iron into the sea and swore never to return to Phocaea until it floated up again. But at the very beginning of the voyage to Corsica more than half of them were seized with such passionate longing to see their city and their old homes once more, that they broke their oath and sailed back to Phocaea. The others kept their oath, and continuing the voyage from the Oenussae, arrived safely in Corsica. For five years they lived at Alalia with the former settlers and built temples in the town: but during that period they caused so much annoyance to their neighbours by plunder and pillage, that the Tyrrhenians and Carthaginians agreed to attack them with a fleet of sixty ships apiece. The Phocaeans manned their own vessels, also sixty in number, and sailed to meet them in the Sardinian sea, as it is called. In the engagement which followed the Phocaeans won.

Herodotus, *The Histories*, 1, 160–166

❋ ❋ ❋

↘ **Why did the Phocaeans colonise?**

↘ **How did they apply pressure on their citizens to become colonists?**

↘ **Does Herodotus contradict Thucydides in any way? If so, how? If not, why not?**

PROCESS OF COLONISATION

It is important for the modern student of colonisation to remember that, in general, the Greek view of colonies was very unlike our modern view. The Greek word for colony was *apoikia* or 'away home'. A colony was not automatically viewed by the Greeks as the possession or territory of the founding mother city. In general the relationship between a mother city and its *apoikia* was religious and sentimental rather than political. Greek colonies tended to quickly develop separate political identities and establish separate citizenship from the mother city. Many colonies thrived on their independent status after foundation and some grew richer and more influential than their parent city-state. As they developed, the different roles and functions of each of the colonies became apparent. For example, Naucratis in Egypt, Pithecusae in Italy, Massilia (modern Marseilles) in France and Emporian in Spain began as trading posts, while Zancle (now Messana) in Sicily and Rhegium in Italy were established to protect valuable trade routes.

↘ **Find each of the colonies listed here on the map. Notice the strategic placement of each city. Why were these trade routes important?**

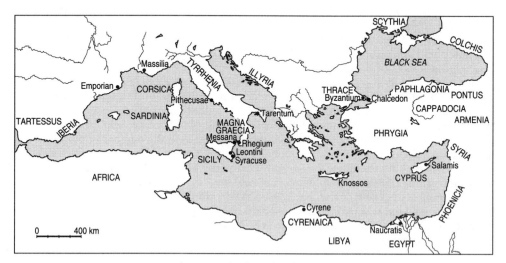

The outreach of Greek colonisation

Others, such as the classic example of Cyrene in north Africa, were set up to accommodate Thera's surplus population, while as mentioned earlier, Taras (Tarentum) in southern Italy was a reflection of Sparta's unique political problems.

STOP AND THINK: DOCUMENT STUDY

Our best and clearest account of the procedure for establishing a colony comes from Herodotus, when he related the story of Thera's foundation of Cyrene. Read it and answer the questions that follow.

During his stay at Delphi, Grinnus consulted the oracle on quite different matters, and received from the Priestess the apparently irrelevant answer that he must found a city in Libya. 'Lord Apollo,' he replied, 'I am too old and inactive to start on such a journey; can you not tell one of these younger men to undertake it instead of me?' And as he spoke he pointed at Battus. For the moment, nothing further occurred; they left Delphi, put the oracle out of their minds, and did nothing about it — for they did not even know where Libya was, and shrank from sending out a party of settlers merely, as it were, into the blue. During the seven years that followed not a drop of rain fell in Thera, and every tree on the island, except one, withered and died. In this difficult situation the Theraeans sent to Delphi for advice, and were reminded about the colony which they had omitted to send to Libya . . .

[T]he party was to represent all the seven villages in Thera, and brothers were to draw lots to determine which should join it. It was to be under the sole authority of Battus . . .

So then they sent Battus off, and he and a party of men sailed for Libya in two fifty-oared galleys; they reached the coast, but, unable to decide what their next move should be, sailed home again to Thera. The islanders, however, refused to allow them to come ashore; they threw things at them as they were making up for the harbour, and shouted that they must put about and go back again; so, as there was nothing else for it, they once more got under way for Libya. This time, they established themselves on Platea, the island off the coast which I mentioned before. It is said to be of the same size as the city of Cyrene is to-day . . . The settlers stayed in Platea for two years; but they failed to prosper in their new home, and all made sail again for Delphi, leaving one man behind on the island. They went to the oracle, and declared that, in spite of the fact that they were living in Libya, they were no better off than before. To this the Priestess replied:

If you know sheep-breeding Libya better than I do,
Not having been there — I have — I marvel much at your cunning!

On this, Battus and his men sailed away once more for Platea, for it was plain that Apollo would not let them off until they established a settlement actually on the Libyan mainland . . . During the lifetime of Battus, the founder of Cyrene, who ruled there for forty years, and of his son Arcesilaus, who ruled for sixteen, the number of people in the town remained equal to that of the original settlers; but under the rule of its third king — known as Battus the Fortunate — an oracle delivered at Delphi was the cause of a great rush amongst the Greeks generally to join the colony. For the people of Cyrene themselves were offering land to new settlers, and the oracle declared that whoever came to delightful Libya after the land was parcelled out, should one day rue it.

In this way the population of the place greatly increased, and it began to encroach upon the territory of its neighbours.

Herodotus, *The Histories*, 4, 148–157

❋   ❋   ❋

⟍ **What were the factors that prompted Thera to colonise?**

⟍ **How were colonists selected?**

⟍ **What was the reaction of Theraeans when colonists sought to return? Why do you think the Theraeans behaved this way?**

⟍ **Did Cyrene eventually prosper? How do we know? Would there be any other sources aside from written ones confirming Herodotus' account?**

In general the first steps in colonisation involved the appointment of an oecist, or official founder. He was selected by the mother city and often became venerated in the *apoikia* as a religious cult figure. The oecist provided one of the religious and sentimental links between the parent state and the colony. Beyond this his active role was as a temporary leader in the early life of the colony.

One of the other common steps in the formative stages of planning was to consult the sage, the Oracle at Delphi. Such advice was regarded as a religious safeguard. The custom was not, however, pure superstition. Many travellers and traders passed through Delphi with gossip and news; it was a clearinghouse of information. The words of the Oracle were often based upon sound intelligence and therefore were useful to would-be colonists.

For the most part the relationship between the mother city and the *apoikia* was not political. Generally when citizens left the mother city they lost citizenship rights in that city and the automatic right to return. A notable exception to this general notion of political independence was Corinth, which, with its keen interest in trade and raw materials, came closest to establishing a colonial empire.

In general, though, the links between colony and parent state were bonds of kinship. They had the same gods and continued to share common religious and public festivals. The symbolic nature of their links was reflected in the gesture of taking a fire from the public hearth in the mother city to light the first public fire in the colony. In some cases the cultural bonds went further; although many colonies became wealthy, especially those in Italy and Sicily, the region that became known as 'Magna Graecia' or Greater Greece seems to have had lingering sense of cultural inferiority. It imported writers and artists from Greece and took real pride in sending contestants to the Olympic Games.

The nature of the relationship between the colonists and the local people of the region they invaded varied. In some cases, if the indigenous population was not organised or advanced, the Greeks would drive them out by military force. Other contacts may have been more peaceful, with shared economic and cultural benefits, while at Naucratis in Egypt the Greeks were tolerated under licence to establish their trading colony.

EFFECTS OF COLONISATION

The effects proved to be generally enduring and far reaching. They can be classified broadly under three headings: social, economic and political. Such a classification is, however, somewhat artificial, since in the real world these categories overlap, the social being influenced by the financial or economic, while in turn reacting with the political and so on. In the simplest terms colonisation affected many of the elements that had caused it, for example:

- one of the most obvious and immediate effects of colonisation, reflecting the tendency of the social, economic and political to overlap, was a resolution of many of the problems of overpopulation and land hunger. The surplus Greek population was spread far and wide.

- with colonisation Greek trade and the Greek economy expanded to an enormous degree. There was, in Thucydides' terms, a marked increase in wealth. This expansion in trade brought in its wake other effects, including the growth in size, wealth and influence of a new merchant class, which began to take a more prominent place in the social, economic and political life of the polis.

- there was a direct link between the two effects listed above and the political life and structure of many city-states. The immediate political problems that had led to colonisation in some city-states were, at least partially, resolved. By easing these political pressures colonisation prolonged the type of government, either monarchical or aristocratic, in some city-states.

  In the long term, however, colonisation, trade and the increase in wealth contributed to tyranny, a new type of government that became common in the Peloponnese during this period.

- Greek culture — religion, architecture, language, crafts and customs — was spread throughout the Mediterranean and Aegean region. In turn the Greeks were exposed to other cultures as never before. This meant new ideas such as the concept of tyranny, the use of coinage and a new alphabet all came from elsewhere.

- the Greek sense of national unity was also encouraged by colonisation. The Greeks noted the unity among the surrounding peoples while the contrast with the 'barbarians', as the Greeks called them, reminded the Greeks of what they had in common.

NOTE: While providing a general sense of unity on one level the colonisation process also aroused some conflict and petty jealousy among the Greek city-states. In this sense colonisation is said by some scholars to have promoted disunity.

STOP AND THINK: ACTIVITIES

↘ **Design and produce a poster to entice would-be colonists to join a colonising party.**

↘ **Draw up a contract between a mother city and an oecist setting down the conditions to apply in establishing a colony.**

↘ **Write a play that examines in some depth the reasons for one specific city-state to send out colonists. The city-state and associated reasons must be historically accurate.**

LIST OF REFERENCES

ANCIENT SOURCES

Hecataeus, of Miletas, *Fragmenta*, La Nuova Italia, Firenze, 1954

Herodotus, *The Histories*, tr. Aubrey de Sélincourt, Penguin, 1972

Hesiod, *Works and Days*, Clarendon Press, Oxford, 1978

Homer, The Epic Cycle, especially *The Odyssey*

Archilochos, Sappho, Alkman: three lyric poets of the late Greek Bronze Age, tr. Guy Davenport, University of California Press c. 1980

Thucydides, *The Peloponnesian War*, tr. Rex Warner, Penguin, 1954 repr. 1980

SECONDARY SOURCES

Bury, J.B. & Meiggs, R., *History of Greece to the Death of Alexander the Great*, 4th ed, Macmillan, London, 1975

Forrest, W.G., *The Emergence of Greek Democracy*, Weidenfeld & Nicolson, London, 1966

Littman, R.J., *The Greek Experiment*, Thames & Hudson, London, 1974

CHAPTER THREE

THE AGE OF TYRANTS

JANE AND BRUCE DENNETT

INTRODUCTION

The so-called Age of Tyrants in Greece coincided with the significant social, economic and political changes that took place in the seventh and sixth centuries BC. Tyranny was a new, revolutionary form of government, unlike anything seen before in Greece. A tyrant was a lone ruler, an autocrat, whose power was supreme. He was also a usurper, someone unlike a king for example, who did not have a legal, traditional or hereditary right to rule.

FOCUS QUESTIONS
✎ **What was the Age of Tyrants?**
✎ **Who were the tyrants?**
✎ **What caused the emergence of tyranny?**
✎ **What were the effects of tyranny?**

Two key points about tyranny must be remembered:

- tyrants appeared all over Greece, at different times and places. Even though the seventh and sixth centuries BC is called the 'Age of Tyrants' because so many emerged during that time, tyrants were not restricted to that period. For example, tyranny was a form of government used by Persia in the late sixth and early fifth century to control the cities established by the Greeks in Asia Minor when they had become part of the growing Persian Empire. Tyrants also appeared in Greek colonies in Sicily and southern Italy in the fifth and fourth centuries BC. In fact evidence is available that shows the survival of tyranny as a form of government in various places right down to the second century BC.
- each tyrant in each polis was in some way unique. Tyranny was an individual response by Greeks to the particular problems of their own city-state. There are some common aspects that will be considered later in the chapter, but it is dangerous to overgeneralise and lump all tyrants together, assuming incorrectly that they were identical.

Tyranny was a political symptom of the wider changes that became apparent in Greek society from the seventh century BC on. Colonisation, increased trade, the growth of new social classes, new methods of warfare, larger cities with bigger urban populations and an overall increase in wealth were a few of the changes that formed the backdrop to the challenge tyrants posed to established governments. *Monarchy*, the rule by one person based upon heredity, had become less common in the seventh century. It was often replaced by *aristocracy*, the rule of a special, elite group, its power based upon a tradition of authority and wealth. Each of these factors was tested during the Age of Tyrants. The would–be tyrant had little respect for traditional attitudes to government, while increased trade meant that new classes of merchants and craftsmen began to match the wealth of the landowning aristocracy. These groups were prepared to support tyrants in order to remove the aristocrats from power and gain some influence over the affairs of the polis. The tyrants' power was therefore based upon three elements:

- *resentment* against aristocratic government
- *performance* — the tyrant had to provide government, at least in the early stages, strong enough to keep his initial supporters satisfied
- *military power* — tyrants were often associated with a new military class called the hoplites.

Tyranny is seen by many scholars as an important transitional phase in the political evolution of the Greek states. Tyrants mark the end of oligarchy — the rule of a few aristocrats — and precede, in some states, democracy, rule by the *demos*, the people. Even so the earliest period of tyranny is important to our understanding of ancient Greek history and civilisation.

STOP AND THINK
✎ **Draw up a table that compares the various forms of government mentioned.**

The word 'tyrant' or *tyrannos* is not Greek; it was derived from a Lydian word.* Our earliest record of it sees it applied to a Lydian ruler, Gyges. It appears that Gyges seized absolute personal power and was therefore a usurper without legal or hereditary authority. Originally the word tyrant did not carry all the negative connotations that it did for later Greek historians and philosophers, nor the evil implications it has today.

Tyranny as a form of government was widespread. Most of the major polis were ruled by tyrants at one time or another. The most useful examples of tyrannies are Pheidon of Argos, the Cypselids of Sicyon, and Theagenes of Megara, while outside southern Greece the Peisistratid tyranny in Athens is also worth consideration.

---

* Lydia was an ancient country in west Asia Minor.

ARCHAEOLOGICAL SOURCES

The tyrants of the seventh and sixth centuries BC proved, on the whole, to be energetic and innovative. Therefore there is an array of archaeological evidence, the physical remains of their presence and achievements. Many tyrants embarked on extensive building programmes, and the remains of these projects verify supposed achievements. Cypselus and his son Periander from Corinth are credited with a number of major public works, the most notable being a slipway across the Isthmus of Corinth to carry ships. Unfortunately the Roman destruction of the city of Corinth in 146 BC wiped out a great deal of useful archaeological evidence of Cypselid construction. Nevertheless archaeologists can point to the site of the Temple of Artemis built by Periander on the island of Corcyra, which is regarded as one of the first examples of monumental Greek architecture. Although little remains, it is possible to link it to the assertion that tyrants often attempted to provide impressive temples and public buildings to win favour, said to be Periander's motive in constructing the Temple of Artemis. There are also the remnants of the Corinthian Treasury built by Cypselus at Delphi. The Treasury is located inside the Apollo Sanctuary and was designed to hold offerings.

Archaeologists have also contributed to the study of tyranny through excavation of the numerous colonial sites established during the Age of Tyrants. Further evidence is available from pottery, coins and weights and measures. Images of hoplite warfare, the new heavily armoured infantry, appear on pottery and are vital to the debate over the date of its earliest appearance. Pottery can also reflect levels of prosperity, trade and artisanship.

Coinage is also significant; for example, the American scholar John Fine in his book *The Ancient Greeks* argues that coinage reflected what he called the growth of 'movable wealth', wealth not linked directly to the ownership of land or direct control of primary produce. Fine says that the extended use of coinage allowed the new classes of artisans, merchants and traders to challenge the wealth and political influence of the old land-owning aristocracies, and in turn influence the emergence of tyranny.

WRITTEN SOURCES

Sources of written material on the Greek tyrants are generally inadequate and must be read with caution. They generally present a negative view of the individual tyrants. One of the few exceptions to this is Aristotle's view of Pisistratus. Nevertheless ancient writers were less than totally objective.

Those sources, however, that appear to be the most useful in forming a picture of the period in question are poets such as Archilochus, Hesiod, Alcaeus, Solon and Theognis, along with historians and philosophers like Herodotus, Thucydides, Ephorus, Aristotle and Plato.

THE POETS

Archilochus: He wrote during the seventh century BC and was regarded by the ancient Greeks as one of their greatest poets. Archilochus provides historians with the earliest written reference to a tyrant. In one of the surviving fragments of his work he describes the Lydian Gyges as a tyrant.

Hesiod: The famous Boeotian poet provides some important insights into the background of tyranny in his *Works and Days*. First we can glean from his poetry some of the sweeping social and economic changes that took place in Greece before the rise of tyranny. Second Hesiod refers to '*dike*', the unwritten ancestral rules and customs that made up Greek law under the aristocracy. These were gradually replaced during the seventh century BC by a codified body of written laws. This step could be seen as one of the first challenges to the power and authority of the aristocratic oligarchies.

Alcaeus: He wrote in the early fifth century BC and provides a valuable insight into the continuous quest for knowledge in ancient history. Up until this century only a handful of quotations from Alcaeus were available, and these had survived only in the works of others. However, fragments of approximately twenty-one papyrus texts were found which included political poems. These political poems made references to one of Alcaeus's political enemies in Mytilene, a man called Pittacus, whom Alcaeus called a tyrant. Strictly speaking this was not true, since Pittacus was an elected official. Hence with Alcaeus in the fifth century we read one of the earlier applications of the word tyrant as a term of abuse. These negative implications were to become common.

Solon and Theognis: Both wrote during the fifth century BC and used the word tyrant in their poetry to signify absolute or complete personal power.

HISTORIANS AND PHILOSOPHERS

Herodotus: He referred to tyrants in *The Histories* but he wrote several generations after the disappearance of the early tyrannies. His work is useful but very anecdotal. His stories highlight the personalities of tyrants, rather than providing a valid political or historical analysis.

Furthermore a great deal of the source information used by Herodotus was heavily biased against tyrants. When writing about the Cypselids in Corinth, much of Herodotus' detail was provided by the aristocratic groups who finally drove the tyrants from power.

Thucydides: He was a great Athenian historian of the fifth century; his references to tyrants, however, are brief and almost invariably unfavourable.

Ephorus: The fragments of his universal history or *Historiai* that remain have been used by both Aristotle and Plato as sources for their own work. Ephorus makes some observations about tyranny, but they should be viewed with caution since exaggeration for literary effect is an acknowledged aspect of his style.

Aristotle: He was one of the truly great intellectual figures of the ancient world. Aristotle wrote *The Politics* in the fourth century BC. It includes an analysis of tyranny as a form of government but Aristotle does not appear to distinguish between the tyrants of the Age of Tyrants (the seventh and sixth centuries) and those of the late fifth century BC. He also used Dionysios of Syracuse as his model of a tyrant and since Dionysios ruled between 406 and 367 BC, we must be careful in drawing too heavily upon Aristotle as a source for the Age of Tyrants.

Plato: Plato taught Aristotle but his works on tyrants tend to be highly theoretical and are of less value than his pupil's.

STOP AND THINK: DOCUMENT STUDY

These are two accounts of the relationship and exchanges of advice between Periander, tyrant of Corinth, and Thrasybulus, tyrant of Miletus. Read them both carefully and then answer the questions that follow.

To begin with, Periander was less violent than his father, but soon surpassed him in bloody-mindedness and savagery. This was the result of a correspondence which he entered into with Thrasybulus, the master of Miletus. He sent a representative to the court of this despot, to ask his opinion on how best and most safely to govern his city. Thrasybulus invited the man to walk with him from the city to a field where corn was growing. As he passed through this cornfield, continually asking questions about why the messenger had come to him from Corinth, he kept cutting off all the tallest ears of wheat which he could see, and throwing them away, until the finest and best grown part of the crop was ruined. In this way he went right through the field, and then sent the messenger away without a word. On his return to Corinth, Periander was eager to hear what advice Thrasybulus had given, and the man replied that he had not given any at all, adding that he was surprised at being sent to visit such a person, who was evidently mad and a wanton destroyer of his own property — and then he described what he had seen Thrasybulus do. Periander seized the point at once; it was perfectly plain to him that Thrasybulus recommended the murder of all the people in the city who were outstanding in influence or ability.

Herodotus, The Histories, 5, 92e–g

❋   ❋   ❋

It is said that to Thrasybulus' messenger, who had come for advice, Periander returned no answer; but while walking in a field, reduced all the stalks to one level by lopping off the tallest. The messenger did not understand the motive for this action, but reported the action to Thrasybulus, who perceived that he ought to remove the outstanding men.

Aristotle, The Politics, 3

❋   ❋   ❋

✎ **In the first account is Periander or Thrasybulus seeking advice? Does the second account agree with the first?**

⬊ **What sign does Thrasybulus give in the first account? What sign does Periander give in the second account?**

⬊ **What do the signs or actions signify?**

⬊ **In your opinion what would be the advantages and disadvantages of carrying through the advice?**

⬊ **In your opinion which of the two accounts is the more emotive (emotional) in its language? Provide quotes to support your answer.**

⬊ **How do these two accounts affect your opinion about the reliability of ancient sources on the question of tyranny?**

STOP AND THINK: MAPPING

⬊ **On a map of Greece and Asia Minor, mark the locations of the major tyrannies:**

- **Argos — ruled by Pheidon**
- **Corinth — ruled by the Cypselids**
  (Cypselus, Periander, Psammetichus)
- **Sicyon — ruled by the Orthagarids**
  (Orthagoras, Myron, Cleisthenes)
- **Megara — ruled by Theagenes**
- **Athens — ruled by the Peisistratids**
  (Pisistratus, Hipparchus, Hippias)
- **Samos — ruled by Polycrates**
- **Miletus — ruled by Thrasybulus**

REASONS FOR THE EMERGENCE OF TYRANNY

There are a variety of theories that have been put forward to explain the appearance of so many tyrants in the seventh and sixth centuries BC. The most significant theories are:

- tyranny arising from an overall increase in wealth,
- the racial theory,
- the hoplite theory,
- conflict within ruling elites.

We shall consider each of these theories in more detail.

TYRANNY AND THE INCREASE IN WEALTH

This theory, dealing with changed social and economic circumstances, bridges the gap between scholars as apparently unrelated as Thucydides and the nineteenth century revolutionary theorist, Karl Marx. Thucydides pointed to a growth in prosperity providing a basis for social and political change, while Karl Marx wrote that any changes in the means of creating wealth — changes in what he called the 'factors of production' — would apply pressure for changes in the ways a community was governed, pressure for changes in the 'factors of relation'. It is possible to see these elements at work in the Greek world of the seventh and sixth centuries BC.

Growth in trade, growing urban populations and the expanded use of coinage altered the fabric of Greek society. The 'new rich', merchants, traders and artisans, began to assert their right to an increased role in the affairs of the state. In doing so they began to challenge the traditional aristocracies. One of the earliest signs of this was pressure from the newly rich 'middle class' for written laws. Tyrants appear to have found in these conditions a fertile breeding ground, casting themselves as the charismatic revolutionaries, usurpers opposing the old order.

TYRANNY AND RACIAL DISPUTES

The fact so many tyrannies did spring up in the Peloponnese provides a reason to consider the theory that the tyrannies were the result of the original pre-Dorian populations supporting tyrants in order to rid themselves of Dorian aristocracies. It may have validity in some cases but it does not explain the tyrannies that emerged outside southern Greece, an area free of the tension between the Dorian and pre-Dorian races. The general validity of this theory is also doubtful when Cypselus' seizure of power in Corinth is examined. Some scholars doubt the significance of racial conflict as an element in Cypselus' accession because there were no specific signs of social reform in Corinth to alter or better the circumstances of the pre-Dorian group. Whether or not this criticism of the racial or pre-Dorian theory is valid, the fact remains that it does appear to be appropriate in the case of Cleisthenes of Sicyon, who apparently made changes to the tribal system of Sicyon that improved the circumstances of the pre-Dorian group.

THE DEVELOPMENT OF HOPLITE WARFARE

It is difficult to date with absolute certainty the widespread application of hoplite warfare. Archaeological evidence provides some clues, for example, a late eighth century BC tomb at Argos contained a hoplite's bronze breastplate and helmet; however pottery from the late eighth and early seventh centuries BC depicts both types of warfare.

It is not until the middle of the seventh century BC (c.650) that Corinthian pottery displays a full hoplite formation. The evidence would appear to indicate a gradual introduction of hoplite tactics; therefore it is difficult to state, as a fact, that tyrants before c.650 BC were the product of the influence of a hoplite class.

The hoplites fought as a unit in a tightly disciplined formation, the phalanx. They were well-armoured with helmet, corselet, greaves, a round shield or hoplon (hence the name hoplite), a short sword and a thrusting spear. The would-be hoplite had to purchase his own armour, hence service as a hoplite was not open to everyone. The new classes of wealthy merchants and artisans, however, did become part of the hoplite class. Advocates of the hoplite theory argue that this group began to agitate for

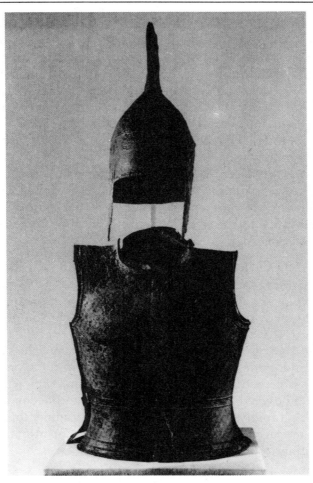

Bronze helmet and breastplate from Argos

greater political influence, influence they felt was compatible with their wealth and their military service. Tyrants are said to have emerged as champions of this class against the old aristocracies.

Nevertheless the hoplite theory like the racial theory does not appear to be universally valid. Even if we accept, for example, that Pheidon of Argos, the first recorded Greek tyrant, was a military figure, it is not possible to claim that his tyrannical power was the product of hoplite support. The problem is the dispute over the date for the advent of hoplite tactics and another dispute over Pheidon's years as a tyrant. Some sources place him around 669 BC and 668 BC when he was meant to have scored a victory at the Battle of Hysiae and taken personal control of the Olympic festival respectively. Herodotus, however, suggests a later date. If the earlier date is true, it is difficult to verify that the hoplites were the key to Pheidon's power.

The universal application of the hoplite theory is also brought into question by a study of Cleisthenes' position in Sicyon. Even allowing for the limited evidence available, Cleisthenes' power appeared to rest far more firmly on his domestic reforms rather than on hoplite support.

Raphael Sealey is one of a number of modern scholars with reservations about the hoplite theory. He argues that the hoplites were an essentially conservative group and were therefore not likely to support the kind of revolutionary political change symbolised by a tyrant. Rather, Sealey suggests, the discipline associated with hoplite warfare and training, where individuality was sacrificed for the good of the whole formation, helped tyrants stay in power, rather than gain power. The tyrant needed an orderly social and military environment in order to consolidate his position. A disciplined body such as the hoplites within the polis could only enhance such a stable environment.

TYRANNY AND CLASHES BETWEEN ELITES

Raphael Sealey offers this theory as an alternative to the racial and hoplite theories, to explain the appearance of tyrannies in Corinth and Athens. However he does not suggest it as a universally applicable theory.

Sealey suggests that the Cypselids' seizure of power at the expense of the Bacchiadae family was not a struggle between a lower class and an upper class, but rather a contest between elements within the Corinthian upper class. Cypselus is depicted as staging a kind of coup, exploiting a growing tide of discontent over the poor performance of the Bacchiads in administering Corinth's rapidly growing colonial and trading interests. Sealey suggests that there are some parallels between the Corinthian situation and Pisistratus coming to power in Athens.

Each of these theories must be acknowledged and applied where and if appropriate. They should not, however, be described as causes of tyranny in the strict sense of the word. At best they are 'pre-conditions', circumstances that, in individual cases, made the rise of certain tyrants possible. The causes are as individual as each of the tyrannies and for the most part, the specific causes are lost due to the limited evidence.

STOP AND THINK: DOCUMENT STUDY
Read these two extracts from the introduction to Thucydides'
***The Peloponnesian War* and answer the questions.**

The old form of government was hereditary monarchy with established rights and limitations; but as Hellas became more powerful and as the importance of acquiring money became more and more evident, tyrannies were established in nearly all the cities, revenues increased, shipbuilding flourished, and ambition turned towards sea-power.

1, 13

❋   ❋   ❋

And in the Hellenic states that were governed by tyrants, the tyrant's first thought was always for himself, for his own personal safety, and for the greatness of his own family. Consequently security was the chief political principle in these governments, and no great action ever came out of them . . .

1, 17

✳   ✳   ✳

✎ **In the first extract, what does Thucydides suggest as a possible reason for the establishment of tyrannies?**

✎ **Which of the theories mentioned previously does this extract support?**

✎ **From the first extract, what does Thucydides say happened after tyrannies were established?**

✎ **From the second extract list the points Thucydides suggests are characteristics of tyranny.**

✎ **After examining both extracts, there is an apparent contradiction in Thucydides' opinion of tyrants. What is it? Support your answer with quotes.**

STOP AND THINK: DOCUMENT STUDY
The extract below is from Aristotle, *The Politics*, 4. Read it carefully and answer the questions that follow.

The earliest constitution (after the kingships) among the Greeks was in fact composed of warriors, of the cavalry in the first place, because it was in them that strength and superiority in war were to be found (for without organized formations a hoplite force is useless, and the ancients had no fund of experience of such things and no tactical procedures for them, so that their strength rested with their cavalry).

✳   ✳   ✳

✎ **According to Aristotle, how were the earliest constitutions or governments (after the kingships) composed or arranged?**

✎ **Why, according to Aristotle, was a cavalry more important in warfare at this early stage?**

 • **Did this situation change? Support your answer by a quote or quotes from the passage.**

✎ **Which of the theories for the emergence of tyranny is Aristotle's account linked to?**

CONCLUSION

Tyranny was a very personal and idiosyncratic style of government. It took its character from both the individual, local factors that produced it, and the personality of the tyrant himself. Nevertheless, while allowing for their individuality, it is possible to draw some general conclusions about the social, economic, racial, military and political elements that established the background, or pre-conditions, that made tyranny possible.

Tyrants often presided over periods of economic expansion and some social reform. They were generally energetic and active rulers, credited with notable public works and enthusiastic support of literature, the arts, and public and religious festivals, possibly because they lacked legitimate authority and had to win and retain support by conspicuous achievements. Tyrants could also be ruthless and repressive in their desire to retain power. In many cases tyrannies in the Greek states demonstrated both these positive and negative qualities.

LIST OF REFERENCES

ANCIENT SOURCES

Archilochus, Sappho, Alkman: three lyric poets of the late Greek Bronze Age, tr. Guy Davenport, University of California Press, c.1980

Aristotle, *The Politics and Athenian Constitution*, ed. and tr. John Warrington, Dent, London, 1959

Herodotus, *The Histories*, tr. Aubrey de Sélincourt, Penguin Classics, 1972

Hesiod, *Works and Days*, Clarendon Press, Oxford, 1978

Thucydides, *The Peloponnesian War*, tr. Rex Warner, Penguin, 1954, repr. 1980

SECONDARY SOURCES

Fine, John, *The Ancient Greeks*, Harvard University Press, Cambridge, Mass, 1983

Page, Denys Lionel, *Sappho and Alcaeus: an introduction to the study of ancient Lesbian poetry*, Clarendon Press, Oxford, 1955

Sealey, Raphael, *A History of the Greek City-states*, University of California Press, 1976

CHAPTER FOUR

SPARTA

JANE AND BRUCE DENNETT

INTRODUCTION

Impressions and images of Sparta and its warriors are one of the truly enduring legacies left by ancient Greece to the modern world. The word 'Spartan' — defined by the *Oxford Dictionary* as 'austere or courageous' — is part of our language. These elements of austerity and courage are inextricably linked with the mystery, myth and propaganda that surround any investigation of ancient Sparta.

However there are important lessons in historical methodology to be gained from a revision of our view of Sparta. The key issue is Sparta's emergence as a powerful, apparently conservative military 'barrack room' state: how and why did this happen? Other lessons concern the need to weigh up carefully written and archaeological sources against each other, seeking points of consensus and noting apparent contradictions. Finally there is a lesson on the need to guard against sweeping generalisations and simplistic explanations. Major events in human history rarely have one cause; they are almost invariably the product of a multiplicity of factors. Any claim, therefore, that the creation of classical Sparta with its unique, mixed constitution, militaristic outlook and austerity — measures that promoted a society whereby all Spartan citizens were equal — was the product of one man or one particular period of history or one crisis must be classed as a myth.

A distinctive Spartan society *did* emerge, but it also contained elements common to other Greek polis of the same period. There were changes but they were far more gradual than the traditional myth would suggest. Finally there is evidence to indicate that some of the reasons for these changes were not unique to Sparta.

FOCUS QUESTIONS

✎ **Was there a great law-giver, Lycurgus, who set out the Spartan constitution?**

⟍ **What was the nature of Spartan government and society?**
⟍ **When did Sparta become the austere, military state of legend and why?**

WRITTEN SOURCES

Until quite recently the principal avenue of enquiry into Sparta was through a detailed study of the assorted fragments of written evidence left to us by the ancient scholars. However there are some problems with the ancient written sources, namely:

- each of the ancient writers brought to the subject of Sparta preconceived ideas. They came either as admirers of Sparta's stability or as critics of its austerity and discipline.
- to a degree the writers from the ancient world reflected the influence of those who had gone before. In other words, myths and misconceptions were often reinforced, or even enhanced, by one writer using the views of a predecessor as a source.
- the Spartans do not appear to have been easy people for outsiders to know. They seem to have been reluctant to disclose a great deal about their way of life, and when they did, the information frequently appears to have included elements of propaganda.

Nevertheless, the ancient authors do have a role to play.

HERODOTUS

The famous author of *The Histories* writing in the middle of the fifth century BC provides one of our earliest surviving accounts of Sparta. He deals far more, however, with Spartan foreign policy than domestic affairs. Furthermore Herodotus appears to spend more time criticising the Spartan constitution than he does describing it. Although he does make reference to the dual Spartan kingship, in general Herodotus is of limited value.

THUCYDIDES

Thucydides produced his great account, *The Peloponnesian War*, late in the fifth century BC. Although, like Herodotus, one of the outstanding authors of the ancient world, he has little to say about the domestic Spartan situation. Nevertheless he was impressed by the '*eunomia*' or 'good order' of Spartan society. It should be noted that such an observation is 'value laden', subjective and perhaps the product of Spartan propaganda.

STOP AND THINK: DOCUMENT STUDY

Consider these two extracts from Thucydides *The Peloponnesian War* and answer the questions that follow.

Suppose, for example, that the city of Sparta were to become deserted and that only the temples and foundations of buildings remained, I think that future generations would, as time passed, find it very difficult to believe that the place had really been as powerful as it was represented to be. Yet the Spartans occupy two-fifths of the Peloponnese and stand at the head not only of the whole Peloponnese itself but also of numerous allies beyond its frontiers. Since, however, the city is not regularly planned and contains no temples or monuments of great magnificence, but is simply a collection of villages, in the ancient Hellenic way, its appearance would not come up to expectation. If, on the other hand, the same thing were to happen to Athens, one would conjecture from what met the eye that the city had been twice as powerful as in fact it is.

1, 10

* * *

... the Spartan constitution goes back to a very early date, and the country has never been ruled by tyrants. For rather more than 400 years, dating from the end of the late war, they have had the same system of government, and this has been not only a source of internal strength, but has enabled them to intervene in the affairs of other states.

1, 18

* * *

- ✎ **How powerful was Sparta in Thucydides' time? What evidence for this power can you find in the extracts?**
- ✎ **Thucydides wrote in the late 400s BC. How old does he suggest the Spartan constitution was?**
- ✎ **Why does Thucydides say the city of Sparta is less impressive than the city of Athens?**
- ✎ **What aspect of the Spartan constitution does Thucydides describe as a source of strength? Do you see this factor as an asset to Sparta?**

XENOPHON

Xenophon wrote a work called *The Constitution of the Lacedaemonians* in the fourth century BC which provides information about the Spartan military system. Although he does give some insight into social customs and the law, he was an unashamed admirer of the Spartan military and the system that produced it.

PLATO AND ARISTOTLE

These were two of the great political thinkers of the fourth century BC but they present Sparta as a kind of 'case study' to highlight their own political theories. Plato was a great admirer of the Spartan system and is unstinting in his praise of its order and stability. In such a view there is a clue to the accumulation of historical perceptions, Plato's views building on the earlier writings of Thucydides.

Aristotle was Plato's pupil and was clearly influenced by his teacher's ideas. Even so, he does criticise some aspects of the Spartan system, especially the system of land ownership and the problems of maintaining a number of landholdings within a small elite citizen group. Aristotle devoted part of Book 2 of his work *The Politics* to the Spartan constitution. He approved of the apparently shared power of the Spartan constitution, describing this as a 'mixed' constitution and suggesting that it may be the cause of Spartan stability.

PLUTARCH

He lived between c. AD 46 and AD 120 and is therefore a much later source than any of the others mentioned above. Nevertheless in Plutarch's *Life of Lycurgus*, Sparta's supposed great law-giver, we have the oldest apparently complete account of the Spartan constitution. Plutarch is a critical source of written evidence but he acknowledges that Lycurgus and his activities are open to doubt and little can be said with certainty on the subject.

PAUSANIAS

He wrote a *Description of Greece* around AD 150 and although this is well after the great days of Sparta it does include useful references to the operation of the Spartan constitution.

POETS — TYRTAEUS, ALCMAN AND TERPANDER

Tyrtaeus was writing around 640 BC at the time of the second Messenian War (a helot revolt). His is war poetry, clearly designed to arouse the martial spirit. Tyrtaeus placed courage in battle above all other qualities.

The works of Alcman and Terpander are quite different from Tyrtaeus' and they appear later. They reflect a varied society. J.T. Hooker in his book *The Ancient Spartans* reviews much of this poetry and concludes that it reflected an atmosphere at variance with the military myth at least into the sixth century BC.

In general the written sources provide reliable information about Spartan government and society during the respective authors' time. They are far less reliable, however, when they attempt to describe or account for events early in Sparta's development.

The most notable myths spawned by the ancient sources are:

- there was a single great law-giver who produced the Spartan system.
- the Spartan system arose out of the need to maintain a strong, militaristic society to control a huge, almost enslaved, subject population (the helots) who constantly threatened to rebel.
- the creation of the Spartan system resulted in a sudden, revolutionary social transformation. Luxury, the arts, crafts, literature and culture were quickly eclipsed by austerity and discipline in a dour military state, a situation that could best be described by the modern English definition of the word 'Spartan'.
- within the Spartan system, full citizens lived side by side in equality.

It is now generally accepted that an individual named Lycurgus did exist, even though some modern scholars assert that he, too is a myth. However, it is no longer accepted that he, acting alone in antiquity, handed down the laws and constitutions of Sparta.

The Spartan system emerged for a variety of reasons, not just pressure from fear of a helot revolt. Modern scholars such as W.G. Forrest in his

History of Sparta imply that economic changes and increased wealth arising from the acquisition of Messenia might have encouraged demands for political change. Others, including Paul Cartledge and John Salmon, point to the emergence of hoplite warfare. They note how it influenced political change in other Greek cities and suggest that it might have done the same in Sparta.

ARCHAEOLOGICAL SOURCES

A review of archaeological evidence has played a key role in revision of a great deal of Spartan history. Archaeological finds assessed and presented by L.F. Fitzhardinge, J.T. Hooker, Paul Cartledge and A.J. Halladay suggest that the creation of the austere Spartan society was not a sudden, revolutionary event. Archaeological expeditions have unearthed pottery, terracottas, ivory and bone carving, bronze work and sculpture of quality down to at least 525 BC. The only possible conclusion is that culture and arts and crafts flourished in Sparta at a time when many of the ancient authors would have us believe they had vanished with the wave of Lycurgus' hand.

Some scholars also link economic factors to the withering away of Spartan culture. They refer to the decline in Sparta's trade with the east that followed Persian expansion into Lydia and Ionian Greece in the middle of the sixth century BC. Another suggestion is that Sparta's retention of iron currency in the form of bars, as opposed to the silver coinage used elsewhere in Greece, also contributed to both a decline in trade and culture. These economic arguments are disputed in some circles, but the fact remains that more than one element was at work in the erosion of Spartan culture.

Increasingly the myth of equality among full Spartan citizens is also being challenged. Historians refer to archaeological remains of luxury goods in Spartan society. They also point to some Spartan competitors in the costly sport of chariot racing at the Olympic Games. J.T. Hooker refers to the Spartan use of propaganda as a factor in perpetuating the myth of equality.

Even so there are still problems associated with the archaeological materials. As noted by Thucydides, Sparta did not have many prominent public buildings and the archaeological record of Sparta as a whole is limited.

Nevertheless an important contribution to the study of Sparta was made by excavation of the sanctuary of Artemis Orthia in Sparta. The archaeological evidence contradicted the ancient sources that maintained Spartan austerity had existed from 900 or 800 BC — archaeological finds reflected a rich and varied cultural life at least to c.650 or 620 BC. The excavations also supported the idea of a long, slow decline in cultural pursuits, not a sudden, revolutionary change.

The debate prompted by these finds has been led by L.F. Fitzhardinge, *The Spartans*; P.A. Cartledge, *Sparta and Laconia*; and J.T. Hooker, *The Ancient Spartans*.

STOP AND THINK: DOCUMENT STUDY
Read the extract below that addresses the birth of the Spartan legend and answer the questions that follow.

The idea of Sparta

... Although, no doubt, elements of the Spartan legend were in existence before the Persian Wars, we can trace its development only as far back as that epoch. And already we are confronted by the two prominent facets of the legend. The ideal is represented by Leonidas, the archetype of the Spartan warrior, who devotes his life to the state and who abhors two things above all: cowardice in battle and disobedience of his country's laws. Pausanias too is deeply versed in the Lycurgan way of life and remains blameless, even heroic, so long as he follows it. But when he turns aside from it, he too becomes an archetype: the simple soldier who once looked with contemptuous incredulity upon the luxury displayed in Mardonius' tent is in the end seduced by that very luxury; and the citizen, who previously merged himself with the state, goes off on a private errand and works against his countrymen. Herodotus heard at Sparta of these men, whose character and career had passed into legend: the noble king who fell at Thermopylae and the flawed regent who met a shameful death in his own city. It is as if a moral tale had been woven about the two figures, to serve as a warning example to future generations of Spartiates; and the tale was spiced with short, pithy sayings, illustrative of Spartan practical wisdom, of the type found in the 'Spartan apophthegms' later collected in Plutarch's *Moralia*.

Thus a suggestion can be made as to the approximate time at which the Spartan legend first became crystallized and as to the manner in which it was enshrined in Hellenic literature: the Spartiates fashioned the legend in the early decades of the fifth century, and Herodotus propagated it in his History. Now there arises a more difficult question: once the legend of the ideal Sparta had come into being, why did it not wither away at the end of the fifth century, when the Spartans manifestly no longer abode by the Lycurgan *kosmos* [world]? Or, if the power of propaganda managed to keep the legend alive even then, how did it survive the disastrous Spartan defeats of 371 and 362, after which Sparta had little means of influencing the opinions of the other Greeks? In order to answer these questions, we have to bear in mind the predilections and prejudices of the writers who were chiefly responsible for the continuation of the Spartan legend in the fifth and fourth centuries. These authors were all Athenians, or at least men who came to live and work at Athens. What was it they saw in Sparta (the very antithesis [opposite] of their own great city, as Thucydides convincingly demonstrates) that led them to throw their weight behind the legend? In one word, it was *orderliness*. The major prose-writers of classical Athens were far from being enamoured of extreme democracy; either (like Thucydides) they favoured a moderately democratic constitution, with restricted franchise, or (like Plato) they had no time at all for what they saw as the riotous excesses of the Athenian democrats.

J.T. Hooker, *The Ancient Spartans*, pp. 230–1.

❋ ❋ ❋

According to Hooker, the legend of the Lycurgan way of life in which the Spartan people were immersed began with Leonidas.

✎ **What was Leonidas' attitude toward the state?**

✎ **What two characteristics of the Spartans did Leonidas loathe?**

✎ **What did Pausanias do to 'turn aside' from the Lycurgan way of life?**

↘ **What reasons does Hooker put forward for the continuation of the legend throughout the fifth and fourth centuries BC?**

↘ **How does this review of the creation of the Spartan legend, and an introduction to the archaeological evidence, influence your view of the reliability of the ancient sources in Sparta?**

AN OVERVIEW OF SPARTAN HISTORY

c.1100–1000 BC	The Dorian race moves into the Peloponnese and settles in the Eurotas Valley.
c.800	Sparta becomes a unified community. Some scholars offer this as a date for the social organisation and laws of Lycurgus.
c.800–730	Sparta gains control of the villages in the surrounding region of Laconia (also referred to as Lacedaemonia).
c.740–720	First Messenian War; in response to its own growing population and the need for land Sparta conquers nearby Messenia and its people become helots.
c.669	Sparta defeated by Argos in Battle of Hysiae.
c.650	Some scholars offer this as an alternative date for the Lycurgan revolution.
c.645–620	Second Messenian War — a revolt by the helot population.
c.550	Sparta defeats Tegea and establishes the Peloponnesian League.
c.546	Sparta defeats Argos.
c.490	First Persian War. Herodotus born.
c.480	Second Persian War. Leonidas dies at Thermopylae.
c.479	Spartans defeat Persians at Plataea.
c.465	Sparta hit by earthquake and a helot revolt.
c.460	Thucydides born.
c.431–404	Peloponnesian War — Sparta defeats Athens.
c.384	Aristotle born.
c.371	Sparta defeated in battle of Leuctra by Thebes.
c.369	Messenian helots freed.

Note the dates of birth for some of the ancient writers and note their relationship in time to many of the events they describe.

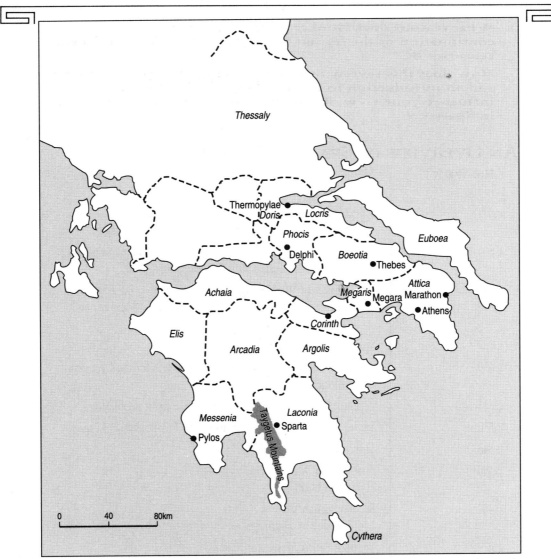

Central Greece and the Peloponnese were connected by the narrow strip called the Isthmus of Corinth. Find the area on the map. Note Sparta is a city-state within the region of Laconia.
How many other regions are there within the geographical area known as the Peloponnese?

The Spartans were the descendants of the Dorian population that moved into southern Greece following the fall of the Mycenaean civilisation and settled in the rich Eurotas Valley. Written sources about Sparta and its history are confined largely to the Spartiates, the full Spartan citizens — those whose mother and father were Spartan citizens — and the helots, the subject population. There is very little on the groups in between.

Sparta became the dominant city in the region. Dorian people from the surrounding villages became *perioeci* (meaning 'dwellers round about').

Their living conditions were better than those of the helots but they still did not have full citizenship rights. The *perioeci* eventually became responsible for trade and commerce in Sparta, allowing the Spartiates to concentrate on martial pursuits.

Sparta solved its problems of overpopulation and land hunger by expanding within the Peloponnese, especially into the nearby region of Messenia. The defeated Messenians became the helots, a resentful subject population, accorded a status similar to that of serfs in the Middle Ages.

GOVERNMENT
POWER AND RESPONSIBILITIES OF ORGANS OF THE SPARTAN CONSTITUTION
Kings

- There were two kings, one from each of the ancient clans, Agiad and Eurypondid. A hereditary position.
- Kings were constitutionally equal.
- Commanded the Spartan army when sent out by the people.
- Only one king left Sparta with the army.
- Unable to finalise a peace treaty but could establish arrangements and conditions for ratification by the Assembly.
- Judicial powers in the case of marriage of an unbetrothed heiress; matters dealing with public roads; adoption of sons.

The Assembly

- All adult Spartiates from the age of twenty.
- Could only vote to accept or reject motions put before it.
- There is some doubt over the right of the ordinary citizen to debate in the Assembly; it is probable that any Spartiate could speak.
- Assembly could not amend motions put before it.
- Elected the Gerousia and the Ephors.
- Power to ratify treaties.
- Power to declare war and choose the king to lead the army.

Gerousia

- 28 members and the two kings.
- Election by the loudest cheer.
- Criminal court, judging cases involving death or exile, and also involving trial of a king.
- Could veto decisions of the Assembly.

The Ephors

- Five Ephors were elected each year. One of them gave his name to the year.
- Any Spartan citizen over thirty years of age was eligible for election.
- Ephors could only hold office once in a lifetime.
- Declared war on the helots each year, putting them to death without trial.
- Had power to fine other magistrates, and power over all citizens, including the kings.
- Judged all civil cases.
- Received foreign envoys.
- Often noted as playing an important role in Gerousia.
- Had power to summon the king before them, and to arrest a king.
- Convened and presided over the Assembly; could put motions before the Assembly.
- Accompanied the king to battle.

STOP AND THINK: DOCUMENT STUDY
Examine these sources and use them to answer the questions that follow.

THE KINGS

I wish to explain with sufficient detail the nature of the covenant between king and state as instituted by Lykourgos [Lycurgus]; for this, I take it, is the sole type of rule which still preserves the original form in which it was first established; whereas other constitutions will be found either to have been already modified or else to be still undergoing modifications at this moment.

He laid it down as law that the king shall offer in behalf of the state all public sacrifices, as being himself of divine descent, and shall lead wherever the state despatches an army. He granted him to receive honorary gifts from the sacrifices, and he assigned him choice land in many of the subject cities, enough to satisfy moderate needs without excess of wealth. And in order that the kings also might dine in public he assigned them a public banquet, and he honoured them with a double portion each at the evening meal, not in order that they might actually eat twice as much as others, but that the king might have wherewithal to honor whomsoever he desired. He also granted each of the kings to choose two messmates called pythioi. He also granted them to receive out of every litter of swine one pig, so that the king might never be at a loss for sacrificial victims if in aught he wished to consult the gods...

All rise from their seats for the king, but ephors do not rise from their seats of office. Monthly they exchange oaths, the ephors in behalf of the state, the king himself in his own behalf. This is the oath on the king's part: 'I will exercise my kingship in accordance with the established laws of the state.' And on the part of the state the oath runs: 'So long as he (who exercises kingship) shall abide by his oath we will not suffer his kingdom to be shaken.'

Xenophon, *Constitution of the Spartans*, 15

❋   ❋   ❋

Of constitutional kingships, (1) the Spartan type is thought by some to come nearest to the true pattern. But this is not really so. The kings of Sparta command the army on foreign expeditions, and may supervise religious worship; beyond that their sovereignty does not extend. This sort of kingship may accordingly be described as an independent and permanent generalship. It has never included the power of life and death, except that in ancient times a king, when on campaign, might execute a subject 'by right of superior force.' In Homer, for instance, we find Agamemnon showing no resentment when abused in the assembly, but when the army goes out to battle he has power even of life and death: 'If I find anyone,' he says, 'flinching from the fight, nothing shall save him from the dogs and vultures, for in my hands is death.' So much for one type of kingship — military command on a life tenure, in some cases hereditary and in others elective.

Aristotle, *The Politics*, 3.1.1 [1285a]

❋   ❋   ❋

Aristotle [Pol. 3.14.4 (1285b)] calls the Spartan kingship a perpetual hereditary generalship, but in the hands of an able king it could be and normally was far more than that. The king, it is true, was at home merely one of the elders, and the political leadership of the assembly was in the hands of the ephors. But the advice of a successful general had immense weight with the assembly, and the kings had the advantage of permanency over their potential rivals. A king might, it is true, be baulked by his colleague, but this in fact very rarely happened, since the colleague of an influential king was very often a minor or an ineffective character. In fact, the number of Spartan commoners who swayed Spartan policy can be numbered on the fingers of one hand — the legendary Chilon, Hetoemaridas, Brasidas, Lysander, Antalcidas. The history of Sparta falls naturally into reigns of a series of great kings — Cleomenes I, Archidamus, Agesilaus, Areus, Agis III, Cleomenes IV, Nabis — who left their imprint, for good or ill, on the fortunes of their country.

A.H.M. Jones, *Sparta*, p. 16

✤ ✤ ✤

THE GEROUSIA

That too was a happy enactment, in my opinion, by which Lykourgos provided for the continual cultivation of virtue, even to old age. By fixing election to the council of elders at the end of life, he made it impossible for a high standard of virtuous living to be disregarded even in old age. So, too, it is worthy of admiration in him that he lent his helping hand to virtuous old age. Thus, by making the elders sole arbiters in the trial for life, he contrived to charge old age with a greater weight of honor than that which is accorded to the strength of mature manhood. And assuredly such a contest as this must appeal to the zeal of mortal man beyond all others in supreme degree. Fair, doubtless, are contests of gymnastic skill, yet they are but trials of bodily excellence, but this contest for the council of elders is an ordeal of the soul itself. In proportion, therefore, as the soul is worthier than the body, so must these contests of the soul be worthier of zealous endeavor than those of the body.

Xenophon, *Constitution of the Spartans*, 10 (1–3)

✤ ✤ ✤

THE ASSEMBLY

After this speech he himself, in his capacity of ephor, put the question to the Spartan assembly. They make their decisions by acclamation, not by voting, and Sthenelaidas said at first that he could not decide on which side the acclamations were the louder. This was because he wanted to make them show their opinions openly and make them all the more enthusiastic for war. He therefore said, 'Spartans, those of you who think that the treaty has been broken and that the Athenians are the aggressors, get up and stand on one side. Those who do not think so, stand on the other side,' and he pointed out to them where they were to stand. Then they rose to their feet and separated into two divisions. The great majority were of the opinion that the treaty had been broken.

Thucydides, *The Peloponnesian War*, 1, 87

✤ ✤ ✤

THE EPHORS

Accordingly the ephors are competent to punish whomsoever they choose; they have power to exact fines on the spur of the moment; they have power to depose magistrates in mid-career — nay, actually to imprison and bring them to trial on the capital charge. Entrusted with these vast powers, they do not, as do the rest of states, allow the elected magistrates to exercise authority as they like, right through the year of office; but, in the style rather of despotic monarchs or presidents of gymnastic games, at the first sign of any transgression they inflict chastisement without warning and without hesitation.

Xenophon, *Constitution of the Spartans*, 8

✤ ✤ ✤

At Sellasia Theramenes and the other ambassadors were asked to define the purpose of their mission. They replied that they had come with full powers to treat for peace and the ephors then gave orders that they should be summoned to Sparta. On their arrival the ephors called an assembly at which many Greek states, and in particular the Corinthians and Thebans, opposed making any peace with Athens. The Athenians, they said, should be destroyed. The Spartans, however, said they would not enslave a Greek city which had done such great things for Greece at the time of her supreme danger. They offered to make peace on the following terms: the Long Walls and the fortifications of Piraeus must be destroyed; all ships except twelve surrendered; the exiles to be recalled; Athens to have the same enemies and the same friends as Sparta had and to follow Spartan leadership in any expedition Sparta might make either by land or sea.

Xenophon, *A History of My Times*, (Hellenica), 2.2, 19–20

✤ ✤ ✤

We come now to a criticism of the Spartan ephoralty, a board of magistrates which enjoys supreme authority in matters of the highest importance. Its members are chosen from the whole people, with the result that very poor men often find themselves elected to an office where their indigence lays them open to bribery. The annals of Sparta contain many such instances, including the recent affair at Andros [It is not certain to what episode Aristotle refers.] when some of the ephors were bribed and did their best to ruin the state. Their power, indeed, is so great, amounting almost to tyranny, that even the kings have been obliged to seek their favour. And in this way, too, not only the royal office, but the constitution as a whole has deteriorated; democracy has superseded aristocracy. It is true, of course, that the ephoralty does hold the state together; their right to share in the highest office keeps the people contented, and this result, whether intended by the legislator or merely accidental, has proved beneficial.

Aristotle, *Politics*, 2.3.4 (1270b)

✤ ✤ ✤

STOP AND THINK
The following tasks are based on your understanding of the information on the Spartan government and constitution. Go back over the introductory table and the supporting documents and work through these tasks.

✎ **Complete this table:**

	Kings	**Gerousia**	**Assembly**	**Ephors**
Eligibility and total number				
Responsibilities				
Political powers				
Judicial powers				
Religious powers				
Privileges or honours				

✎ **List the advantages and disadvantages of membership of each of the bodies under the constitution. Which government body would you wish to be part of? Why?**

✎ In small groups write and present a play where the constitutional processes of the Spartan government are re-enacted. Some guidelines to follow:

- decide on a motion to be voted on
- convene the Gerousia to discuss it and prepare for its presentation
- convene the Assembly
- present the bill to the Assembly
- discuss the bill in the Assembly
- vote on the bill.

What will be the result? Will it be vetoed?

✎ **Use this quote from Aristotle, *The Politics*, 2.2.6 (1265b) as the basis of a discussion. Do you agree with him?**

Some, in fact, hold that the best constitution is a mixture of all existing schemes. This is why they admire the Spartan regime. It is a compound, they say, of oligarchy, monarchy, and democracy; the kings form the monarchical, the council of elders the oligarchical element, while democracy is represented by the ephors, who are chosen from among the people. Others maintain that the ephorality is tyrannical, and that the democratic element is to be found in the system of common meals and the general pattern of everyday life.

✳ ✳ ✳

ECONOMIC AND SOCIAL ORGANISATION

STOP AND THINK: DOCUMENT STUDY
Review the extracts below and answer the questions that follow.

It is agreed that leisure is an essential of every well-ordered state: the citizens must be free from the necessity of supplying their own day-to-day requirements. But it is difficult to see how this can be arranged. The penestae in Thessaly have often risen against their masters, as have the helots against the Spartans, for whose misfortunes they continually lie in wait. Nothing like this has ever happened in Crete, [1269b] for the probable reason that here the neighbouring cities, even when at war with one another, never ally themselves with disaffected serfs, because they themselves have dependent populations and it does them no good to countenance rebellion. But when the helots first revolted, all Sparta's neighbours (Argives, Messenians, Arcadians) were her enemies; and the original revolt of the serfs in Thessaly was due to that country being still at war with the neighbouring Achaeans, Perrhaebians, and Magnesians. Besides, the management of slaves is likely to prove difficult at the best of times. Unless kept in hand, they become insolent and consider themselves as good as their masters; if harshly treated they are embittered and conspire against them. Now results of this kind go to show that a state has yet to learn the right method of handling its subject population.

Aristotle, *The Politics*, Book 2B.1.1 (1296a–b)

✳ ✳ ✳

✎ **Why was Sparta more at risk from an internal revolt than other cities?**

✎ **Using information from earlier in the chapter, what 'essential tasks' would helots free Spartans from?**

In the next place, he declared an outlawry of all needless and superfluous arts; but here he might almost have spared his proclamation; for they of themselves would have gone after the gold and silver, the money which remained being not so proper payment for curious work; for, being of iron, it was scarcely portable, neither, if they should take the means to export it, would it pass amongst the other Greeks, who ridiculed it. So there was now no more means of purchasing foreign goods and small wares; merchants sent no shiploads into Laconian ports; no rhetoric-master, no itinerate fortune-teller, no harlot-monger, or gold or silver-smith, engraver, or jeweller, set foot in a country which had no money; so that luxury, deprived little by little of that which fed and fomented it, wasted to nothing and died away of itself.

Plutarch, *Life of Lycurgus*, 9.4

✽ ✽ ✽

✎ **Why, in Plutarch's view, was it unnecessary for Lycurgus to 'outlaw' 'all needless and superfluous arts'?**

✎ **What happened to luxury in Sparta?**

✎ **What support is there in this passage for any of the modern economic theories for the growing austerity in Sparta?**

STOP AND THINK: DOCUMENT STUDY
Read the extracts from Plutarch and Xenophon below, then complete the tasks that follow.

Lycurgus was of another mind; he would not have masters bought out of the market for his young Spartans, nor such as should sell their pains; nor was it lawful, indeed, for the father himself to breed up the children after his own fancy; but as soon as they were seven years old they were to be enrolled in certain companies and classes, where they all lived under the same order and discipline, doing their exercises and taking their play together. Of these, he who showed the most conduct and courage was made captain; they had their eyes always upon him, obeyed his orders, and underwent patiently whatsoever punishment he inflicted; so that the whole course of their education was one continued exercise of a ready and perfect obedience. The old men, too, were spectators of their performances, and often raised quarrels and disputes among them, to have a good opportunity of finding out their different characters, and of seeing which would be valiant, which a coward, when they should come to more dangerous encounters. Reading and writing they gave them, just enough to serve their turn: their chief care was to make them good subjects, and to teach them to endure pain and conquer in battle. To this end, as they grew in years, their discipline was proportionately increased; their heads were close-clipped, they were accustomed to go barefoot, and for the most part to play naked.

Plutarch, *Life of Lycurgus*, 16.1–6

✽ ✽ ✽

I recall the astonishment with which I first noted the unique position of Sparta among the states of Hellas, the relatively sparse population, and at the same time the extraordinary power and prestige of the community . . .

Take, for example — and it is well to begin at the beginning — the whole topic of the begetting and rearing of children. Throughout the rest of the world the young girl, who will one day become a mother (and I speak of those who may be held to be well brought up), is nurtured on the plainest food attainable, with the scantiest addition of meat or other condiments; while as to wine they train them either to total abstinence or to take it highly diluted with water. And in imitation, as it were, of the handicraft type, since the majority of artificers are sedentary, we, the rest of the Hellenes, are content that our girls should sit quietly and work wools. This is all we demand of them. But how are we to expect that women nurtured in this fashion should produce a splendid offspring?

Lykourgos pursued a different path. Clothes were things, he held, the furnishing of which might well enough be left to female slaves. And, believing that the highest function of a free woman was the bearing of children, in the first place he insisted on the training of the body as incumbent no less on the female than on the male; and in pursuit of the same idea he instituted contests in running and feats of strength for women as for men. His belief was that where both parents were strong their progeny would be found to be more vigorous.

And so again after marriage. In view of the fact that immoderate intercourse is elsewhere permitted during the earlier period of matrimony, he adopted a principle directly opposite. He laid it down as an ordinance that a man should be ashamed to be seen visiting the chamber of his wife, whether going in or coming out. When they did meet under such restraint the mutual longing of these lovers could not but be increased, and the fruit which might spring from such intercourse would tend to be more robust than theirs whose affections are cloyed by satiety. By a further step in the same direction he refused to allow marriages to be contracted at any period of life according to the fancy of the parties concerned. Marriage, as he ordained it, must only take place in the prime of bodily vigor, this too being, as he believed, a condition conducive to the production of healthy offspring. Or, in the case of an old man wedded to a young wife, considering the jealous watch which such husbands are apt to keep over their wives, he introduced a directly opposite custom; that is to say, he made it incumbent on the aged husband to introduce some one whose qualities, physical and moral, he admired, to play the husband's part and to beget him children. Or again, in the case of a man who might not desire to live with a wife permanently, but yet might be anxious to have children of his own worthy the name, the lawgiver laid down a law in his behalf; such an one might select some woman, the wife of some man, well born herself and blest with fair offspring, and, the sanction and consent of her husband first obtained, raise up children for himself through her.

These and many other adaptations of a like sort the lawgiver sanctioned. As, for instance, at Sparta a wife will not object to bear the burden of a double establishment, or a husband to adopt sons as foster-brothers of his own children, with a full share in his family and position, but possessing no claim to his wealth and property.

So opposed to those of the rest of the world are the principles which Lykourgos devised in reference to the production of children. Whether they enabled him to provide Sparta with a race of men superior to all in size and strength I leave to the judgment of whomsoever it may concern.

After this exposition of the customs in connection with the birth of children, I wish now to explain the systems of education in fashion here and elsewhere. Throughout the rest of Hellas the custom on the part of those who claim to educate their sons in the best way is as follows. As soon as the children are of an age to understand what is said to them they are immediately placed under the charge of paidagogoi, who are also attendants, and are sent off to the school of some teacher to be taught grammar, music, and the concerns of the palestra. Besides this they are given shoes to wear which tend to make their feet tender, and their bodies are enervated by various changes of clothing. As for food, the only measure recognized is that which is fixed by appetite.

But when we turn to Lykourgos, instead of leaving it to each member of the state privately to appoint a slave to be his son's tutor, he set over the young Spartans a public guardian, the paidonomos (educator) as he is called, with complete authority over them. This guardian was selected from those who filled the highest magistracies. He had authority to hold musters of the boys, and as their overseer, in case of any misbehaviour, to chastise severely. The legislator further provided the educator with a body of youths in the prime of life and bearing whips, to inflict punishment when necessary, with this happy result that in Sparta modesty and obedience ever go hand in hand, nor is there lack of either.

Instead of softening their feet with shoe or sandal, his rule was to make them hardy through going barefoot. This habit if practised would, as he believed, enable them to scale heights more easily and clamber down precipices with less danger. In fact, with his feet so trained the young Spartan would leap and spring and run faster unshod than another shod in the ordinary way.

Instead of making them effeminate with a variety of clothes, his rule was to habituate them to a single garment the whole year through, thinking that so they would be better prepared to withstand the variations of heat and cold.

Again, as regards food, he counseled such moderation as to avoid that heaviness which is engendered by repletion, and yet not to remain altogether unacquainted with the pains of penurious living. His belief was that by such training in boyhood they would be better able when occasion demanded to continue toiling on an empty stomach. They would be all the fitter, if the word of command were given, to remain for a long stretch without extra dieting. The craving for luxuries would be less, the readiness to take any victual set before them greater, and in general the regimen would be found more healthy; under it they would increase in stature since, as he maintained, a diet which gave suppleness to the limbs must be more beneficial than one which added thickness to the bodily parts by feeding.

On the other hand, in order to guard against a too great pinch of starvation, though he did not actually allow the boys to help themselves without further trouble to what more they needed, he did give them permission to steal this thing or that in the effort to alleviate their hunger. It was certainly not from any real difficulty of supplying them with nutriment that he left them to provide themselves by this crafty method, nor can I conceive that any one will so misinterpret the custom. Clearly its explanation lies in the fact that he who would live the life of a robber must forgo sleep by night, and in the daytime he must employ shifts and lie in ambuscade; he must prepare and make ready his scouts, and so forth, if he is to succeed in capturing the quarry.

It is obvious that the whole of this education tended, and was intended, to make the boys craftier and more inventive in getting supplies, while at the same time it cultivated their warlike instincts. An objector may retort: 'But if he thought it so fine a feat to steal, why did he inflect all those blows on the unfortunate who was caught?' My answer is: for the selfsame reason which induces people, in other matters which are taught, to punish the malperformance of a service. So they, the Spartans, visit penalties on the boy who is detected thieving as being but a sorry bungler in the art. So to steal as many cheeses as possible was a feat to be encouraged; but, at the same moment, others were enjoined to scourge the thief, which would point a moral not obscurely, that by pain endured for a brief season a man may earn the joyous reward of lasting glory. Herein, too, it is plainly shown that where speed is requisite the sluggard will win for himself much trouble and scant good.

Furthermore, and in order that the boys should not want a guide even if the paidonomos himself were absent, he gave to any citizen who chanced to be present authority to lay upon them injunctions for their good, and to chastise them for any trespass committed. By so doing he created in the boys of Sparta a rare modesty. And indeed there is nothing which, whether as boys or men, they respect more highly than these guides. Lastly, and with the same intention, that the boys must never be without a guide, he laid down the rule that, if by chance there were no grown man present, the sharpest of the twenty-year-olds was to serve as guide of each group. Thus the boys of Sparta are never without a guide.

Xenophon, *Constitution of the Spartans*, 1, 2

* * *

On Spartan women, education and marriage:
- **What was the difference, according to Xenophon, between the upbringing of women in Sparta as opposed to other Greek cities? What was the purpose of the Spartan method?**
- **Why and how did Lycurgus make it difficult for newly married Spartan men and women to meet?**
- **What controls were there over the age of marriage?**
- **From these passages, what appears to be the prime purpose of a Spartan woman?**
- **Even though what was expected of Spartan women may seem quite foreign or even unacceptable to us today, it was common practice for many of them. Think carefully about Sparta and its people and write a speech that might have been delivered by a Spartan woman in support of these State ideals.**
- **Write a dialogue between a Spartan woman and an Athenian woman which presents the differences and similarities in their lives. You will need to research.**

On Spartan education:
- **For each aspect of education drawn from the sources and listed below, write a statement underneath explaining its purpose.**

Children were not to be educated by masters bought out of the market.

_____
_____

Children were not to be educated by their parents.

_____
_____

Children were removed from families at age seven and enrolled in companies where they lived according to strict guidelines.

_____
_____

The captain of the company had great power over each member.

_____
_____

Elderly Spartans often 'raised quarrels and disputes' among the young Spartans.

_____

_____

Young Spartans' hair was close cropped; they were accustomed to being barefoot; they played naked.

_____

_____

- **Explain the following quote from Plutarch: 'Reading and writing they gave them, just enough to serve their turn . . . '**
- **Draw up your own brief comparative table on the education of the Athenians and the Spartans. (You will need to do some research to compare them.)**
- **Look closely at the language used by Plutarch and Xenophon. Find examples of language which indicate the objectivity and/or bias of the author.**

Research Essay

Using the ancient sources from pages 69–73 as a guide, prepare a project using primary written and archaeological sources, as well as secondary sources, on the life of the ancient Spartans. Focus on:

- **the social classes**
- **education**
- **housing and family life**
- **status of women**
- **military service.**

DEBUNKING MYTHS

THE MYTH OF LYCURGUS

Ancient sources describe Lycurgus as a real figure and they place him and his reforms deep in Spartan antiquity. Such a myth is clearly not sustained by modern research. At best modern scholars refer to Lycurgus as a 'shadowy figure' (Forrest) or even a Spartan invention (Beloch). Modern historians do dispute the date of Lycurgan reforms, whether they were the product of a single figure or a group. N.G.L. Hammond argues for 800 BC, K.J. Beloch supports 550 BC, while W.G. Forrest suggests dates around 600 or 675 BC. Forrest supports his view by pointing out that writing had not been rediscovered in Greece until c. 750 BC and thinks it is unlikely that a detailed constitution could have been prepared before that time.

There is so much doubt about Lycurgus that even if such a figure existed, there is not enough evidence to credit him with the creation of the Spartan system.

The ancient Greeks in arguing for the legendary Lycurgus cite dates from c. 1100 to 776 BC. If they are right and Lycurgus did all they claim, then why is the claim for Lycurgan austerity in Sparta from c. 1100 BC or c. 776 BC directly contradicted by the archaeological evidence that shows art, poetry and culture flourishing long after the ancient scholars claim they vanished?

STOP AND THINK: RESEARCH
Find out as much as you can about the legendary figure of Lycurgus. Draw up two columns: on the left list the facts, things we know for certain about him, and on the right list the speculation, areas of doubt. Examine the completed lists. What conclusions do you draw from them as a historian about Lycurgus and our knowledge of him?

THE MYTH THAT THE SPARTAN SYSTEM WAS CREATED TO PREVENT A HELOT REVOLT

Clearly military strength to protect Sparta against threats, both internal and external, was a significant causal factor in the evolution of the Spartan system. However, to isolate Sparta from developments in the rest of Greece and to isolate a single cause for so significant an event are unsound historically.

Throughout Greece in the seventh and sixth centuries BC economic changes produced political change. Aristocracies challenged old monarchies and the aristocracies were in turn challenged by new merchant and commercial classes. To deny that similar elements had a part in the Spartan reforms is unrealistic.

One of the most significant changes in Greece was the emergence of hoplite warfare (see pages 52–54). Many scholars including Antony Andrewes argue that this new style of fighting diminished the power and influence of the old aristocracies, leading to political change and the appearance of tyranny. Even though it is acknowledged that Sparta did not become a tyranny, John Salmon and Paul Cartledge, in important articles in the *Journal of Hellenic Studies* in 1977, indicated that economic factors and hoplite warfare could have influenced the Spartan political changes of the period.

It would be foolish to ignore the significance of Spartan fears of a helot revolt, but it would also be irresponsible to ignore the presence of other, contributing causal factors. To ignore the range of interacting elements in a causal mix is to perpetuate a kind of historical myth.

THE MYTH THAT SPARTAN CULTURE DISAPPEARED BOTH EARLY IN ITS HISTORY AND SUDDENLY

Archaeological evidence from the dig at Artemis Orthia clearly debunks the myth of Spartan austerity before the middle of the sixth century BC. More significantly, however, the work of L.F. Fitzhardinge, among others, establishes that Spartan culture eroded slowly; it did not vanish suddenly as we might assume from ancient accounts of the prohibition of luxury.

Fitzhardinge marshals an impressive array of evidence, for example:

- painted pottery of the highest quality was found dating from c.630 BC down to c.500 BC,
- terracottas of good quality were found dating from c. 650 BC,
- fine sculpture in marble and other stone was found dating from c. 650 BC to 500 BC,
- ivory and bone carving was found and dated down to c. 600 BC,
- bronze work and small lead figures were found down to 550 BC.

Peasant boy riding a horse
Cup from the workshop of Euphronios c. 500 BC

Terracotta mask showing an old woman

Mourning youth from Yeraki

Bone relief of Orthia

Soldier from Dodona

The presence of these items reflects a sense of culture, even luxury, and a consumer's instinct at odds with the ancient sources. The archaeological evidence also indicates a gradual withering away of crafts, not a sudden stop. This has led scholars such as A.J. Halladay to speculate about the cause. Was the death of Spartan culture due to government edict, dislocation of trade, or poverty? J.T. Hooker often refers to Spartan propaganda and it should not be ignored as an element in sustaining the myth that Sparta was austere by choice rather than economic circumstances.

THE MYTH OF SPARTIATE EQUALITY

Spartan propaganda and the biased accounts of ancient writers who saw Sparta as a model of good and stable government created this myth. Any careful review of the written and the archaeological evidence yields examples of inequalities. Equality, through education and the public masses, may have been the ideal but it was not the reality. Not all Spartiates had land of equal quality or productivity; therefore, not all Spartiates had equality of resources.

CONCLUSION

The lesson to be learnt from our on-going investigation of Sparta is the fact that it is on-going. Reviews of past assumptions need to be constantly made in the light of new theories and new evidence. The methodology of ancient history is a constant quest for a clearer picture of the past. An assessment of written and archaeological remains must function together, to test, and then to contradict or verify conclusions.

LIST OF REFERENCES

ANCIENT SOURCES

Aristotle, *The Politics and Athenian Constitution*, ed. and tr. John Warrington, Dent, London, 1959

Herodotus, *The Histories*, tr. Aubrey de Sélincourt, Penguin Classics, 1972

Pausanias, *Description of Greece*, tr. J.G. Frazer, Biblo & Tanner, New York, 1965

Plutarch, *Lives*, Loeb Classical Library, Heinemann, 1926.

Thucydides, *The Peloponnesian War*, tr. Rex Warner, Penguin Classics, 1954 repr. 1980

Xenophon, 'Constitution of the Spartans' in Lewis, Naphtali, *Greek Historical Documents, The Fifth Century B.C.*, A.M. Hakkert Ltd, Toronto, 1971

——— *A History of My Times (Hellenica)*, tr. Rex Warner, Penguin, 1966 repr. 1986

SECONDARY SOURCES

Andrewes, Antony, *Greek Society*, Penguin, 1967 repr. 1979

Barrow, R., *Sparta*, George Allen & Unwin, London, 1975

Cartledge, Paul, *Sparta and Lakonia: a regional history 1300–362 B.C.*, Routledge & Kegan Paul, London, 1979

Fitzhardinge, L.F., *The Spartans*, Thames & Hudson, London, 1980

Forrest, W.G., *History of Sparta*, 2nd ed, Duckworth, London, 1980

Hammond, N.G.L., *A History of Greece to 322 B.C.*, 2nd ed, Clarendon Press, Oxford, 1967

Hooker, J.T., *The Ancient Spartans*, Dent, London, 1980

Jones, A.H.M., *Sparta*, Blackwell, Oxford, 1967

CHAPTER FIVE

THE PERSIAN WARS

JANE AND BRUCE DENNETT

INTRODUCTION

Between 559 BC and 539 BC the Achaemenid Dynasty in Persia had gradually established a formidable empire. By 540 BC the Persian ruler Cyrus had brought the Ionian Greek cities of Asia Minor under his control. These events brought the Greeks and the Persians into contact for the first time and eventually led to conflict between the European Greek states and the mighty eastern empire. In 499 BC the Greek cities on the coast of Asia Minor attempted to throw off Persia's despotic rule. The revolt was ended with difficulty in 494 BC. Soon afterwards the Persians began a series of campaigns to subdue the city-states on the Greek mainland and make European Greece part of the Persian empire. In 492 BC a possible invasion was thwarted when a Persian fleet was severely damaged by storm off the coast near Mt Athos. Two years later the Persians tried again, only to be surprisingly defeated at the Battle of Marathon. Unrest within the empire delayed Persia's last and most determined bid to conquer Greece until 480 BC. Between 480 and 479 BC there were a number of battles. The Persians had a costly victory at Thermopylae, Artemisium was indecisive, then the Greeks triumphed with victories at Salamis, Plataea and Mycale.

Although this was one of the most famous periods of Greek history and one that has attracted a great deal of attention from scholars, both ancient and modern, there are still many aspects of the Persian Wars that are open to speculation. One of the difficulties in obtaining a completely accurate version of the Persian Wars stems from the Greek tendency to glorify and mythologise events. The Greeks used the conflict as the foundation for inspirational lessons for later generations. These motives and the influence of hindsight tend to cloud the truth. Historians not only argue about the exact location of battles, but about the size of armies and motives behind many of the actions on both sides. Investigation of areas of disagreement and uncertainty demands a careful review of both the archaeological remains and the written sources available to us.

 How did the Greeks manage to survive against the might of the Persian empire?

 What really happened at Marathon, Salamis and the other famous battles?

ARCHAEOLOGICAL SOURCES

The body of archaeological evidence on the period of the Persian Wars provides a significant proportion of our information. Sources are in the form of reliefs, paintings and inscriptions on temples, tombs, memorials and palaces. Coins, designs on pots, the study of battle sites and the Athenian burial mound have also yielded valuable information.

RELIEFS

Carvings or mouldings that stand out from the surface of walls in the Persian palaces of Susa and Persepolis depict noblemen, officials bearing tribute and images of the 'Immortals', the 10 000-strong elite guard of the Persian army. These reliefs and the well-preserved palace at Persepolis are very useful.

The reliefs show tribute-bearers bringing offerings to the 'Great King', the Persian ruler, from all parts of the far-flung empire. The image of these tribute-bearers reflects the extensive and demanding system of taxation imposed by Persian kings on their conquered subjects.

Relief images also capture the appearance and armament of the finest Persian troops, the 'Immortals'. Excavation of their barracks at Susa confirms their special status; an unusually large number of wine bottles was unearthed and this find appears to corroborate the works of ancient writers such as Herodotus, who refers to them going to war with servants, concubines and special provisions.

Evidence for distinctions within the Persian forces is important, because it seems that the Immortals and the cavalry were the only troops of real 'quality' in the army. The remainder relied strictly on 'quantity', weight of numbers, since both their training and armament appear to have been poor. Images on pots, paintings and statues of Greek soldiers, the heavily armoured hoplites, abound. These provide valuable insights into many of the battles and the tactics favoured by the Greeks.

STOP AND THINK: EXAMINING EVIDENCE

Examine the pictures on the opposite page carefully.

 List the most obvious differences in weapons and armour between the two.

 Which of the two would, in your opinion, be better suited to fighting at close quarters in confined spaces? Why?

A Greek hoplite (above) and an immortal

PAINTINGS AND INSCRIPTIONS

Among the earliest archaeological sources providing evidence of the battle of Marathon in 490 BC is a picture in the Poecile Stoa in the Agora in Athens. It seems to have been a tribute to the warriors of Marathon and depicts three phases of the battle. The work is attributed to Micon and Paeanus and is dated around 460 BC.

ATHENIAN EPIGRAMS

An indication of the controversy that can arise with archaeological evidence becomes obvious when we consider the two famous Athenian epigrams. Classified by archaeologists as inscription A and B, these couplets were uncovered in the late nineteenth century. Initially both were thought to refer to Marathon; however, work by B.D. Merit in the 1950s indicates that the lettering for inscription A is dated around 485–470 BC, while B is dated between 475 and 460 BC. The most likely explanation appears to be that inscription A celebrated Greek valour in the second Persian War (480–479 BC), while inscription B was added later as a tribute to the Athenians at Marathon in the first Persian War. This view is based upon an examination of linguistic differences and emphasis. There is also a theory that inscription B was added for political reasons to remind Athenians of the greatness of Miltiades, the hero of Marathon. Miltiades' son Cimon was actively involved in Athenian politics at the time and such a reference would aid his cause.

SERPENT COLUMN

After their victory at Plataea the Greeks made an offering to the god Apollo at Delphi. It took the form of a golden tripod of three intertwined serpents on top of a bronze column. The column was taken to Constantinople many years later by the Roman emperor Constantine, where it survives today. Some of the original inscriptions on the column were removed but we can still read a list of the Greek cities that took part in the second Persian War under the heading 'These fought the war'. The inscriptions have been used as clues to the membership and relationships of cities within the Hellenic League of 481 BC, an alliance formed by the Greeks to meet the Persian threat.

TROEZEN INSCRIPTION

An inscription on a marble slab found in the 1930s came to prominence in 1959 through the work of Professor M. Jameson. The inscription itself was dated to the third century BC and was meant to be a copy of a decree by the Athenian leader Themistocles in the fifth century BC. If reliable, this find would change our interpretation of many of the key events of the second Persian War. Before 1959 the Athenian decision to evacuate their city after the Persian victory at Thermopylae was thought to be an emergency measure taken in haste after an unexpected defeat and in the face of the rapidly advancing Persians. This is the view presented by the famous Greek historian Herodotus. However, if the Troezen Inscription and its Themistocles Decree is reliable, then the evacuation of Athens was planned well in advance and indicates the view that Themistocles, at least, did not expect the Greeks to hold Thermopylae. We must also conclude therefore that Themistocles anticipated the great naval battle of Salamis.

There is considerable argument between historians about the authenticity of the Troezen Inscription and hence about which version of events after Thermopylae is the most accurate. This is clearly one of the most delicate areas of historical investigation. There is no dispute about the essential facts: the Athenians did evacuate their city; it was occupied and burned by the Persians; and a major Greek naval victory did follow at Salamis. These facts, however, are not the issue — the question is one of motives, plans and intentions and these, understandably, are far more difficult to determine.

COINS

A number of coins are also available for study with inscriptions and images that commemorate aspects of the Persian Wars.

TEMPLES AND MEMORIALS

The Athenian victory at Marathon was marked by building a treasury at Delphi with reliefs that are well preserved. The Greeks also apparently laid the foundations for a temple on the Acropolis that was never completed.

BATTLE SITES

A study of each of the main battlefields from an archaeological and a topographical point of view can provide valuable insight for the historian. N.G.L. Hammond in particular, among the modern scholars, has made frequent use of each of the areas of research in the examinations of the battles of Marathon and Salamis. For example, Hammond draws conclusions about the site of the battle of Marathon and the disposition of troops from the Athenians' funeral mound and significant finds of large numbers of Persian arrowheads.

Hammond's views on these battles will be considered later, but his methodology provides a useful model for the young scholar. Hammond attempts to relate and cross-check the archaeological and topographical evidence, such as the relief on the Poecile Stoa, with the Athenian epigrams and the accounts from the ancient authors. He considers when they appear to be compatible and when they are contradictory.

WRITTEN SOURCES

There are a number of useful written works on the Persian Wars and they should be considered not only in their own right but against the work of the archaeologist.

HERODOTUS

He wrote his work *The Histories* within fifty years of the events in question. Herodotus had access to a great oral tradition about the Persian Wars.

There were still many witnesses and participants available for interview. In large part, Herodotus' account is a synthesis of those recollections. His work has all the strengths and weaknesses that you might imagine come with such an approach to gathering information: pro-Athenian bias, selective or faulty memory on one side, first-hand experience. Herodotus is generally reliable when it comes to the principal events, even though he is prone to exaggerate the size of the Persian armies brought against Greece. He is not, however, as useful when it comes to analysis, particularly his judgements about causes for events or tactics in battles. Herodotus follows the Greek tradition of explaining causes in terms of a 'just grievance' by pointing to the events that occur on each side to generate the excuses for action, rather than looking for the deeper causes. Therefore Herodotus' views on 'causation' tend to be superficial. This weakness is, nevertheless, counterbalanced by the fact that Herodotus was an Ionian Greek, born at Halicarnassus on the coast of Asia Minor, on the fringes of the Persian empire. This contact provided him with an excellent background in Persian history and culture.

PLUTARCH

He wrote his most significant accounts of the Persian Wars and the leading figures, such as Themistocles, several centuries after the conflict. Nevertheless he is a capable historian and is likely to have had access to material left by some very early Attic historians, known as the Atthidographers.

AESCHYLUS

He was a notable Athenian playwright. His famous work *Persae* or *The Persians* deals with the Greek victory at Salamis. Aeschylus experienced both Persian Wars firsthand: he fought at Marathon and, at the very least, was a witness to Salamis. His play includes a detailed account of Salamis, even though there are a few discrepancies between his version and that provided by Herodotus. Overall, Aeschylus' real value is as an insight into the Athenian mind and the Athenians' view of themselves and their world. Aeschylus is inclined to exaggerate the events associated with Salamis and we must be careful not to take all his claims literally. His focus on Athens' role in defeating Xerxes by ignoring the other states and the other battles that were part of the second Persian War is conscious and determined and we must be aware of it.

BACKGROUND TO THE PERSIAN WARS

THE RISE OF PERSIA

Under a series of strong and capable rulers, Cyrus, Cambyses and Darius, Persia had become one of the most powerful and extensive empires in the history of the ancient world. Persian dominance extended over the Greek cities of Asia Minor, where they appointed local tyrants and levied taxes. Persian influence also spread in stages to some of the Ionian Greek islands of the Aegean: Samos, Cheos and Lesbos. According to Herodotus political contacts were also made with mainland Greek cities, including Athens and Sparta.

By about 520 BC the Persian empire extended from Libya in the west to the borders of India in the east, and from the Black Sea in the north to Arabia in the south. In 472 BC Aeschylus goes to some lengths to list the size and variety of the Persian hordes descending upon Greece, but it remains unlikely that the Greeks ever really understood the real might of the empire that attacked them.

The Persian ruler, the Great King, did not attempt to administer the day-to-day affairs of so vast a realm. Instead the empire was divided into a series of almost autonomous provinces, known as *satrapies*, of which there were approximately twenty, each ruled by a *satrap*. (The word translated as protector or defender of the kingdom.) Although they were largely independent, they were still subject to visits from the Great King's inspectors. In war each satrap was required to raise and lead an army; in peace he had to maintain law and order and levy taxes.

IONIAN REVOLT

The Ionian Greeks of Asia Minor were recognised as among the most cultured, politically aware and sophisticated of people. Major cities such as Miletas, Priene, Phocaea and Cyme were centres of commerce, literature, philosophy and science.

There are a number of possible theories concerning the causes of a revolt of the Ionian cities in 499 BC:

- Herodotus implies that there were internal disputes among the leading Greek political figures in a number of cities and that these disputes contributed to the revolt by focusing the discontent of some on the nature of their government. Persian control was the most obvious aspect of that administration.
- One very popular theory was that the Ionians rebelled because of their hatred of tyranny. The philosophical and political sophistication of many Ionian writers and thinkers supports this view. However, the fact that once the revolt had begun most cities allowed their tyrants to go free raises doubts about the intensity of their hostility to tyranny.

- Persia had a tradition of firm, and in some cases harsh, taxation demands. In Ionia however their administration does not appear to have been unreasonable.
- The spread of Athenian pottery towards the close of the sixth century has led to speculation about the economic and commercial decline of some Ionian city states. If this was the case, discontent and frustration could understandably have boiled over into violence and rebellion. It would have been easy for the Ionian Greeks to blame the Persians for their problems.

STOP AND THINK: RESEARCH EXERCISE

Make a list in point form of the key events of the Ionian Revolt of 499–494 BC.

The Ionians were finally defeated in 494 BC with the fall of Miletus. It had been no easy task — there were a number of major battles including a large naval engagement at Lade in 494 BC. This resulted in a Persian victory and should be remembered as we go on to consider later conflicts between the Greeks and Persians.

PERSIAN EYES TURN TO GREECE

Herodotus, displaying the concept of 'just grievance', suggests that Persian plans to invade Greece were the result of a series of violent actions and reactions, not the least of which was the support offered to the Ionians by European Greek city states such as Athens and Eretria.

STOP AND THINK: DOCUMENT STUDY

During the Ionian Revolt an Athenian force supported the revolt briefly and took part in the burning of the Persian-controlled city of Sardis.
  Read the two extracts and answer the questions that follow.

In the conflagration at Sardis a temple of Cybebe, a goddess worshipped in that part of the world, was destroyed, and the Persians later made this a pretext for their burning of Greek temples...
  After this battle the Athenians would have nothing more to do with the Ionian rebellion, and in spite of frequent appeals from Aristagoras refused to help him. But the Ionians, in view of the injury they had already done Darius, pressed on the war with no less vigour, even without Athenian aid.

Herodotus, *The Histories*, 5, 104

✦ ✦ ✦

. . . news was brought to Darius that Sardis had been taken and burnt by the Athenians and Ionians, and that the prime mover in the joint enterprise was Aristagoras of Miletus. The story goes that when Darius learnt of the disaster, he did not give a thought to the Ionians, knowing perfectly well that the punishment for their revolt would come; but he asked who the Athenians were, and then, on being told, called for his bow. He took it, set an arrow on the string, shot it up into the air and cried: 'Grant, O God, that I may punish the Athenians'. Then he commanded one of his servants to repeat to him the words, 'Master, remember the Athenians', three times, whenever he sat down to dinner.

Herodotus, *The Histories*, 5, 105

✳ ✳ ✳

✎ **From the two extracts select three quotes that best illustrate Herodotus' argument that the attempted invasions of Greece would be acts of revenge?**

✎ **From the second extract, which Ionian city supported Athens in burning Sardis?**

✎ **What was Darius' attitude to the possible result of the revolt?**

✎ **How do these extracts support Herodotus' concept of 'just grievances'?**

In 492 BC what may have been an invasion attempt led by Darius' son-in-law, Mardonius, ended when his fleet was severely damaged by storm off the coast of Chalcidice near Mt Athos. Herodotus claims that the objective of this fleet was the punishment of Athens and Eretria.

WHY THE PERSIANS ATTACKED GREECE

Herodotus is quite definite about his view of the underlying causes for the Persian campaigns against Greece in 490 and 480–79 BC — revenge. In 490 BC it was revenge for intervention in the Ionian revolt; in 480–79 BC it was revenge, the 'just grievances' in Persian eyes, for the defeat suffered at the hands of Athenian hoplites at Marathon.

STOP AND THINK: DOCUMENT STUDY

Examine the extract from Herodotus and answer the questions that follow:

When the news of the battle of Marathon reached Darius, son of Hystaspes and king of Persia, his anger against Athens, already great enough on account of the assault on Sardis, was even greater, and he was more than ever determined to make war on Greece. Without loss of time he dispatched couriers to the various states under his dominion with orders to raise an army much larger than before; and also warships, transports, horses, and grain. So the royal command went round; and all Asia was in an uproar for three years, with the best men being enrolled in the army for the invasion of Greece . . .

Herodotus, *The Histories*, 7, 1–2

✳ ✳ ✳

✎ **What are the two Persian grievances referred to?**

✎ **How does the passage give the impression that Darius took these events personally?**

✎ **How does the extract reflect Darius' determination to punish Greece?**

✎ **Write out the speech that Darius might have delivered to the messenger who brought the news of the Persian defeat at Marathon. Try to show his emotions in the speech.**

Even though there is a place for Herodotus' view of the reasons for Persian aggression, some alternative factors need to be considered, for example:

- the pattern of Persian history and the values exhibited by the Persian ruling class appeared to value conquest. When this is linked with a steadily growing Persian awareness of the Greeks and their skills as engineers, builders, artisans, scientists, and doctors, European Greece may have become an attractive target.
- some historians argue that the Scythian expedition that added Thrace to Persia's empire back in 514 BC reflected an interest in opening a land route that might one day be used for an invasion of Greece.
- it is possible that the Persian empire, through its rulers, had come to assume that growth and expansion was a natural state. Acquisition had become the norm, an ingrained tendency. Expansion of the empire had gained a certain momentum and that energy was directed at the apparently divided and vulnerable European Greeks.

THE FIRST PERSIAN WAR AND MARATHON, 490 BC

Historical evidence about the internal political situation in Athens at this time is limited; however, the factionalism that was often so apparent in later

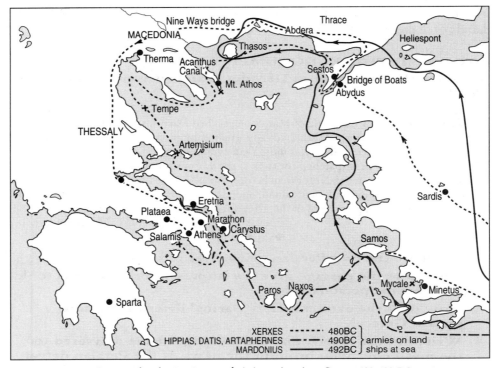

Routes taken by Persians on their incursions into Greece 492–480 BC

years was common. The Athenian policy of hostility towards Persia does not appear to be a reflection of any specific or planned foreign policy. One element that might have contributed to Athenian animosity was the fact that her hated local rival, Aegina, was seen as a Persian ally.

The Persian invasion advanced on Marathon by sea taking Naxos, Carystus and finally Eretria — which was besieged for six days until it was betrayed from within — on the way. It is estimated that the Persians had about 20 000 troops, including 800 cavalry. The Persians may have selected Marathon, north of Athens, as their landing place for a variety of reasons:

- it was the nearest point of land, after leaving Eretria on the island of Euboea for the Greek peninsula, that offered an easy route to Athens.
- there was a beach suitable for landing, good water and pasture for the horses.
- some historians suggest that Hippias, a former tyrant of Athens, who was now part of the Persian camp, suggested the landing site in the hope that he might find support among the Greeks of eastern Attica.

THE BATTLE

When news reached Athens concerning the Persian advance, the Greeks marched out to meet the invader. This appears to have been an unusual step, and it is likely that this action was prompted, at least in part, by Athenian fears that they might be betrayed from within as the Eretrians had been. By the time they reached Marathon the Athenians knew that there would be no immediate aid from Sparta. A messenger had returned saying that the Spartan force would be delayed due to a religious festival.

The Athenian commander was the polemarch Callimachus. However, one of the other ten strategoi (military leaders) was Miltiades, strongly praised by Herodotus for his leadership and the victory. Once at Marathon the Persians held their place on the plain, while the Athenians kept to the high ground between the invaders and Athens. Both sides held these positions for seventeen days before battle was joined. Details of the battle itself are not really in dispute: Herodotus' account (set out below) is compatible with the archaeological picture in the Poecile Stoa. Herodotus' account would also have been read and, if necessary, challenged by Marathon veterans.

STOP AND THINK: DOCUMENT STUDY
Read Herodotus' account of the battle and answer the questions below.

The struggle at Marathon was long drawn out. In the centre, held by the Persians themselves and the Sacae, the advantage was with the foreigners, who were so far successful as to break the Greek line and pursue the fugitives inland from the sea; but the Athenians on one wing and the Plataeans on the other were both victorious. Having got the upper hand, they left the defeated enemy to make their escape, and then, drawing the two wings together into a single unit, they turned their attention to the Persians who had broken through in the centre. Here again they were triumphant, chasing the routed enemy, and cutting them down until they came to the sea, and men were calling for fire and taking hold of the ships. It was in this phase of the struggle that the War Archon Callimachus was killed, fighting bravely, and also Stesilaus, the son of Thrasylaus, one of the generals; Cynegirus, too, the son of Euphorion, had his hand cut off with an axe as he was getting hold of a ship's stern, and so lost his life, together with many other well-known Athenians. The Athenians secured in this way seven ships; but the rest got off, and the Persians aboard them, after picking up the Eretrian prisoners whom they had left on Aegilia, laid a course round Sunium for Athens, which they hoped to reach in advance of the Athenian army. In Athens the Alcmaeonidae were accused of suggesting this move; they had, it was said, an understanding with the Persians, and raised a shield as a signal to them when they were already on board.

While the Persian fleet was on its way round Sunium, the Athenians hurried back with all possible speed to save their city, and succeeded in reaching it before the arrival of the Persians. Just as at Marathon the Athenian camp had been a plot of ground sacred to Heracles, so now they fixed their camp on another, also sacred to the same god, at Cynosarges. When the Persian fleet appeared, it lay at anchor for a while off Phalerum (at that time the chief harbour of Athens) and then sailed for Asia.

In the battle of Marathon some 6400 Persians were killed; the losses of the Athenians were 192.

Herodotus, *The Histories*, 6, 115–116

✳ ✳ ✳

> ✎ **Summarise in your own words the stages of the battle as described by Herodotus.**
> ✎ **Where did the Persian ships go after the battle?**
> ✎ **What were the Persian and the Athenian losses in the battle?**
> ✎ **What evidence from the passage might be said to justify Athenian fears of betrayal from within?**

To match the length of the Persian line, since they were outnumbered at least two to one, the Athenians deliberately thinned the centre of their line. As the Persians advanced, the Athenian centre gave ground, but the Athenian troops moved forward and then turned in on the centre. The Persians now faced encirclement; they began to flee and were pursued to the boats.

Although few of the facts about the phases of the battle itself are in dispute, historical controversy about Marathon still exists. The main areas of dispute are:

SITE OF THE MAIN CLASH OF ARMS

The modern scholar N.G.L. Hammond argues that the main clash of arms and the site of most casualties is marked by the Athenian funeral mound at Marathon. He suggests that this is where the Persians broke through the Athenian centre. He uses the archaeological finds produced by the excavation of the mound. Hammond believes that when the Athenian centre gave way this was the site of most of their casualties. He also points to a number of Persian arrowheads found near the mound that helps support his view.

Another modern scholar A.R. Burn argues that most of the fighting and most of the casualties were suffered after the Athenian encircling man-oeuvre had begun and as the Persians retreated to the boats. Burn points to the fact that Herodotus lists most of the Greek casualties at the fighting for the boats.

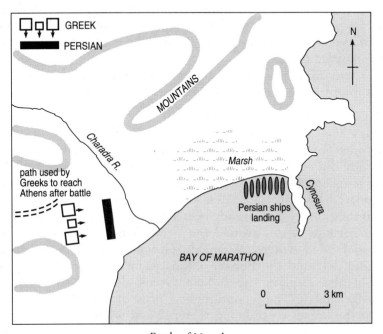

Battle of Marathon

DISPOSITION OF THE GREEK AND PERSIAN FORCES

There are two possible views about the alignment of both sides at Mara-thon. The most widely accepted view has both sides at right angles to the sea. Hammond's view, however, has the Persians with their backs to the sea and the Athenians facing them. Hammond's view is based upon the line from Herodotus (appearing in the immediately preceding extract) where he says the fugitives from the broken Greek centre were pursued inland from the sea.

WHY DELAY SEVENTEEN DAYS?

Athenian side   Herodotus claimed that the Greeks were waiting until it was Miltiades' turn to take charge. He cites a tradition of alternating command. However, it is possible that this tradition was not in use at the time of Marathon. Furthermore Callimachus appeared quite willing to cooperate and heed Miltiades' advice; hence there was no reason to wait for Miltiades' day of command, if such a procedure actually existed.

An alternative may have been the Athenian hope that the Spartans might still arrive as promised, following their delay for religious reasons.

Finally, the Athenians appeared ready to bide their time until circumstances changed.

Persian side   As you will have noted from the exercise on page 80, the Persians were not as heavily armoured as the Greeks; their weapons and tactics were better suited to the plain of Marathon. The Persians hoped that the Greeks would advance onto the open plain where the Persian cavalry and archers would be most effective. However the Greeks recognised this fact and remained in the hills.

The Persians may also have accepted the delay in the hope that the Athenians might be betrayed as the Eretrians had been.

ABSENCE OF THE PERSIAN CAVALRY

The cavalry was one of the elite units of the Persian army and might, therefore, have been expected to play a significant part in the battle. The fact that they did not has raised the question: what happened to them?

There are essentially two theories that attempt to answer this question. One, supported by historians such as A.R. Burn and George Wilcoxon, argues that the cavalry had already been put back on the Persian ships before the battle, perhaps to sail around the Greek army and land behind them, near an undefended Athens. When the Greeks became aware of this they attacked and defeated the Persian infantry, now denied cavalry support. This would also explain the sudden Greek decision to attack after a seventeen-day delay. The second theory, presented by N.G.L. Hammond, claims that the horses were being watered and when they returned it was difficult or impossible for them to take effective part in the battle.

After their defeat at Marathon the Persians withdrew. Before sailing away, however, they apparently attempted to sail to Athens and attack the undefended city. A forced march by the Athenians thwarted the plan. At this moment a signal was flashed from the Acropolis. No one knows why. There was speculation that it was part of a betrayal and the Alcmaeonids were blamed. Others argue that it might have been a signal to the Athenians that the Persians were finally on their way.

INTER-WAR YEARS

After the battle at Marathon Athens was torn by internal strife. Many key political figures were ostracised and exiled, including Hipparchus, 487–86 BC; Megacles, 486–85 BC; Xanthippus, 485–84 BC; and Aristides, 483–82 BC.

Miltiades, the hero of Marathon, died in disgrace accused of corruption after an ill-fated military expedition against the island of Paros in 489 BC.

Themistocles rose to prominence as an Athenian political leader. When silver was discovered at Laurium in 483 BC Themistocles successfully argued that it be used to pay for the building of an Athenian navy. Two hundred ships were built within the next three years.

Throughout the 480s Athens was constantly at war with its neighbour, Aegina.

STOP AND THINK: DOCUMENT STUDY
Read the extract below from Plutarch and answer the questions that follow.

In the first place he was the only man who had the courage to come before the people and propose that the revenue from the silver mines at Laurium, which the Athenians had been in the habit of dividing among themselves, should be set aside and the money used to build triremes for the war against Aegina. This conflict, at that moment the most important in all Greece, was at its height and the islanders, thanks to the size of their fleet, were masters of the sea. This made it all the easier for Themistocles to carry his point. There was no need to terrify the Athenians with the threat of Darius and the Persians, who were far away and whom few people seriously imagined would come and attack them; he had only to play upon the enmity and the jealousy the people felt towards the Aeginetans to make them agree to the outlay. The result was that the Athenians built a hundred triremes with the money, and these ships actually fought at Salamis against Xerxes.

After this he continued to draw on the Athenians little by little and turn their thoughts in the direction of the sea. He told them that their army was no match even for their nearest neighbours, the Boeotians, but that with the power they would command in their fleet they could not only drive off the barbarians, but become the leaders of all Greece.

Plutarch, *Themistocles*, 4

✳ ✳ ✳

✎ **Before Themistocles, what did Athens do with the profits from its silver mines?**

✎ **What did Themistocles suggest should be done with the profits?**

✎ **What enemy did Themistocles point to? What enemy and threat does Plutarch suggest he had in mind?**

✎ **What arguments did Themistocles use to support his case for a fleet?**

✎ **Have another close look at the passage. Write out some short sections that highlight Themistocles' political skills. What skills do your chosen sections bring out?**

RENEWED PREPARATIONS FOR WAR

Persia

Their plans were disrupted for a time by a revolt in Egypt and the death of Darius, both in 486 BC.

Xerxes succeeded his father. Even though the preparations for the second invasion were more systematic than the first, Xerxes is not generally as well regarded a ruler as Darius.

Over a four-year period the Persians set about consolidating a land approach to Greece. The army would march through Thrace and Macedonia into northern Greece, supported by an accompanying fleet.

To make this land route possible they:

- built a 'boat bridge' across the Hellespont.
- put another bridge across the Strymon River.
- established regular supply depots along the 'line of march'.

To help safeguard the fleet a canal was dug through the Chalcidic peninsula of Mount Athos. This was intended to avoid the dangerous waters that saw storm damage to Mardonius' fleet in 492 BC.

Xerxes gathered a vast army — between 80 000 and 100 000 men.

In 481 BC Xerxes sent messengers to a number of Greek cities demanding 'earth and water...' — tokens of submission to Persian authority.

Greece

The Greeks recognised the Persian preparations for what they were and realised that unity was the key to their survival.

In 481 BC a league or alliance of Greek states was formed to meet the Persian threat. For convenience we will call it the Hellenic League of 481.

The League did not always have wholehearted support, but it did manage to provide a framework of unity. It made agreements to:

- end wars between its members, especially between Athens and Aegina.
- send spies to Asia.
- send envoys to Crete, Syracuse and Corcyra with requests for aid.

The League also sent envoys to Argos in the Peloponnese because it was feared Argos might ally with Persia.

A Greek force was sent north to Thessaly with the idea of opposing the Persians there but withdrew to Thermopylae.

The Greek strategy is still in dispute among modern scholars. They either:

- planned to hold northern Greece at Thermopylae with military force, or
- really intended to use their fleet as the key weapon of defence, probably at Salamis.

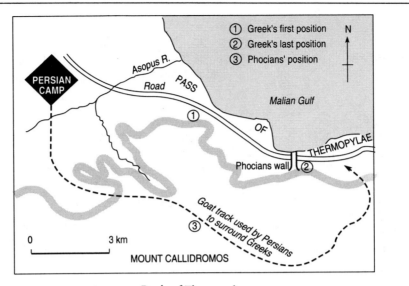

Battle of Thermopylae

THERMOPYLAE

The narrow pass at Thermopylae was held by 7000 hoplites under the Spartan King Leonidas. This was a coastal position and they were supported by a Greek fleet, made up mostly of Athenian ships at Artemisium. The fleet was needed to stop the Persian fleet sailing around the Greek position in the pass and landing Persian forces to cut off their supplies.

As the battle progressed it appeared that the Greeks under Leonidas could have held, had it not been for a traitor Ephialtes who guided the Persians along a path, the Anopaea, that outflanked the Greeks in the pass. Some Greeks fled or were ordered away by Leonidas, but he and 300 Spartans stayed and died. Leonidas' decision to remain could have been:

- in the vain hope that the Persian flanking force that had travelled down the path might itself be trapped between the 300 Spartans and the main Greek force south of Thermopylae.
- to honour, as Herodotus says, a prophecy that Sparta would be plundered unless a Spartan king died.

While the events at Thermopylae were unfolding a limited and indecisive naval engagement took place at Artemisium. If either side gained an advantage in this naval battle, modern scholars feel it was probably the Persians. Nevertheless, a storm blew up and inflicted damage on both fleets. In this instance, however, the Persians were clearly the losers. The storm lessened the advantage in numbers enjoyed by the Persian fleet, a factor that would prove important at Salamis.

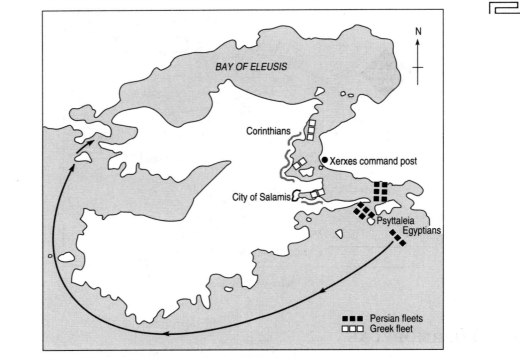

Battle of Salamis

SALAMIS

Following the defeat at Thermopylae the Peloponnesians withdrew from Boeotia and Attica, and began consolidating a defensive position across the Isthmus of Corinth. Athens was, therefore, exposed to the Persian army. Themistocles ordered an evacuation of Athens and struggled to convince his allies that the fleet should stay and fight at Salamis.

Accounts by ancient writers such as Herodotus, Aeschylus and Plutarch show a pro-Athenian bias and it is difficult to discern the truth behind the Greek tactics. As mentioned earlier, disputes over the Troezen Inscription further complicate the issue.

It has been widely acknowledged that the key element of Greek strategy was the fleet and that Leonidas was simply meant to hold Thermopylae while the fleet sought a decisive battle. This view had developed because:

- Athens played a key role in naval operations and many of the surviving histories are pro-Athenian.
- the Greeks were not as badly outnumbered at sea as they were on land.
- the naval battle at Salamis proved to be so decisive.

Nevertheless, there is an alternative point of view and its key arguments are:

- the largely Athenian Greek fleet was still new and untested in battle.

- the opposing Persian fleet included Phoenician and Egyptian ships and was highly regarded.
- the last time the Greeks and Persians had fought at sea was at the Battle of Lade during the Ionian Revolt, and the Persians had won.
- it is wrong to argue from hindsight — to see Salamis as decisive and assume that this had been the Greek plan all along.
- besides, at Artemisium, the Greek fleet did not appear to seek a 'showdown' battle. On the contrary, it appeared happy to support the land forces.

Regardless of the cause — by chance or by design — the battle of Salamis became the key to the Greek victory in the second Persian War. A naval triumph for Persia would have allowed the Persian army to strike at will, anywhere in Greece. This strategic advantage would almost certainly have guaranteed the Persians victory. The Greeks, however, won and with the victory went Xerxes' plans of conquest.

Herodotus and Aeschylus present Themistocles as the brilliant leader who fooled the hapless Xerxes into fighting in the narrow waters of the straits of Salamis. Themistocles is meant to have sent a messenger posing as a traitor to Xerxes, to tell him that the Greek fleet was about to retreat and that unless he acted they would get away. In response Xerxes rushed his fleet after them and into a trap.

Xerxes emerges from this account of events in a poor light. Nevertheless, there are some points that can be made in his defence:

- he had good reason to have confidence in his fleet, even though the narrow straits of Salamis lessened his advantages in ship numbers and manoeuvrability.
- he faced the onset of winter and in the ancient world that would end the campaign until the following spring. Xerxes was, therefore, prepared for a quick and decisive battle that might bring victory before the winter.
- a victory in 480 BC would appeal to Xerxes because, it is important to remember, he had commitments to a vast empire. For him, the campaign against Greece was just one problem; by contrast, for the Greeks it was the only problem.

Given these factors, it was not an unreasonable decision on Xerxes' part to fight at Salamis. His problem is that history often judges losers harshly.

Following the defeat at Salamis Xerxes returned to Persia, leaving General Mardonius in charge of the army.

STOP AND THINK: DOCUMENT STUDY
On the following pages you will find three separate accounts of the Battle of Salamis, by Herodotus, Aeschylus and

Plutarch. Read all three and make a list of all the points of agreement and the points of disagreement between them. Then write your own description of the battle based upon the common features of the accounts.

The whole fleet now got under way, and in a moment the Persians were on them. The Greeks checked their way and began to back astern; and they were on the point of running aground when Ameinias of Pallene, in command of an Athenian ship, drove ahead and rammed an enemy vessel. Seeing the two ships foul of one another and locked together, the rest of the Greek fleet hurried to Ameinias' assistance, and the general action began. Such is the Athenian account of how the battle started; the Aeginetans claim that the first to go into action was the ship which fetched the Sons of Aeacus from Aegina. There is also a popular belief that the phantom shape of a woman appeared and, in a voice which could be heard by every man in the fleet, contemptuously cried out: 'Fools, how much further do you propose to go astern?'

The Athenian squadron found itself facing the Phoenicians, who formed the Persian left wing on the western, Eleusis, end of the line; the Lacedaemonians faced the ships of Ionia, which were stationed on the Piraeus, or eastern, end. A few of the Ionians remembered Themistocles' appeal and deliberately held back in the course of the fighting but most not at all. I could if I wished give a long list of officers in the enemy fleet who captured Greek ships, but the only ones I will mention are Theomestor, the son of Androdamas, and Phylacus, the son of Histiaeus, both of them Samians. My reason for naming these two is that Theomestor in reward for this service was invested by the Persians with the lordship of Samos, and Phylacus was enrolled in the catalogue of the King's Benefactors and presented with a large estate. The Persian word for King's Benefactors is *orosangae*.

These two officers, as I say, had some success; but the greater part of the Persian fleet suffered severely in the battle, the Athenians and Aeginetans accounting for a great many of their ships. Since the Greek fleet worked together as a whole, while the Persians had lost formation and were no longer fighting on any plan, that was what was bound to happen. None the less they fought well that day — far better than in the actions off Euboea. Every man of them did his best for fear of Xerxes, feeling that the king's eye was on him.

I cannot give precise details of the part played in this battle by the various Greek or foreign contingents in the Persian fleet; I must, however, mention Artemisia, on account of an exploit which still further increased her reputation with Xerxes. After the Persian fleet had lost all semblance of order, Artemisia was chased by an Athenian trireme. As her ship happened to be closest to the enemy and there were other friendly ships just ahead of her, escape was impossible. In this awkward situation she hit on a plan which turned out greatly to her advantage: with the Athenian close on her tail she drove ahead with all possible speed and rammed one of her friends — a ship of Calynda, with Damasithymus, the Calyndian king, on board. I cannot say if she did this deliberately because of some quarrel she had had with this man while the fleet was in the Hellespont, or if it was just chance that that particular vessel was in her way; but in any case she rammed and sank her, and was lucky enough, as a result, to reap a double benefit. For the captain of the Athenian trireme, on seeing her ram an enemy, naturally supposed that her ship was a Greek one, or else a deserter which was fighting on the Greek side; so he abandoned the chase and turned to attack elsewhere. That, then, was one piece of luck — that she escaped with her life; the other was that, by this very act she raised herself higher than ever in Xerxes' esteem. For the story goes that Xerxes, who was watching the battle, observed the incident, and that one of the bystanders remarked: 'Do you see, my lord, how well Artemisia is fighting? She has sunk an enemy ship.' Xerxes asked if they were sure it was really Artemisia, and was told that there was no doubt whatever — they knew her ensign well, and of course supposed that it was an enemy ship that had been sunk. She was, indeed, lucky in every way — not least in the fact that there were no survivors from the Calyndian ship to accuse her. Xerxes' comment on what was told him is said to have been: 'My men have turned into women, my women into men.'

Amongst the killed in this struggle was the Ariabignes, the son of Darius and Xerxes' brother, and many other well-known men from Persia, Media, and the confederate nations. There were also Greek casualties, but not many; for most of the Greeks could swim, and those who lost their ships, provided they were not killed in the actual fighting, swam over to Salamis. Most of the enemy, on the other hand, being unable to swim, were drowned. The greatest destruction took place when the ships which had been first engaged turned tail; for those astern fell foul of them in their attempt to press forward and do some service before the eyes of the king. In the confusion which resulted, some Phoenicians who had lost their ships came to Xerxes and tried to make out that the loss was due to the treachery of the Ionians. But the upshot was that it was they themselves, and not the Ionian captains, who were executed for misbehaviour. While they were speaking, a ship of Samothrace rammed an Athenian; the Athenian was going down, when an Aeginetan vessel bore down upon the Samothracian and sank her, but the Samothracian crew, who were armed with javelins, cleared the deck of the attacking vessel, leapt aboard, and captured her. This exploit saved the Ionians; for when Xerxes saw an Ionian ship do such a fine piece of work, he turned to the Phoenicians and, ready as he was in his extreme vexation to find fault with anyone, ordered their heads to be cut off, to stop them from casting cowardly aspersions upon their betters.

Xerxes watched the course of the battle from the base of Mt Aegaleos, across the strait from Salamis; whenever he saw one of his officers behaving with distinction, he would find out his name, and his secretaries wrote it down, together with his city and parentage.

The Persian Ariaramnes, who was a friend of the Ionians and was present during the battle, also had a share in bringing about the punishment of the Phoenicians.

When the Persian rout began and they were trying to get back to Phalerum, the Aeginetan squadron, which was waiting to catch them in the narrows, did memorable service. The enemy was in hopeless confusion; such ships as offered resistance or tried to escape were cut to pieces by the Athenians, while the Aeginetans caught those which attempted to get clear, so that any ship which escaped the one enemy promptly fell amongst the other. It happened at this stage that Themistocles, chasing an enemy vessel, ran close by the ship which was commanded by Polycritus, the son of Crius, the Aeginetan. Polycritus had just rammed a Sidonian, the very ship which captured the Aeginetan guard-vessel off Sciathus — the one, it will be remembered, which had Pytheas on board, the man the Persians kept with them out of admiration for his gallantry in refusing to surrender in spite of his appalling wounds. When the ship was taken with him and the Persian crew on board, he got safe home to Aegina. When Polycritus noticed the Athenian ship, and recognized the admiral's flag, he shouted to Themistocles and asked him in a tone of ironic reproach if he still thought that the people of Aegina were Persia's friends.

Such of the Persian ships as escaped destruction made their way back to Phalerum and brought up there under the protection of the army.

Herodotus, *The Histories*, 8, 85–92

✦ ✦ ✦

At once ship into ship battered its brazen beak.
A Hellene ship charged first, and chopped off the whole stern
Of a Phoenician galley. Then charge followed charge
On every side. At first by its huge impetus
Our fleet withstood them. But soon, in that narrow space,
Our ships were jammed in hundreds; none could help another.

They rammed each other with their prows of bronze; and some
Were stripped of every oar. Meanwhile the enemy
Came round us in a ring and charged. Our vessels heeled
Over; the sea was hidden, carpeted with wrecks
And dead men; all the shores and reefs were full of dead.
   Then every ship we had broke rank and rowed for life.
The Hellenes seized fragments of wrecks and broken oars
And hacked and stabbed at our men swimming in the sea
As fishermen kill tunnies or some netted haul.
The whole sea was one din of shrieks and dying groans,
Till night and darkness hid the scene. If I should speak
For ten days and ten nights, I could not tell you all
That day's agony. But know this: never before
In one day died so vast a company of men.
ATOSSA: Alas! How great an ocean of disaster has
   Broken on Persia and on every eastern race!
MESSENGER: But there is more, and worse; my story is not half told.
   Be sure, what follows twice outweighs what went before.
ATOSSA: What could be worse? What could our armament endure,
   To outweigh all the sufferings already told?
MESSENGER: The flower of Persian chivalry and gentle blood,
   The youth and valour of our choice nobility,
   First in unmoved devotion to the king himself,
   Are sunk into the mire of ignominious death.
ATOSSA: My friends, this evil news is more than I can bear. —
   How do you say they died?
MESSENGER: Opposite Salamis
   There is an island — small, useless for anchorage —
   Where Pan the Dancer treads along the briny shore.
   There Xerxes sent them, so that, when the enemy,
   Flung from their ships, were struggling to the island beach,
   The Persian force might without trouble cut them down,
   And rescue Persian crews from drowning in the sea:
   Fatal misjudgement! When in the sea-battle Heaven
   Had given glory to the Hellenes, that same day
   They came, armed with bronze shields and spears, leapt from their ships,
   And made a ring round the whole island, that our men
   Could not tell where to turn. First came a shower of blows
   From stones slung with the hand; then from the drawn bow-string
   Arrows leapt forth to slaughter; finally, with one
   Fierce roar the Hellenes rushed at them, and cut and carved
   Their limbs like butchers, till the last poor wretch lay dead.
This depth of horror Xerxes saw; close to the sea
On a high hill he sat, where he could clearly watch
His whole force both by sea and land. He wailed aloud,
And tore his clothes, weeping; and instantly dismissed
His army, hastening them to a disordered flight.
This, then, brings you new grief to mingle with the first.

Aeschylus, *The Persians*

✳ ✳ ✳

In his tragedy *The Persians*, the poet Aeschylus writes of the numbers of the barbarian ships as though he knew these for a fact:

But Xerxes, as I know well, had a thousand ships
At his command; the vessels built for speed
Numbered two hundred and seven, so stands the count.

The Athenian contingent was 180 strong and each ship had eighteen men to fight on deck, four of these being archers and the rest infantry-men.

Themistocles appears to have chosen the time for the battle as judiciously as he had the place. He was careful not to let the triremes engage the barbarian ships head on, until the time of day when the wind usually blows fresh from the sea and sends a heavy swell rolling through the narrows. This breeze was no disadvantage to the Greek ships, which were comparatively small and lay low in the water, but it caught the Persian vessels, which were difficult to manoeuvre with their high decks and towering sterns, and swung them round broad-side on to their opponents, who dashed in eagerly to the attack. The Greek captains kept a watchful eye on Themistocles, because they felt that he saw most clearly what were the right tactics to follow, and also because he had ranged opposite him Xerxes' admiral, Ariamenes, a man of great courage, who was both the most stalwart and the most high-principled of the king's brothers. He was stationed on a huge ship, from which he kept discharging arrows and javelins, as though he were on the wall of a fortress. Ameinias of Decelea and Socles of the deme of Paeania, who were both sailing in the same vessel, bore down upon his and met it bows on, and as the two ships crashed into each other and were held by their bronze beaks, Ariamenes tried to board their trireme; but the two Athenians faced him, ran him through with their spears, and pitched him into the sea. Artemisia, the queen of Caria, recognized his body, as it floated about with the wreckage, and she had it brought to Xerxes.

At this point in the battle it is said that a great light suddenly shone out from Eleusis and a loud cry seemed to fill the whole breadth of the Thriasian plain down to the sea, as though an immense crowd were escorting the mystic Iacchus in procession. Then, from the place where the shouting was heard, a cloud seemed to rise slowly from the land, drift out to sea, and descend upon the triremes. Others believed that they saw phantoms and the shapes of armed men coming from Aegina with hands outstretched to protect the Greek ships. These, they believed, were the sons of Aeacus, to whom they had offered prayers for help just before the battle.

The first man to capture an enemy ship was Lycomedes, the commander of an Athenian trireme, who cut off the Persian's figure-head and dedicated it to Apollo the Laurel-bearer at Phlya. The rest of the Greeks now found themselves on equal terms with their enemies, since the Persians could only bring a small part of their whole fleet into action at a time, as their ships constantly fouled one another in the narrow straits; and so, although they held out till the evening, the Greeks finally put them to utter rout. Thus they gained 'that noble and famous victory', as Simonides says, 'the most glorious exploit ever achieved at sea by Greek or barbarian, and they owed it to the courage and determination of all those who fought their ships, but not least to the surpassing skill and judgement of Themistocles.'

Plutarch, *Themistocles*, 3, 14–15

✳ ✳ ✳

PLATAEA 479 BC

Following Salamis the Persian army under Mardonius retreated north and wintered on the Plain of Thessaly. There was still uncertainty in the Greek union, the key division being between the interests of the northern Greeks and the Peloponnesians. The Peloponnesians were reluctant to risk their

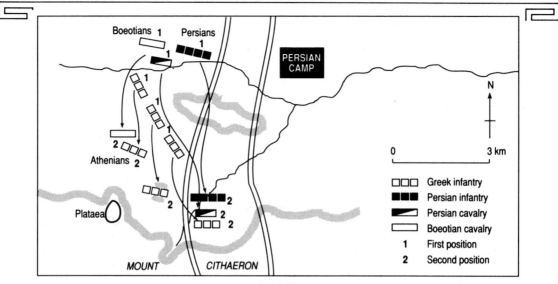

Battle of Plataea

forces defending north Greece while the northern Greeks were unwilling to commit themselves to resistance without determined Peloponnesian support.

During the winter after Salamis Mardonius attempted unsuccessfully to lure Athens away from the League with promises of a generous separate peace. Had he been successful, the position of Greece and the Peloponnese would have been grave. Nevertheless the Peloponnesians still only made token promises of support while continuing to defend their southern area by fortifying the Isthmus of Corinth.

It was not until Mardonius marched south again that Athens, Megara and Plataea all sent ambassadors to Sparta demanding that an army march north. Once again Athens was evacuated and ravaged.

After debate a Spartan army of 5000 marched north under Pausanias. This brought the Greek army to 100 000 with the addition of the other Peloponnesians and the western and northern states. Once this Greek army took the field Mardonius withdrew from Attica and established a defensive position on the northern bank of the Asopus River.

Mardonius was in no hurry to join battle because:

- the longer the Greeks were together in the field the more chance there was of disagreements and jealousies dividing them.
- he wanted the Greeks to attack him so that they would be forced to fight where he wanted, on a plain, where his cavalry would provide him with an advantage.

By contrast, the Greeks preferred to fight in the more rugged country south of the Asopus. Therefore the armies faced one another for days, while the Persians launched the odd cavalry raid.

Disputes in the Persian camp between Mardonius and Artabazus appear to have prompted the Persians to attack, and as at Salamis, the Persians would again fight in conditions favouring the Greeks.

In the battle itself the discipline of the Spartan hoplites proved effective. The Persians were defeated and Mardonius was killed.

Plataea was, above all, a Spartan success, but Athenian sources and later Herodotus set about unjustly emphasising the Athenian role and providing only grudging praise for the Spartans. These views are suspect since they impose highly doubtful interpretations on a number of aspects of the battle.

Plataea and Salamis were two vital battles, and they ended the Persian threat. They were triumphs for Sparta and Athens respectively. After Plataea Greek victories at Mycale and Sestus followed in quick succession.

BATTLE OF MYCALE, AUGUST 479 BC

According to Herodotus the Persians suffered another defeat on the same day as their defeat at Plataea. This took place at Mycale, a small bay on the Ionian coast, and was supposedly spurred on by news of an impending Ionian revolt against Persian dominance of the Greeks. The victorious Athenians then moved on to Sestus which they seized, finally ridding the Aegean of the Persians.

REASONS FOR GREEK VICTORY

- The Greeks managed a unified response to Persian aggression when it mattered most. Greek unity was always fragile, but it proved equal to the task.
- Greek leadership proved superior to the Persians'. On the strategic level, Themistocles recognised the importance of unity and the Athenian need for a fleet, whereas the Persians underestimated the Greeks. Tactically the Persians fought on sites chosen by the Greeks at Thermopylae and Salamis, giving the Greeks an advantage, at Marathon the Greeks attacked at the crucial moment, and errors were made by the Persians at Plataea.
- A committed fighting force — the Greeks were fighting for survival, for their homes; victory over Persia was their prime concern. By contrast, the Persian troops, many of whom were conscripts or mercenaries, lacked commitment. The Persian leaders Darius and Xerxes also often had other concerns over and above the campaign against Greece.
- Logistics — the problems of communication and supply — posed enormous problems for the Persians. For the Greeks the problem was not as great because they had shorter lines of supply and communication.
- The Persians had to win decisive victories to force the Greek states to surrender. By contrast, the Greeks had only to hold. If the Greeks held firm, Persian supply problems would force them to retire. The pressure

for decisive victories may have led to Persian errors, for example, Salamis.
- The quality of the Greek hoplites, in terms of fighting ability and arms, proved consistently superior under Greek conditions.
- Luck, fortune, or in Aeschylus' words, 'the Gods favoured the Greeks'. Stories of Mt Athos in 492 BC, the Hellespont and at Artemisium all helped the Greeks and hindered the Persian cause.

STOP AND THINK: PUTTING IT ALL TOGETHER

⟍ **Rule up a chart using headings as shown below. In each of the columns provide the required information:**

- **name the six battles of the Persian Wars. List them in the order in which they took place.**
- **categorise each battle as a land or sea battle.**
- **find out the year and month of each battle.**
- **find out the leaders of each of the forces in each battle.**
- **what was the outcome of each battle?**

BATTLE LAND/SEA DATE LEADERS OUTCOME

⟍ **Group Task**
In groups of four or five select one of the battles of the Persian Wars, then form a team of investigative journalists. Write a report of the battle for a feature article in a Greek popular weekend newspaper. The article should:

- **examine the preparedness of both sides**
- **investigate any preliminary activities or action**
- **describe the site of the battle**
- **provide details of action: tactics, manoeuvres**
- **provide descriptions and accounts of outstanding individuals**
- **give the results, including casualties, territory gained and lost**
- **analyse the aftermath.**

⟍ **Write a paragraph on the significance of each of the following in bringing about the final result of the Persian Wars:**

- **weapons and armoury**
- **leadership**
- **knowledge of the terrain of battle sites**
- **Greek unity**
- **Greek attitude to Persian dominance**
- **risk taking and ingenuity**
- **naval forces**
- **availability of supplies and resources**
- **size of armies**
- **types of fighting forces within each army**

LIST OF SOURCES

ANCIENT SOURCES

Aeschylus, *The Persians*, tr. A.J. Podlecki, Prentice-Hall, Englewood Cliffs, NJ, 1970

Herodotus, *The Histories*, tr. Aubrey de Sélincourt, Penguin Classics, 1972

Plutarch, *The Rise and Fall of Athens: nine Greek lives*, tr. Ian Scott-Kilvert, Penguin Classics, 1960 repr. 1973

SECONDARY SOURCES

Bengston, H., *The Greeks and the Persians*, Weidenfeld & Nicolson, London, 1970

Burn, A.R., *Persia and the Greeks: the defence of the west*, Edward Arnold, London, 1962

Hammond, N.G.L., *A History of Greece to 322 B.C.*, 2nd ed, Clarendon Press, Oxford, 1967

Hignett, C., *Xerxes' Invasion of Greece*, Oxford, 1963

Horsley, G.H.R. (ed), *Hellenika*, Macquarie Ancient History Association, 1982

Wilcoxon, George Dent, *Athens Ascendant*, Iowa State University Press, 1979

CHAPTER SIX

PERICLES

GARY KENWORTHY

INTRODUCTION

Just as Athens dominated the affairs of the Aegean during the fifth century BC so too, according to the ancient writers, did Pericles dominate the affairs of Athens. One of our two main sources, Thucydides, summed up Pericles' value to his city:

> • • • and, so far as the general needs of the state as a whole were concerned, they regarded Pericles as the best man they had. Indeed, during the whole period of peace-time when Pericles was at the head of affairs the state was wisely led and firmly guarded, and it was under him that Athens was at her greatest.
>
> *The Peloponnesian War*, 2, 65

✳ ✳ ✳

So invaluable was Pericles to the democracy of Athens that he was elected to the position of strategos (general) sixteen times between 445 and 430 BC. His strength of character and political skill, as the leader of the 'radical' democratic faction after 459 BC, is reflected in his ability to maintain his influence on the Athenian political scene for some thirty-five years.

Pericles has also been blamed for helping to create tensions between Athens and Sparta, through his imperialistic foreign policies, which led to the Peloponnesian War in 431 BC.

What can we make of these claims? In order to assess them we must examine the available sources and answer the following questions.

FOCUS QUESTIONS

➤ **What were the early influences on Pericles' thoughts?**

➤ **How did the Athenian democracy work in the period 460–430 BC?**

➤ **How was it possible for one man, Pericles, to dominate the Athenian democracy?**

➤ **To what extent were his policies responsible for the outbreak of the Peloponnesian War?**

Bust of Pericles

THE SOURCES

The sources available to us on the life and career of Pericles are, considering his prominence, limited. This in itself can cause problems in that we may be unable to assess the claims of one source properly, due to the lack of corroborating evidence, over the claims of another. Luckily what does survive can be seen as generally reliable.

THUCYDIDES (460/50–400? BC)

Thucydides held Pericles, who belonged to a conservative political family from Athens, to have been the greatest of all the leading figures of the Peloponnesian War. During his exile from Athens, Thucydides wrote an incomplete history of the war in eight books, and Books 1 and 2 make mention of Pericles but do not provide a complete and sharply drawn picture of the man. However Thucydides does record several supposed speeches of Pericles within his text that provide a good indication of his motives. Generally Thucydides is regarded as reliable and thorough in his research, the first of the scientific historians.

ARISTOPHANES (477–385? BC)

An Athenian contemporary of Pericles, Aristophanes is regarded as the greatest poet of Old Attic Comedy. Of his plays, eleven survive, many of which deal with contemporary political and social issues, e.g. *The Wasps*, which ridicules the enthusiasm of old men for jury duty. Writing mainly caricatures, his favourite methods are parody, satire and exaggeration and his favourite targets are prominent politicians such as his enemy Cleon.

ARISTOTLE (384–322 BC)

Born in Stragirus in the Chalcidice Aristotle, a philosopher, wrote many works; of these the most relevant to the topic is *The Athenian Constitution* written around 329 BC. Despite a problem with the authorship of the text its value lies in the fact that it is an historical account of the development of the Athenian democracy and an analysis of how the constitution worked in Aristotle's day. It is distinctly anti-Democratic in outlook.

PLUTARCH

A Greek biographer who lived sometime between AD 46 and 120, he is best known for his *Parallel Lives* of Greeks and Romans, of which Pericles and Fabius Maximus form a pair. His accounts are not meant as strict works of history, as he states himself. His aim is to write biography with a moral purpose and so, whilst following a chronological approach, he often digresses to include an anecdote with which to illustrate a particular aspect of his subject's character. Plutarch refers to approximately twenty different authorities on Pericles' life as his sources. Unfortunately his work really only covers the last twenty years of Pericles' life.

EUPOLIS (460?–415?)

Although regarded as one of the greatest poets of the Old Attic Comedy, all that remains of his work are fragments. He was a contemporary of Pericles, but little is known of his politics. He was chiefly a satirist, as was Aristophanes.

KEY EVENTS IN THE LIFE OF PERICLES

494 BC	Pericles born.
484	Archons chosen by lot.
484	Rich silver strike at Laurion mines.
483	Themistocles' naval bill passed. Athenian fleet built.
480/79	Xerxes, King of Persia, invades Greece. Pericles evacuated to Salamis. Athens sacked and burnt. Battles of Salamis and Plataea.
479	Pericles' father, Xanthippus, admiral at Mycale.
478	Delian League formed. Fortification of Athens begins (the Long Walls).

477	Cimon's campaigns begin.
476/5	Cimon captures Eion.
474	Pericles' first military service. Cimon captures Scyros.
472	Pericles, as *choregos*, pays for the production of Aeschylus' play, *The Persians*. Athenians reduce Carystus.
471	Themistocles ostracised.
469	Pericles' first speech in the Ecclesia. Becomes prominent as Ephialtes' lieutenant. Naxos revolts.
468/7	Battle of Eurymedon. Ephialtes becomes democratic faction leader.
466	Attacks made by Ephialtes and the democrats on the power of the Areopagus.
465	Pericles prosecutes Cimon. Revolt of Thasos.
464	Pericles elected strategos (general). Earthquake leads to helot revolt in Laconia.
463	Pericles leads Athenian fleet on sweeps in the Levant. Cimon sent to help Spartans besiege helots at Mt Ithome. Spartans insult Athens by returning the troops before the completion of operations.
462	Ephialtes' reforms of the Areopagus passed.
461	Pericles introduces decree to allow payment of jurors in Heliaea. Cimon ostracised. Alliance of Athens with Argos and Thessaly.
460/59	Athenian expedition to Egypt. Ephialtes assassinated. Pericles becomes chief radical democratic leader at Athens.
459	Spartans capture Mt Ithome. Messenian helots settled at Naupactus. Megara allies with Athens. Battles at Helieis and Cecryphalia against Peloponnesians.
458	Zeugitae admitted to archonship. Boule chosen by lot from all citizens. Archons and Boule members paid. Battle of Aegina in the Megarid.
457	Fall of Aegina. Spartans send forces to restore Theban control of Boeotia. Pericles strategos at the Battle of Tanagra. Athenian loss. Pericles proposes recall of Cimon. Battle of Oenophyta results in Athenian control of Boeotia. Long Walls completed at Athens.
455	Athenian fleet active in Corinthian Gulf under Tolmides.
454	Athenian disaster in Egypt. Defeat by Persians. Delian League treasury moved to Athens.
453	Pericles strategos. Brings home western fleet. Tribute lists begin.
452/1	Argos signs thirty-year truce with Sparta. Athens signs five-year truce with Sparta and Peloponnesians. Pericles and Cimon reach friendly agreement.

451/0	Citizenship law introduced by Pericles.
450	Cimon dies in Cyprus. Pericles instrumental in establishing *cleruchies* (colonies) at Naxos, Andros and Carystus.
449	Peace with Persia signed.
448	Pericles general. Active in central Greece. Abortive plan for an Hellenic council proposed by Pericles. Sparta refuses to join. Parthenon begun.
447	Battle of Coronea. Boeotia lost to Athens. Megara and Euboea revolt.
446	Pericles as strategos subdues Euboea. Pericles responsible for establishment of colonies in Chersonese, Lemnos and Imbros.
445	Athens signs thirty-year peace with Sparta. Thucydides, son of Melesius, main opponent to Pericles.
444	Pericles not elected strategos.
443	Thucydides ostracised.
442	Pericles director of Festival of Dionysus.
440	Revolt of Samos and Byzantium. Pericles strategos.
439	Pericles strategos. Campaigns at Samos. Subdues the island.
438	Pericles strategos. Commands Black Sea expedition. Parthenon finished.
437	Pericles establishes colony of Amphipolis in Chalcidice.
436	Phormio, Athenian strategos, in northwestern Greece.
435	Epidamnus incident. Work starts on Propylaia. Corcyra defeats Corinthians in sea battle.
433	Pericles opposes diplomatic concessions with Spartans. Athenian fleet sent to help Corcyra. Athens allies with Corcyra. Angers Corinth. Battle of Sybota.
432	'Megarian decree' issued. Revolt of Potidaea from Thebans.
431	Peloponnesian War begins. Pericles delivers Funeral Oration.
430	Pericles leads expedition to Argolis. Pericles reappointed strategos. Potidaea surrenders. Pericles deposed from position of strategos and fined. Plague hits Athens.
429	Pericles dies of plague.

FAMILY BACKGROUND

HIS PARENTS

Pericles' family background was extremely distinguished. His father, Xanthippus, belonged to a prominent political family and was a rising politician who had served as strategos in 479 at the Battle of Mycale. His mother, Agariste, was a member of the famous Alcmaeonid family, long involved in the political history of Athens. Pericles' great-uncle was the famous Cleisthenes, who had reformed the government of Athens in 507 and according to Herodotus 'enlisted the people in his party', thereby democratising it to an extent.

STOP AND THINK: RESEARCH TASKS

Using the library and any other source available answer the following questions:

✎ **What was the 'curse' of the Alcmaeonids? What happened to put the family under this curse? How was it used by the political enemies of the Alcmaeonids to restrict their political power within Athens?**

✎ **Which tyrant was related to Pericles' mother, Agariste? Is this significant to Pericles' political outlook? Explain your answer.**

✎ **Briefly outline the political reforms instituted by Cleisthenes at Athens. How did these lead the Athenian political system towards democracy?**

✎ **Read the following extract:**

When the tyranny [Peisistratid] had been overthrown, strife broke out between Isagoras, a friend of the tyrants, and Cleisthenes of the Alcmaeonid family. As Cleisthenes was getting the worse of the party struggle, he attached the people to his following, by proposing to give political power to the masses.

Aristotle, *The Athenian Constitution*, 20

❋ ❋ ❋

- **According to this source why did Cleisthenes reform the Athenian system of government?**
- **Do you think that the author favoured these changes? Explain your answer.**
- **What other reasons might Cleisthenes have had in proposing these changes?**
- **Do you think that his motives were purely selfish? Explain your answer.**
- **Is this extract a reliable source of evidence on this issue?**

EARLY INFLUENCES

THE PERSIAN INVASIONS

The Persian invasions of Greece in 490 and 480–479 BC and the subsequent victory of the Greeks over the stronger Persian forces led to a rise of Greek national pride. The confidence gained by these victories was nowhere more apparent than at Athens. The Athenians, who had played a prominent part in the success, were able to capitalise on this spirit via the astuteness of political leaders such as Themistocles and Aristides, and assume a dominant political and diplomatic role in the Aegean through the formation of the Delian League in 478.

Having endured the humiliation of evacuating Athens in the wake of the Persian invasion, Pericles, as a youth and a member of a politically active family, would have based his opinion regarding the greatness of Athens on the Greek victories at Salamis and Plataea. This is expressed in his famous Funeral Oration. (Thucydides, Book 2, 34–46) The ensuing years, with the military successes of Cimon (477–472 BC) only lent weight to these convictions. With these successes came the temptation of the possibility of imperial exploitation and a means of ensuring a political career.

THE INTELLECTUAL CLIMATE OF ATHENS

Another result of the Greek victories over the Persians was the influx into Athens of leading thinkers and artists from the Ionian cities. The Athens of Pericles' youth was alive with the teachings of various philosophers. Pericles, according to Plutarch, came under the influence of a number of these.

STOP AND THINK: DOCUMENT STUDY

Read these extracts and answer the questions that follow. All come from Plutarch's *Life of Pericles*, 4, 5.

A His teacher in music [this included poetry and other subjects], most writers agree, was Damon, although according to Aristotle he had a thorough musical training at the hands of Pythocleides. This Damon appears to have been a sophist of the highest order . . . in fact it was he who trained Pericles for his political contests, much as a masseur or trainer prepares an athlete . . . he was ostracised on the grounds of being a great intriguer and supporter of tyranny.

B Pericles also studied under Zeno the Eleatic . . . Zeno had perfected a technique of cross-examination which enabled him to corner his opponent by the method of question and answer.

C But there was one man more closely associated with Pericles than any other, who did most to clothe him with a majestic bearing that was more potent than any demagogue's appeal and who helped to develop the natural dignity of his character to the highest degree. This was Anaxagoras of Clazomenae, whom the men of his time used to call Intelligence personified . . . he was the first to dethrone Chance and Necessity and set up pure intelligence in their place as the principle of law and order . . .

D From it [Anaxagorus' teachings] he derived not only a dignity of spirit and a nobility of utterance which was entirely free from the vulgar and unscrupulous buffooneries of mob oratory, but also a composure of countenance.

> ✎ **What was a 'sophist' (extract A) and a 'demogogue' (extract C)?**

> ✎ **What aspects of the teachings of each of the three philosophers above would have helped Pericles in his political career?**

✎ **What evidence is there in these extracts that Plutarch was trying to be a 'good' historian?**

✎ **What problems might we expect with Plutarch's sources of information on Pericles?**

Plutarch also makes mention (*Life of Pericles*, 13) of Pericles' friendship with the sculptor and architect of the Parthenon, Pheidias. We know also of a close association with the playwrights Sophocles and Aeschylus and with the greatest of the sophists, Protagoras.

STOP AND THINK: LIBRARY RESEARCH

✎ **Using the library find out more about the following people: Damon, Zeno the Eleatic, Anaxagoras of Clazomenae, Pheidias, Sophocles, Aeschylus, Protagoras.**

  • **Why are they famous? What might Pericles have learnt from them?**

THE POLITICAL CLIMATE OF ATHENS 484–469 BC

The political scene in Athens during these years saw the rise and fall of many of the most famous names in Athenian political history. Men such as Themistocles, Aristides and Cimon and their political activities and ideas must have affected the political outlook and career of Pericles.

STOP AND THINK: DOCUMENT STUDY

Plutarch (*Life of Pericles*, 7) gives us a good insight into Pericles' first step into the political arena. Read these extracts and answer the questions that follow.

A As a young man Pericles was inclined to shrink from facing the people. One reason for this was that he was considered to bear a distinct resemblance to the tyrant Pisistratus.

B The fact that he was rich and that he came of a distinguished family and possessed exceedingly powerful friends made the fear of ostracism very real to him, and at the beginning he took no part in politics but devoted himself to soldiering, in which he showed great daring and enterprise.

C However, the time came when Aristides was dead, Themistocles in exile, and Cimon frequently absent on distant campaigns. Then, at last, Pericles decided to attach himself to the people's party and to take up the cause of the poor and the many instead of that of the rich and the few, in spite of the fact that this was quite contrary to his own temperament, which was thoroughly aristocratic.

D He was afraid, apparently, of being suspected of aiming at a dictatorship; so when he saw that Cimon's sympathies were strongly with the nobles and that he was the idol of the aristocratic party, Pericles began to ingratiate himself with the people, partly for self preservation and partly by way of securing power against his rival.

↘ **Why, according to these extracts, did Pericles go into politics?**

↘ **Do you think that there might have been other reasons?**
(*Clue*: **Look at Pericles' family background.**)

↘ **What light do extracts A and B throw on Pericles as a skilful future political candidate?**

↘ **According to extract D why didn't Pericles, an aristocrat himself, join that political 'party'?**

↘ **How does extract C contradict extract D regarding Pericles' motives for joining the 'people's' party?**

↘ **What light do these extracts throw on the way politics operated at Athens? How did a person become politically significant?**

THE DEVELOPMENT OF ATHENIAN DEMOCRACY 508–433 BC

BACKGROUND

The word 'democracy' comes from a Greek word that literally translated means 'rule by the people'. Cleisthenes used the word '*isonomia*' — 'equality' — to describe his system of reformed Athenian government. These reforms, and the basis of Athenian democracy, were born of the political chaos that erupted on the expulsion of the Peisistratid tyrants in 509 BC. The political dogfight that arose between Isagoras' and Cleisthenes' parties forced the latter to enlist the support of the masses by 'promising to give political power to them'. (Aristotle, *The Athenian Constitution*, 20.1) In what amounted to a virtual state of civil war Isagoras and his supporters were ousted from power and Cleisthenes, 'as champion of the masses' reformed the government, making it more democratic or 'equal'.

The basis of Cleisthenes' democratic reforms was the creation of ten new tribal divisions to replace the previous four. In these all citizens were redistributed based upon where they lived, not on family connections as previously. This was designed to break up the political power of some of the old aristocratic factions by dividing their support base. (See W.G. Forrest, *The Emergence of Greek Democracy*, pp. 187–200 for a fuller discussion of this issue.)

His reforms, however, did not destroy the old Solonic social classes (the Pentacosiomedimnoi, the Hippeis, the Zeugitae and the Thetes) or the restrictions on the eligibility of members of these various classes to positions such as the archonship or the Areopagus (see table on page 116).

During the period 508–433 BC the democratisation of the Athenian government was completed through the work of successive 'popular' leaders.

STOP AND THINK: LIBRARY RESEARCH

➘ **Who was Solon? What reforms did he make to the Athenian constitution? Why was he famous in Athenian political history?**

➘ **What reforms did Cleisthenes make to the Athenian constitution? How were his reforms viewed by his contemporaries?**

THE OFFICE OF STRATEGOS

In 501–500 BC the office of strategos (general) was elevated to commander in chief of the Athenian forces on land and sea. Ten were elected annually, one from each tribe. The number sent on each campaign was decided by the Ecclesia (see table on page 116). As well as military powers they also had some civil powers. One of these was the power to convene and preside over meetings of the Ecclesia. However, there is some uncertainty as to whether they gained this power now or later. Eventually they became the chief executive officers of the state.

THE WORK OF ARISTIDES (530?–467? BC)

Aristides, as leader of the people's party, reputedly introduced in 487 BC a decree to the Ecclesia whereby 'every citizen would have a share in the government and the archons would in future be elected from the whole body of voters'. (Plutarch, *Life of Aristides*, 22) Plutarch seems to have misunderstood this action, for in practice what occurred is that five hundred candidates from those citizens 'eligible' were to be first elected, fifty from each tribe, as candidates for selection by lot for the archons' positions. Previously only the highest social class was eligible for this magistracy. Aristides now widened the base for eligibility by throwing open the archonship to those of the second highest social class, the Hippeis, as well. This opened the position to more citizens but not to all. Selection by lot also weakened the desire for aspiring politicians to hold this position, for although they might gain initial selection, the final one was by sheer chance — the odds being little better than fifty to one. The use of selection by lot was seen as fairer because the choice of candidate was therefore in the 'laps of the gods'. As a result the position of strategos was now seen as the key political position. The power of the Ecclesia was also increased.

As well as this Aristides supposedly is responsible for having changed the basis of the census at Athens. The previous social divisions had been based upon land ownership alone; Aristides changed this to include all property. This still did not open up the higher magistracies to all citizens but it did increase the number of citizens eligible for the archonship and eventually the Areopagus, thus weakening the hold on the government by the old aristocracy.

	ECCLESIA	BOULE	AREOPAGUS	HELIAEA	THE STRATEGOI	THE ARCHONS	OTHER MAGISTRATES
MEMBERSHIP	• All male citizens over the age of 18 could attend meetings and vote on issues • Met approximately forty times a year	• All male citizens above 30 years of age eligible for selection by lot • 50 citizens chosen from each tribe for one year, total 500 • Usually worked in committees (called *prytaneis*) of 50 for a tenth of the year (35/36 days) • Citizens could not sit on this body more than twice, and not in consecutive years • Members lived at public expense while in working *prytaneis*	• All ex-archons were eligible for membership • Membership for life	• Citizens over 30 years of age • 6000 jurors chosen by lot each year to be available for service • Jurors were chosen on the day a court was to sit, by lot, from the list of 6000 • Paid for service	• Citizens only • 10 in number • One elected annually from each tribe by popular vote • Re-election allowed Began term of office probably on the first day of Hekatombaion	• Citizens only (some doubt over eligibility of the Thetes) • Chosen from whole citizen body by lot • 9 in all • Paid for service	• Aristotle gives a total of 700 magistracies • They were usually organised in boards of 10, elected by lot, one from each tribal division and holding annual tenure
RESPONSIBILITY / POWERS	• Passed legislation • Elected magistrates • Heard accounts of retiring magistrates • Acted as the final court of appeal • Empowered strategoi • Heard reports from strategoi approximately ten times a year • Guardian of the constitution • Right to punish public officials • Tried cases where public interest was threatened	• Drafted bills for presentation to Ecclesia • Supervised election of strategoi • Inspected cavalry and naval ships • Managed the public boards • Tried magistrates accused of mismanagement • Checked qualifications of newly allotted officials • Heard some criminal trials and some trials where public interest was threatened	• Heard deliberate homicide cases and arson cases • Care of sacred olive groves • Had some say in the supervision of property of the Eleusinian deities • Could call magistrates to account for illegal or irregular acts in the fulfilling of their responsibilities or failing to carry out duties	• Juries heard civil cases. No counsels or cross-examination allowed. Each plaintiff spoke independently. Time was predetermined for a speaker — measured by a water clock (the *klepsydra*) • Jurors made judgement by voting with a pierced brass ballot for guilty and an unpierced one for not guilty • Tried officials who had failed to give a satisfactory account of their administration • Jurisdiction in most cases dealing with religious impiety	• Commanded military and naval expeditions • Could conduct preliminary negotiations with foreign states • Could convene the Ecclesia • Responsible to the Ecclesia and could only act under its instructions	• Administrative only: *Polemarch:* Military Archon *Eponymous:* President of the State *Archon Basileus:* Religion *The Six Thesmotheta:* Jury Courts	• Jobs varied from corn commissioners to superintendents of the docks • All were subject to monthly and annual scrutiny. As the empire increased, so did the number of these minor officials to serve overseas

STOP AND THINK

✎ **Find out more about Aristides. What is he famous for?**

- **How democratic were the reforms of Aristides? (*Clue*: Why were only the two richest of the social classes given access to the archonship?)**
- **Was he merely using the support of the people to further his own political career?**

✎ **Who really were favoured by these reforms? What might this mean for the future of Athenian foreign policy?**

✎ **How would the changes in the selection procedures for the archonship have made the position of strategos more significant?**

THE ASCENDANCY OF THE AREOPAGUS

During the period following the Greek victories over the Persians and the formation of the Delian League, Athens and its popular politicians became too preoccupied with the great military matters of the day (see the key events time-line, page 108) to concentrate on further democratic reform. Perhaps also the leaders of the party of the people saw no need for further change because under the reforms of Aristides, the Areopagus would eventually be controlled by people 'friendly' to his party's policies. As a result the Areopagus, with its body of largely conservative aristocratic ex-archons, gained control of the government of Athens. This came about through its powers to try and punish magistrates for misconduct during their time in office, and its duty to supervise the administration of the state and its laws. Couple to this its judicial power and one can see the importance of its position.

EPHIALTES' REFORMS (495?–462/1 BC)

Ephialtes became the leader of the people's party in 468–67 and set out to attack the power of the Areopagus. He prepared the way for its reform by accusing and successfully impeaching individual Areopagites for corruption and fraudulent practices. (Aristotle, *Athenian Constitution*, 25)

Taking advantage of Cimon's absence on campaign he introduced a series of laws, reportedly with some assistance from Themistocles (Aristotle, *Athenian Constitution*, 25), which stripped the Areopagus of its major powers. Under these the Areopagus lost:

- the power to punish magistrates for misconduct,
- the power to supervise the administration of the state,
- the duty of seeing that the laws were obeyed, and
- the right to investigate the lives of private citizens.

These powers were transferred to the Boule, the Ecclesia and the Heliaea. The only functions retained by the Areopagus were its powers of jurisdiction over cases of intentional homicide and the supervision of religious ceremonies.

STOP AND THINK

✎ **To what extent were these reforms more democratic than those of Aristides?**

✎ **What effect would these reforms have had on the positions of archon and strategos?**

Ephialtes' reforms gave more control of the state to the masses and earned him the ire of the aristocrats and others: he was assassinated in 462–61. Whether or not he had intended to take his reforms further is uncertain, but his successor as leader of the people's party, Pericles, certainly did.

PERICLES' REFORMS

Pericles was, according to the sources, responsible for a number of democratic reforms.

At the same time as the attack on the Areopagus (461 BC) Pericles proposed a bill for the payment of jurors. This served two purposes: it gained Pericles popular support for the attack on the Areopagus and would also encourage citizens to undertake jury service. The result was, by modern standards, the democratisation of the law courts. Every citizen who wished could place his name on a list from which a list of 6000 jurors was selected by lot, a set number from each tribe. The courts were empanelled from this final list. This meant also that one faction could not, theoretically, dominate these courts.

STOP AND THINK

✎ **Most ancient sources saw this reform as a bad one. Would you agree with them? Why?**

✎ **Theoretically anyone could end up on a jury panel, just as happens today. However, could one faction or party dominate the panels or not? Explain your answer.**

In 458 BC Pericles proposed a bill that abolished the previous system of the choice of archons and minor officials. These had been chosen by lot from a select number of candidates who had been previously elected from the two upper social classes by each tribe. Pericles' reform admitted the third class, the Zeugitae, to the archonship and eliminated the initial tribal election. Henceforth all archons, along with the members of the Boule, were selected by lot. This move once more weakened the power of the old aristocracy and opened up the running of the government to the middle class. To ensure the success of these reforms and a more representative body of candidates, Pericles also introduced a payment for service as an archon or as a member of the Boule.

STOP AND THINK: GIVE YOUR OPINION

◢ **How did these reforms open up the running of government?**

◢ **Why is payment for service so important to democratic government?**

◢ **Was Pericles a true democratic reformer or did he have other motives for the changes he made? Explain your answer.**

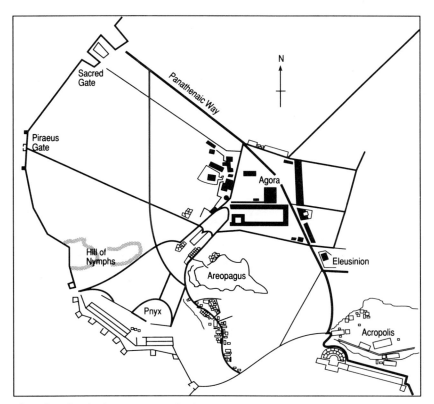

The political and religious centre of Athens
What major buildings did Pericles have constructed on the Acropolis?
How did he pay for these buildings?
How might this add to his popularity amongst the voting citizens of the city?
Do his building programme and imperialistic foreign policy shed any light on his character as a politician? Why?

Note: The eligibility of the lowest class, the Thetes, for the office of archon was never formally conferred upon them. However, sometime in the late part of the fifth century BC, possibly due to their importance in the navy, the distinction between them and the Zeugitae became fainter. In time they were enrolled as Zeugitae and not as Thetes and as such became eligible to hold the office of archon.

In 451 BC Pericles introduced a decree that was passed by the Ecclesia. This decree revised the citizenship rolls and restricted the admission of new citizens depending upon their parentage. In future no child could become an Athenian citizen unless both parents were already citizens and legally wedded.

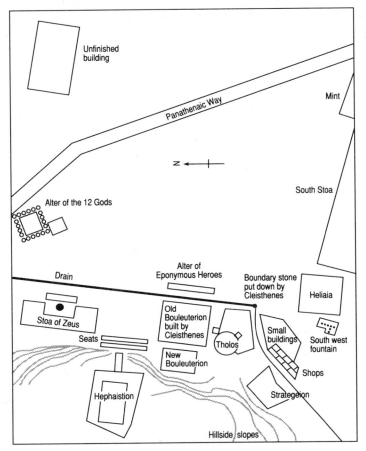

A plan of the Athenian Agora in the time of Cleisthenes
What was the Agora?
Which buildings in the Agora were politically important?
What is a stoa?
What was the strategion used for?
Why would political buildings be placed in or near the Agora?

STOP AND THINK: GIVE YOUR OPINION

> **Why would Pericles and the Assembly wish to limit the number of citizens in Athens? (*Clue*: What proposals had been carried in 461 and 458 BC?)**

> **How democratic does this appear to be? Explain your answer.**

THE ATHENIAN DEMOCRACY (458–430 BC)

By 458 BC the development of the Athenian democracy had reached its height. How then did it function during the period of Pericles 'domination' of Athens' government?

Rostrum at Pnyx

STOP AND THINK: RESEARCH

Ecclesia

- **Meetings of the Ecclesia were held at the Pnyx. Find out where it was. How difficult would it have been for all citizens of Attica to attend meetings of the Ecclesia?**
- **Which groups of people would have been favoured by the location of meetings of the Ecclesia?**
- **How might the need to vote in person be used by Athenian politicians to ensure the success of their policies?**

Boule

- **How democratic was this body? Explain your answer.**
- **What was its general purpose within the government?**
- **Could it be controlled by one person or political party?**

Areopagus

- **The powers and responsibilities of the Areopagus centred largely on control of the lives and morals of the citizens. What social values were the Areopagus protecting?**
- **Compare the powers and responsibilities of the Areopagus with those of the Ecclesia and the Boule. What are the significant differences?**
- **Why would a group of already proven ex-magistrates have such limited powers?**

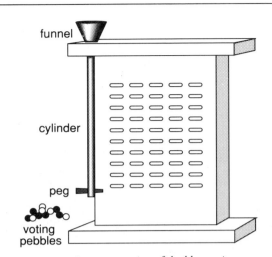

A reconstruction of the kleroterion

A kleroterion or allotment machine
This device was invented to minimise the risk of jury bribing. Each juror carried an identification ticket which he placed in a box to indicate his desire to sit on a jury panel that day. These were then pulled out at random and each placed in one of the slots on the kleroterion. A number of black and white balls were then fed in, and were released one at a time. If the first ball out was white, the citizens named on the tickets in the first row of the kleroterion were jurors for the day; if it was black they were dismissed.

A juror's ticket from the 4th century BC

The Heliaea

- **How democratic was this body?**
- **Many of the ancient writers criticise the quality of the jurors and their verdicts. Find a copy of Aristophanes' *The Wasps* and read it. What type of person is presented in the play as likely to seek the position of juror? Why? Write down any interesting pieces of information from the play on the procedures followed in the Heliaea.**
- **Could these courts be used as a weapon against a political opponent? How?**

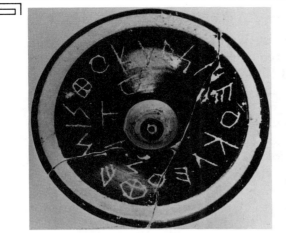

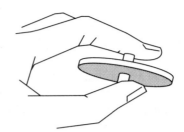

A reconstruction showing how a juror's ballot was held.

An ostraka with 'Out with Themistocles' written on it.
This was used during an ostracism.
What was an ostracism?
What were the constitutional requirements for an ostracism to take place?
How was an ostracism conducted?
How could ostracism have worked to support Athenian democracy?

The Magistrates

- **What was incorporated into the constitution to enable active participation of any person who chose to participate?**
- **Why is it unlikely that a poor man could be elected strategoi. Would a poor person want to be strategoi?**
- **One way of controlling the state would have been to gain control of the army. Who served in the Athenian army? Could one strategos take control of the army?**
- **What safeguards were there against one man assuming too much power in one of these positions?**

The Athenians were at great pains to minimise corruption in the legal system. Look carefully at each of the stages of juror selection and voting and provide a reason for each of the procedures adopted. Could you think of any ways it could be thwarted?

To sum up:

Having looked at the workings of the political institutions of Athens during the period 458–430 BC answer these questions:

- **Which group ultimately controlled the Athenian government during this period? Provide a detailed explanation for your answer.**
- **If an Athenian citizen had a burning desire to be the most powerful person in the world, what would he have to do to first, achieve the position, and second, maintain the position?**

PERICLES' DOMINATION OF ATHENIAN DEMOCRACY

The Athenian system of government during the period 460–430 BC is often referred to as the best example of the democratic form. Periclean democracy had universal suffrage for all adult male citizens, direct elections of magistrates and public officials for annual terms, and accountability of these officials via an assessment by the people of their actions whilst in office. The Ecclesia, or assembly of citizens, held the final say on most issues and could decide directly on issues such as war or treaties. The Heliaea, or jury courts, whose members were drawn by lot from the citizen body held almost total judicial power and some legislative. Despite these achievements, Thucydides, a contemporary writer, described the relationship between Pericles and Athens in what appears to be a contradictory way:

So, in what was nominally a democracy, power was really in the hands of the first citizen.

The Peloponnesian War, 2, 65

❊   ❊   ❊

Just what Thucydides meant by this is a little obscure. Nonetheless during the period 448–430 BC Pericles did, from all accounts, dominate the political scene at Athens, and was elected strategos fifteen times from 446 to 430 BC.

An analysis of the workings of the government during the period shows that Pericles had no special place within it that was not constitutionally legal. In fact during Pericles' political career the government became more democratic than it had been previously. How then, if the government was democratic, was he able to dominate it and maintain his position within it?

STOP AND THINK: DOCUMENT STUDY
Look at the sources presented below. Answer the questions and make up your own mind on this issue.

A . . . he [Pericles] had first distinguished himself when, as a young man, he prosecuted Cimon in the examination after his generalship.

Aristotle, *The Athenian Constitution*, 27

❊   ❊   ❊

B The reason for this was that Pericles, because of his position, his intelligence, and his known integrity, could respect the liberty of the people and at the same time hold them in check. It was he who led them, rather than they who led him, and, since he never sought power from any wrong motive, he was under no necessity of flattering them: in fact he was so highly respected that he was able to speak angrily to them and to contradict them. Certainly when he saw that they were going too far in a mood of over-confidence, he would bring them back to a sense of their dangers; and when they were discouraged for no good reason he would restore their confidence.

Thucydides, *The Peloponnesian War*, 2, 65

❊   ❊   ❊

C **F**rom it he derived not only a dignity of spirit and a nobility of utterance which was entirely free from the vulgar and unscrupulous buffooneries of mob-oratory, but also a composure of countenance that never dissolved into laughter, a serenity in his movements and in the graceful arrangement of his dress which nothing could disturb while he was speaking, a firm and evenly modulated voice, and other characteristics of the same kind which deeply impressed his audience.

Plutarch, *Life of Pericles*, 5

*   *   *

D **I**n eloquence no man could equal him —
When Pericles arose and took the floor,
By ten good feet our common orators
As by an expert runner were outstripped.
Not only voluble, but with persuasion
Sitting upon his lips. He bound a spell,
And had this power alone of orators,
To prick men's hearts and leave behind the sting.

Eupolis, fragment 94

*   *   *

E . . . men who were well on in years remarked on the charm of Pericles' voice and the smoothness and fluency of his speech . . . The fact that he was rich and that he came of a distinguished family and possessed exceedingly powerful friends made the fear of ostracism very real to him, and at the beginning of his career he took no part in politics but devoted himself to soldiering, in which he showed great daring and enterprise.

Plutarch, *Life of Pericles*, 7

*   *   *

F **P**ericles . . . took care not to make himself too familiar a figure, even to the people, and he only addressed them at long intervals. He did not choose to speak on every question, but reserved himself . . . for great occasions, and allowed his friends and other public speakers to deal with less important matters.

Plutarch, *Life of Pericles*, 7

*   *   *

G **M**oreover, Pericles was the first man to provide payment for jury service, as a political measure to counter the generosity of Cimon . . . Some people allege that it was as a result of this that the courts deteriorated, since it was always the ordinary people rather than the better sort who were eager to be picked for jury service. After this judicial corruption began.

Aristotle, *The Athenian Constitution*, 27

*   *   *

H **A**t the beginning of his career . . . Pericles had to measure himself against Cimon's reputation, and he therefore set out to win the favour of the people. He could not compete with the wealth or the property by means of which Cimon captured the affections of the poor; for the latter supplied a free dinner every day to any Athenian who needed it, provided clothes for the old, and took down the fences on his estates so that anyone who wished could pick the fruit. So finding himself outmatched in this kind of popular appeal, Pericles turned his attention to the distribution of the public wealth . . . and before long, what with the allowances for public festivals, fees for jury service, and other grants and gratuities, he succeeded in bribing the masses wholesale.

Plutarch, *Life of Pericles*, 9

*   *   *

I **P**ericles therefore chose this moment [c. 448 BC] to hand over the reins of power to the people to a greater extent than ever before and deliberately shaped his policy to please them. He constantly provided public pageants, banquets and processions in the city, entertaining the people like children with elegant pleasures; and he sent out 60 triremes to cruise every year, in which many of the citizens served with pay for eight months and learned and practised seamanship at the same time. Besides this, he dispatched 1,000 settlers to the Chersonese, 500 to Naxos, 250 to Andros, 1,000 to Thrace . . . and others to the new colony named Thurii . . . In this way he relieved the city of a large number of idlers and agitators, raised the standards of the poorest classes, and, by installing garrisons amongst the allies, implanted at the same time a healthy fear of rebellion.

Plutarch, *Life of Pericles*, 11

✳ ✳ ✳

J **S**o he boldly laid before the people proposals for immense public works and plans for buildings, which would involve many different arts and industries and require long periods to complete, his object being that those who stayed at home, no less than those serving on the fleet or the army or on garrison duty, should be enabled to enjoy a share of the national wealth . . . and so through these various demands the city's prosperity was extended far and wide and shared among every age and condition in Athens.

Plutarch, *Life of Pericles*, 12

✳ ✳ ✳

✎ **Construct a chart, using the headings shown below, and complete it.**

Extract	Author	Reason given for Pericles' popularity	Problem with source

✎ **How did Pericles increase his reputation when young?**

✎ **What personal qualities made him popular among the people?**

✎ **Which extracts give evidence of his political ability? What do they say?**

✎ **Which extracts complement or support one another? Explain why.**

✎ **What problem regarding reliability appears in extract G? Can you explain why this might be so?**

✎ **Could Pericles be accused of buying the people's affection for his own political ends? Use evidence from the extracts to support your view.**

PERICLES' POSITION

Before we can fully assess Pericles' position within the Athenian system of government we must look at the position held by him during the period in question.

Pericles was an Athenian citizen and a member of the upper classes, from a politically distinguished family. He therefore had the same rights as every other citizen; he could vote and stand for election to any of the magistracies; he could participate in the Boule or Heliaea, if selected by lot, and in the Ecclesia.

He did stand, and was elected by his tribe, as one of the ten strategoi. He was elected sixteen times, fifteen times between 445–430 BC (re-election was not forbidden), and Cimon held the position at least ten times. This position had become, as we have already seen, the key political position within Athens during this period. The main role of the strategos was military; however, he could call meetings of the Ecclesia and give advice that carried considerable weight. The citizens could and did, on occasion, refuse to listen to this advice, and it was also the duty of the strategos to carry out policy decided upon by the citizens even if he regarded it as unsound.

A strategos was, like all magistrates, subject to public scrutiny. He could be brought to trial or even fined if any part of his work was suspect or unsuccessful. Pericles was in fact fined and removed from office in 431–30 BC by the citizens as a result of the hardships of the first two years of the Peloponnesian War. They blamed him for having persuaded them to undertake the war.

A safeguard against any citizen regarded as a danger to the state's welfare was ostracism. This meant exile from Attica for ten years. Each year in the sixth prytany the question whether an ostracism should be held was put to the Ecclesia. If one was to be held it was supervised by the archons and Boule in the Agora. Each citizen voted on a piece of pottery (known as an *ostraka*) and if the total number of votes equalled 6000 or more the citizen with the largest number of votes was exiled. Many famous political figures had been ostracised in the past, Themistocles, Cimon and even Pericles' father, Xanthippus, to name but a few. During Pericles' time several of his own associates, notably Damon, his music teacher, were either ostracised or attacked politically. Pericles, however, was never ostracised.

STOP AND THINK: RESEARCH

➘ **Using Plutarch's *Life of Pericles*, find out the names of Pericles' political opponents. How did he deal with them? Was this legal?**

➘ **Why might Plutarch overemphasise Pericles' power within the Athenian system of government?**

➘ **Using any other information you find and extracts A–J above, explain how Pericles was able to dominate the democracy in Athens between 460 and 430 BC?**
Use the following headings as guidelines in your answer:

- **his personal abilities**
- **his political methods and policies**
- **his position as strategos.**

➘ **Having assessed the work of Pericles as a politician working within the confines of a democratic system, choose one leading Australian politician and compare the methods used to win votes today. Has anything really changed?**

PERICLES' POLICIES AND OUTBREAK OF THE PELOPONNESIAN WAR

There are many reasons that have been advanced by various historians for the outbreak of the Peloponnesian War in 431–30. Among them is one that places the blame and responsibility on the imperialistic foreign policies adopted by Pericles prior to the start of the war. It is important to note, however, when apportioning blame or responsibility that any control that Pericles exercised over the foreign policy of Athens came through the majority support of its citizens voting within the Ecclesia. In order to assess Pericles' responsibilities we must examine our available sources carefully.

STOP AND THINK: DOCUMENT STUDY

Read the following extracts and answer the questions that follow.

A **. . .** why should we blame it all on the Spartans? It was Athenians . . . it was them who started the whole thing. They started bringing charges against the Megarians. First it was their woollies, and before long, whenever they saw anyone with a watermelon, or a young hare or a piglet, or some garlic and rock-salt, 'Ah!' they said, 'Megarian contraband', and had them confiscated and put under the hammer that very day. Well, that was minor — just our national sport, as you might say, but then some young chaps got drunk and, for a lark, went to Megara and kidnapped their tart Simaetha. Well, this raised the Megarians' hackles, and they stole two of Aspasia's girls in retaliation. And that, gentlemen, was the cause of the war that has been raging throughout Greece these six years: it was all on account of three prostitutes. Because Pericles, Olympian Pericles, sent Pericles' mistress out thunder and lightning and threw all Greece into confusion. He began making laws written like drinking songs,

> No Megarian shall stand
> On sea or on land
> and from all of our markets
> they're utterly banned.

Well, pretty soon the Megarians were starving by slow degrees, and not unnaturally asked their allies the Spartans to try and get the decree reversed . . . they asked us, more than once, but we refused, and so the shields began to clash . . .

Speech of Dikaiopolis, Aristophanes, The Acharnians, 2, 514–38

✦ ✦ ✦

B **A** few years later, when the clouds were already gathering for the Peloponnesian war, Pericles persuaded the Athenians to send help to Corcyra in her war with Corinth and so bring over to their side an island with a powerful navy at a time when the Peloponnesians had all but declared war on them.

Plutarch, Life of Pericles, 29

✦ ✦ ✦

C **I**n spite of all this a succession of embassies was sent to Athens . . . In fact, it seems likely that the Athenians might have avoided war on any of the other issues, if only they could have been persuaded to lift their embargo against the Megarians and come to terms with them. And since it was Pericles who opposed this solution more strongly than anyone else and urged the people to persist in their hostility towards the Megarians, it was he alone who was held responsible for the war.

Plutarch, Life of Pericles, 29

✦ ✦ ✦

D **P**ericles' answer... was that the Athenians were not obliged to give the allies any account of how their money was spent, provided that they carried on the war for them and kept the Persians away... It is no more than fair that after Athens has been equipped with all she needs to carry on the war, she should apply the surplus to public works, which, once completed, will bring her glory for all time, and while they are being built will convert the surplus to immediate use. In this way all kinds of enterprises and demands will be created which will provide inspiration for every art, find employment for every hand, and transform the whole people into wage earners, so that the city will decorate and maintain itself at the same time from her own resources.

Plutarch, *Life of Pericles*, 12

❋ ❋ ❋

E **P**ericles, however, constantly strove to curb this extravagant spirit of conquest, to restrain the desire to meddle with foreign states and to devote Athens' main strength to guarding and consolidating what she had already won. He considered that to hold the Spartans in check was one of the prime objectives of Athenian policy, and he set himself to oppose them in every way; he showed this in many of his decisions...

Plutarch, *Life of Pericles*, 21

❋ ❋ ❋

F **A**nd now you must make up your minds what you are going to do — either to give way to them [the Peloponnesians] before being hurt by them, or, if we go to war — as I think we should do — to be determined that, whether the reason put forward is big or small, we are not in any case going to climb down nor hold our possessions under a constant threat of interference.

Thucydides, *The Peloponnesian War*, 1, 141

❋ ❋ ❋

G **T**his was Pericles' speech. The Athenians considered that his advice was best and voted as he had asked them to vote. Their reply to the Spartans was the one he had suggested...

Thucydides *The Peloponnesian War*, 1, 145

❋ ❋ ❋

✎ **According to extract A what caused the Peloponnesian War?**

✎ **What was the Megarian decree? When was it passed?**

✎ **What problems might exist with the reliability of extract A?**

✎ • **What complaints did the Corinthians have against Athens according to these extracts?**
  • **Were there any other reasons for complaint that you can discover between Corinth and Athens? (*Clue*: Read Thucydides, *The Peloponnesian War*, 1, 67–72.)**

✎ **Using the library research the following questions.**

  • **Why did the people of Aegina consider themselves oppressed by Athens?**
  • **What was the Peloponnesian League? How did it work? Who were its members?**

✎ **Which extracts indicate that Pericles played a leading role in pushing Athens and Sparta towards conflict? Use evidence from the extracts to support your choices.**

Thucydides (2, 13) tells us that the allies of Athens supplied an average yearly income of 600 talents (estimated to be approximately US $600 000 per year).

- According to the extracts how did Pericles make use of this money?
- What do extracts D and F tell us about Pericles' attitudes towards Athens' allies?
- According to extract D why did Pericles use this money in this way?
- What other reasons might Pericles have had for using the money in this way?

Of the three ancient works quoted here which would you consider the most reliable? Explain your answer.

Using whatever evidence is available to you, assess in essay form the extent to which Pericles' policies were responsible for the outbreak of the Peloponnesian War. You will need wider reading.

PERICLES' IMPORTANCE TO ATHENS

Pericles succeeded in enabling Athens to rise to the height of material prosperity by the expansion of her economy. He opened up the Athenian government to the people, thereby completing its democratic development, and made the city the cultural centre of Greece. This was not achieved without a cost. The cost, however, was borne by the supposed allies and eventually, because of the Peloponnesian War, by all the Athenians themselves. Nonetheless Pericles, a patriot to the end, best sums up the greatness of the city that he had largely built in the Funeral Oration, delivered by him at the end of the first year of the Peloponnesian War (Thucydides, 2, 37–47), when he says, 'In a word, then, I say that our city as a whole is the school of Hellas . . .'.

STOP AND THINK: ACTIVITIES AND ADDITIONAL RESEARCH

Produce a series of full page news-stand posters where you show what you consider to be the most important events and changes in Periclean Athens.

Assume the role of Pericles. Write your statement of 'My Life and My Works' which will be reproduced on a column of stone in the Agora. State clearly where your account concludes. It may be continued after your death by a supporter or friend.

Assume the role of a Periclean supporter. You have had a speech written for you by a demographer which you will deliver to the Ecclesia in 437 BC, a year of great commercial expansion for Athens. Your intention in this speech is to point out to the Athenian citizens what Athens has gained from the leadership of Pericles.

Note: **You must be factual; however a reasonable amount of flattery would be quite acceptable. Remember also that the people you are addressing are well aware of the present situation and the events of the past. You may admit poor decisions in some areas but your intention is to reawaken an awareness of the greatness of Athens because of the policies of Pericles.**

One of Pericles' greatest achievements was his reconstruction and extension of the city of Athens.

- **Why was this undertaken?**
- **How was it financed?**
- **What was the attitude of the member states of the Athenian empire towards this programme?**
- **List all of the architectural monuments of the Athenian empire included in this programme.**
- **Draw or obtain pictures of at least five of these monuments and list their most outstanding architectural features. How was each monument used, and how important was it?**

LIST OF REFERENCES

ANCIENT SOURCES

Aeschylus, *The Persians*, tr. A.J. Podlecki, Prentice-Hall, Englewood Cliffs, NJ, 1970

Aristophanes, *The Complete Plays of Aristophanes*, ed. Moses Hadas, Bantam, 1981

Aristotle, *The Politics and Athenian Constitution*, ed. and tr. John Warrington, Dent, London, 1959

Plutarch, 'Life of Aristides' and 'Life of Pericles' in *The Rise and Fall of Athens: nine Greek lives*, tr. Ian Scott-Kilvert, Penguin Classics, 1960 repr. 1980

Thucydides, *The Peloponnesian War*, tr. Rex Warner, Penguin Classics, 1954 repr. 1980

SECONDARY SOURCES

Barrow, R., *Athenian Democracy*, Inside the Ancient World series, Macmillan, 1982

—— *The Athenian Citizen: Excavation in the Athenian Agora*, Book 4, American School of Classical Studies, Athens, 1960

Bowra, C.M., *Periclean Athens*, Weidenfeld & Nicolson, London, 1971

Burn, A.R., *Pericles and Athens*, English University Press, 1966

Forrest, W.G., *The Emergence of Greek Democracy, 800–400 BC*, Weidenfeld & Nicolson, London, 1966

Jones, A.H.M., *Athenian Democracy*, Blackwell, Oxford, 1978

CHAPTER SEVEN

THE PELOPONNESIAN WAR

Kate Cameron and Dianne Hennessy

During the Persian invasion of 480–479BC Sparta and Athens and twenty-nine other Greek states fought together to repel the mighty invader. At the beginning of the war those Greeks who had come together as the Hellenic League handed leadership of land and sea forces to Sparta who was acknowledged as the leading power among the Greeks. The Athenians may well have resented Sparta's pre-eminent position, especially as leader of the sea forces, because Athens provided the largest proportion of the fleet. Also the Athenians were justifiably proud of having defeated the Persians at Marathon ten years earlier, unaided by Sparta.

Despite this initial ill-feeling and some serious disagreements over strategy during the war, these two states and their Hellenic allies defeated the Persians and drove them from Greek soil. Athens' prestige grew through its part in the war, particularly because of its outstanding leadership and the strength and ability of its fleet, especially at Salamis. The Spartans' participation too inspired other Greeks, and under Spartan leadership the decisive land victory was won at Plataea.

Spartan prestige, however, was seriously diminished by the conduct of one of their most successful generals, Pausanias. He was recalled to Sparta by the ephors for his treasonable conduct in Byzantium (478 BC) and was eventually starved to death. Sparta too was reluctant to fight too far from home because of the fear of helot revolts, and when it looked as if the campaign against Persia was going to be conducted further afield, Sparta did not seek to regain leadership of the Greek forces continuing the war into Asia.

Athens then assumed leadership of the campaign. From this position it was able to assemble a confederacy of Greek states from the Aegean and Ionia which looked to Athens for protection and even for revenge against the Persians. This confederacy became known as the Delian League.

By the end of the war, although Sparta's reputation as leader of the Greeks had been seriously challenged by the Athenians, its position as most powerful state on the mainland was still secure. Athens' main interests at this time were in the Aegean and Ionia and so it seemed that each state enjoyed its own sphere of influence at the head of its own alliance system.

Within fifty years these two states and their allies were at war with each other, engaged in a long and bitter struggle which had catastrophic results for Greece. Thucydides tells us that:

> The Peloponnesian War . . . not only lasted for a long time, but throughout its course brought with it unprecedented suffering for Hellas. Never before had so many cities been captured and then devastated, whether by foreign armies or by the Hellenic powers themselves . . . never had there been so many exiles; never such loss of life.
>
> Thucydides, *The Peloponnesian War*, 1, 23

HOW DID SUCH A WAR COME ABOUT?

The Peloponnesian War was not fought between Athens and Sparta alone. Each was involved in a web of alliances with other Greek states and this made the conflict far more extensive. In order to understand what caused the conflict, some consideration needs to be given to the nature of these alliances and the relationships that existed within and between them.

SPARTA AND THE PELOPONNESIAN LEAGUE

The Peloponnesian League developed as a result of a change in Spartan foreign policy that occurred around the middle of the sixth century. Until then Sparta had engaged in military conquest and annexation of the territory around it and enslavement of the conquered population. After this time the Spartans realised their resources were fully extended in controlling the areas they had already acquired and so they decided to ensure the co-operation of their neighbours through military alliances rather than military conquest.

Each state which entered into an alliance with Sparta took an oath 'to have the same enemies and the same friends as Sparta had and to follow Spartan leadership in any expedition Sparta might make by land or sea'. In return, the Spartans agreed to defend their ally if it was attacked. All the Peloponnesian states, except Argos and Achaea, entered into such alliances, as did the states of Corinth and Megara.

The Peloponnesian League did not hold regular meetings. Representatives of the allies met in a League Congress to discuss issues affecting League forces, such as the declaration of war or the conclusion of a peace. Members had an equal vote and debate was open. There were no financial or military obligations on members, except when the League was at war.

Sparta's supremacy within the League was evident: League members swore individual treaties with Sparta; Sparta convened and conducted meetings of the League Congress; meetings were held at Sparta and Sparta commanded all League forces. Sparta would only call a meeting of the League Congress once the Spartan Assembly had decided on a particular course of action. If the majority of the League Congress disagreed, however, Sparta had to accept that decision and abandon the original course of action.

Generally all allies were bound by a majority decision of the League Congress except for the proviso 'unless something to do with the gods or heroes prevented it'. (Thucydides, 5, 30) Such an exemption might apply if following a majority decision meant that an ally would breach a pre-existing treaty, or interrupt a religious festival or sacred truce.

In theory the Peloponnesian League came into effect only in times of war. It was a military alliance where members acknowledged Sparta's leadership in military matters, but were otherwise autonomous.

In practice, however, Sparta did intervene in the internal politics of League members, propping up pro-Spartan oligarchies and actively discouraging democracies and tyranny. The terms of the oath sworn to enter the League — 'to have the same enemies and friends as Sparta' — virtually meant that allies surrendered control of their foreign policy to Sparta.

As leader of this powerful alliance, Sparta was secure in its position in the Peloponnese, knowing that it could be assured of help from its allies to put down revolts of the helots. The Peloponnesian League enabled Sparta to continue living according to its own institutions.

ATHENS AND THE DELIAN LEAGUE

The Delian League was formed in 478–77 BC towards the end of the Persian War when Athens assumed leadership of the Greek forces who were determined to drive the Persians from the Aegean. The purpose of the League was to protect Greek cities rescued from the Persians and to seek compensation for their losses by ravaging the territory of the King of Persia. (Thucydides, *The Peloponnesian War*, 1, 96) States which joined the League swore an oath with Athens to have the same enemies and friends. (Aristotle, *Athenian Constitution*, 23.5) Iron bars were then sunk into the sea to signify the permanence of the oath — that it should last until the bars rose to the surface.

There were over 150 members of the League, including the Greek cities of Asia, the islands off the Asian coast as far south as Rhodes, towns on the Propontis, towns in Thrace and Chalcidice, most of the Cyclades and the island of Euboea, except for Carystus. Sparta was not a member of the Delian League.

Meetings of the League were held at Delos where a treasury was established to hold the contributions made by members. These contributions were made each year and formed a type of permanent war fund.

Representatives from each allied state attended meetings where each had an equal vote. Athens had only one vote, but was often able to influence the vote of smaller states.

Although the League was a confederacy of autonomous states with equal voting power, Athens' authority over its allies was clear from the beginning: League members swore individual oaths to Athens; an Athenian, Aristides, assessed how much each state should contribute to the League's treasury each year; treasury officials were Athenians, and Athens commanded all League forces. Nevertheless, it was a voluntary confederacy and members were keen to have Athens' leadership.

For the first few years of the League's operations Athens respected the autonomy of her allies, requiring only that they maintain their annual contributions. In return Athens fulfilled her obligations. Under the Athenian general Cimon, League forces drove the Persians from the Aegean and from coastal Asia Minor. In 469 BC the Greeks defeated the Persian army and fleet at Eurymedon. It seemed that Greece was free from the Persian threat.

STOP AND THINK: PUTTING IT ALL TOGETHER
Draw up a chart highlighting the main features of the two alliances. Use the sub-headings provided.

	PELOPONNESIAN LEAGUE	**DELIAN LEAGUE**
Leader		
Members		
Oath		
Purpose		
Contributions		
Gains for the allies		
Gains for the leader		
Primary sources		

SPARTA AND ATHENS 479–460: CORDIAL RELATIONS
At the end of the Persian War the Athenians hastened to rebuild the walls which had been destroyed by the Persians. The Spartans, who had suffered no invasion or damage, objected. They sent an embassy to Athens requesting not only that Athens should not rebuild her walls, but also that she should join Sparta in dismantling the fortifications of other cities outside the Peloponnese, so that they could not be used by the Persians in the event of another attack.

Themistocles felt that Athens needed to be fortified in order to protect its own citizens and to safeguard its position within Greece. Thucydides gives the details of how Themistocles tricked the Spartans, delaying their return until the walls were 'high enough to be defended'. This implies that Themistocles suspected Sparta might attack to stop the reconstruction of the walls. This did not eventuate, however, and the Spartans 'showed no open signs of displeasure towards Athens'. (Thucydides, 1, 92)

From this incident on, for about the next sixteen years, relations between Sparta and Athens appear to have been quite friendly. Each was involved in its own affairs and the affairs of its respective league.

Sparta turned its interest north of the Peloponnese to Thessaly and central Greece where it intended to punish those cities who had submitted to the Persians, in accordance with an oath originally taken by members of the Hellenic League. Another way in which Sparta sought to punish those who had not fought against the Persians was to try to expel them from the Amphictyonic League, a religious association which controlled Delphi. Sparta's efforts were frustrated when the Athenian, Themistocles, delivered a persuasive speech which brought about the defeat of the Spartan motion.

In 473 BC Sparta was alarmed when her traditional enemy, Argos, entered into a treaty with Tegea. Sparta attacked Tegea, then defeated the combined forces of Tegea and Argos. Argos was again the source of trouble for Sparta when Themistocles went into exile there after his ostracism from Athens in 472 BC, and allegedly carried on anti-Spartan activities there and in other parts of the Peloponnese.

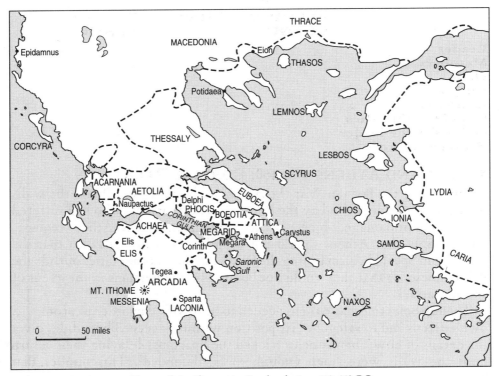

Places of significance in Greek relations 479–460 BC

While Sparta's supremacy was being challenged within its sphere of influence, Athens was asserting its position in the Aegean. Under the direction of the Athenian Cimon, the Delian League recaptured Eion on the Strymon River in 476–75 and cleared the Persians from Caria. League forces also conquered the island of Scyrus and established a cleruchy there.

In 472 BC the Delian League turned its attention to the city of Carystus on Euboea, which had not originally joined the League. It was now forced to do so. Athens argued that Carystus' strategic position was too important to allow it to fall into Persian hands, so in the interests of all League members it must be forced to join. According to Thucydides a war followed and Carystus surrendered.

The next action of the League was against one of its own members, the island of Naxos, which tried to secede from the League in 469 BC. After a siege Naxos was forced back into the League. Thucydides explains that Athens insisted members of the League should meet their obligations and that it was prepared to bring severe pressure on allies who would not do so. Thucydides also describes the way that many League members became reluctant to provide military service in the form of men and ships and agreed instead to pay money. As a result the Athenian navy grew strong at their expense. League members lost the ability to defend themselves, making them more reliant than ever on Athens.

In 468 BC Cimon led League forces on a campaign against the Persians in southern Caria. He then defeated the Persian fleet and army which stood at the mouth of the Eurymedon River in Pamphylia. It was a great victory and to many Greeks it seemed that the Persian threat had been eliminated. However, the League was not dissolved and when Thasos tried to secede in 465 BC, it was attacked. Cimon led League forces to defeat the Thasian fleet, then besieged the city. Thasos appealed to Sparta for help. According to Thucydides (10, 1) Sparta promised to relieve the pressure on Thasos by invading Attica, but an earthquake and helot revolt prevented it from carrying out the promise. After two years of siege, Thasos was forced to surrender, its walls were destroyed and its fleet was confiscated by Athens.

Cimon's pro-Spartan sympathies were well known and in the early years of the League, the respect shown to him by the Spartans made him a valuable negotiator amongst the Greek states. However, as the Delian League grew in strength, some Athenians saw Sparta as a rival rather than a friend. When Sparta asked for Athens' help to put down a helot revolt, Ephialtes, representing the anti-Spartan faction,

. . . opposed the request and exhorted the Athenians not to attempt to rescue or restore a city which was their rival but rather to let Sparta's pride be trampled underfoot. Cimon, on the other hand, put Sparta's interests before his own country's aggrandisement and persuaded the Athenians to send a large force of hoplites to her aid.

Plutarch, *Cimon,* 16.

✳   ✳   ✳

According to Thucydides, the Spartans grew afraid of Athenian enterprise and its unorthodox methods. They were also suspicious that the Athenians, being of a different nationality (i.e. Ionian, not Dorian), might become sympathetic to the people of Ithome and support some revolutionary policy there. (Thucydides, 1, 102) Whatever the reason, the Spartans sent the Athenians home but kept all the other allies with them.

The Athenians were humiliated by this treatment and denounced the original treaty of alliance which had been made against the Persians. In 461 BC Cimon was ostracised. These events marked the end of the period of cordial relations between Athens and Sparta.

STOP AND THINK

⟍ **List the events that indicate Sparta's distrust of Athens.**

⟍ **List the events that show Athens' distrust of Sparta.**

⟍ **Draw up a two-columned chart of events. Include events that show any challenges to Sparta's position in one column, and events that show the strengthening of Athens' position in the other.**

⟍ **Take any single event where there was conflict between Athens and Sparta. Research further into the event. Prepare a *pair* of speeches that indicate clearly the opposing viewpoints.**

SPARTA AND ATHENS 460–445 BC: HOSTILITIES

The ostracism of Cimon in 461 BC indicated a change in Athens' relationship with Sparta and its allies. The Athenian radical democratic faction, which had expressed anti-Spartan sentiments before, now gained increasing support and reached a position of influence in affairs. While the hostilities against Persia were continued and the Delian League was maintained, Athens now embarked on another branch of foreign policy which brought it into direct conflict with Sparta and its allies. Athens withdrew from its longstanding alliance with Sparta and entered into alliances with Sparta's enemy, Argos, and with Thessaly.

The Spartan rejection of Athenian hoplites from Mt Ithome had been a great humiliation to Athens, but was it enough to warrant this change in policy? Was this change part of an aggressive imperialism on Athens' part — an attempt to expand its empire into central Greece? Or was it an act of self-defence against a perceived threat from Sparta?

People like Ephialtes no doubt would have reminded the Assembly of Sparta's past interference in Athens' affairs, of its demand that Athens pull down rather than rebuild its fortifications at the end of the Persian War, and of Sparta's four invasions of Attica in the last decade of the sixth century. Perhaps Sparta's promise to help Thasos by invading Athens also became known at this time. If the Athenians did regard Sparta as a real threat, it was important that they ally themselves with appropriate and strategically placed land-based powers. Athens' strength was in her navy; her army was no match for the armies of Sparta and the Peloponnesian League.

Few modern historians accept this self-defence motive, and see this phase of Athens' actions as a new aspect of imperialism, a deliberate attempt to build up a land empire in central Greece, an area dominated by Sparta's allies.

Some historians suggest that Athens' actions in central Greece were motivated by rivalry with Corinth over trade. Through its control of the Delian League Athens had greatly increased its sea power and had used it to extend trade and so enhance its own prosperity. Proponents of this theory suggest that any expansion of Athenian trade west of the Aegean would bring it into competition with Corinth, an important ally of Sparta.

STOP AND THINK: WHAT DO YOU THINK?

As you read the following outline of events consider which motive you would attribute to Athens: self-defence, expansion of empire, or competition with Corinth? It is important that you keep referring to the map on page 141 where issues of strategic advantage are readily apparent.

The following events are from Thucydides, *The Peloponnesian War*, 1, 102–15. The dates given are approximate because there is disagreement among historians about the exact sequence of some of the events.

461	Sparta dismissed Athenian troops from Mt Ithome.
	Athens denounced the treaty made with Sparta against the Persians.
	Athens entered into alliances with Argos, Sparta's enemy, and Thessaly.
	Athens received the Messenian rebels whom the Spartans had exiled from Mt Ithome, and settled them in the town of Naupactus which Athens had recently taken.
460	Megara abandoned its alliance with Sparta because of a border dispute with Corinth and joined the Delian League. This gave Athens control of Megara's two ports, Pagae on the Corinthian Gulf and Nisaea on the Saronic Gulf.
	Athens built walls from Megara to Nisaea and garrisoned them with Athenian troops. According to Thucydides, this was the start of Corinth's 'bitter hatred' for Athens.
458	Athens and a Delian League fleet of 200 ships engaged in a campaign against Cyprus but abandoned it to go to Egypt to help a Libyan prince expel the Persians who ruled there.
	An Athenian fleet landed at Haliae where they were defeated by a force of Corinthians and Epidaurians.
	Soon after there was a sea battle at Cecryphalia between the Athenian and Peloponnesian fleets. The Athenians were victorious.

457	War broke out between Athens and Aegina. Allies from both sides were involved in a major naval battle which the Athenians won.
	At the same time Corinth and its allies invaded Megara, in the belief that Athens would be unable to help Megara because its forces were occupied in Egypt and Aegina. However the Athenians raised a force of reserves and eventually defeated the Corinthians.
	The Athenians began building two long walls from Athens down to its two ports, Phalerum and Piraeus.
	The Phocians started a campaign against Doris. The Spartans and their allies came to the aid of the Dorians and defeated the Phocians. They returned to the Peloponnese through Boeotia.
	The Athenians and their allies attacked the Peloponnesian forces in Boeotia but were defeated at the Battle of Tanagra.
	The Athenians returned to Boeotia two months later, defeated the Boeotians in a battle at Oenophyta, then conquered all of Boeotia and Phocis which were forced to join the Delian League.
	Aegina was forced to surrender, to destroy its fortifications, to hand over its fleet to Athens and to become a tribute-paying member of the Delian League.
	An Athenian force sailed around the Peloponnese and burnt the Spartan dockyards at Gytheum. The same force captured the Corinthian city of Chalcis in Aetolia and attacked the city of Sicyon.
	Meanwhile, fifty triremes from Athens and the Delian League set out to relieve the forces in Egypt which, unbeknown to them, had already been defeated by the Persians. The relieving forces were also defeated. At about this time Athens transferred the treasury of the Delian League from Delos to Athens.
454	Pericles led another Athenian force against Sicyon and defeated the troops who opposed him. On their return voyage they sailed westward along the Corinthian Gulf. They forced Achaea to join the Delian League.
451	A five-year truce was made between Athens and the Peloponnesians.
448–7	In a campaign known as the 'Sacred War', Sparta took the temple at Delphi from the control of the Phocians and gave it back to the Delphians. As soon as the Spartans retired the Athenians took the temple again and gave it back to the Phocians.
446	Boeotia revolted from Athens.
	Euboea revolted but was crushed by Athens.
	Megara revolted from Athens.
	Peloponnesian forces under the Spartan King Pleistoanax invaded Attica, laying waste the country as far as Eleusis. After this, they returned home.
445	Athens made a Thirty Year Truce with the Spartans.

STOP AND THINK

Look closely at the map to answer these questions:

⬩ **What strategic advantages would Athens gain from:**

- **an alliance with Argos?**
- **an alliance with Megara?**
- **controlling the port city of Naupactus?**

⬩ **Why would Corinth object to Athens installing a garrison at the Megarian port of Nisaea?**

⬩ **At what time did Athens control the largest area in central Greece?**

⬩ **Which mainland states or cities had joined — or been forced to join — the Athenian alliance?**

⬩ **What event made it easier for the Peloponnesians to invade Attica in 447 BC?**

⬩ **What do you see as Athens' motives for its actions during this period?**

⬩ **How would you describe Corinth's role in these events?**

⬩ **What role was played by Sparta?**

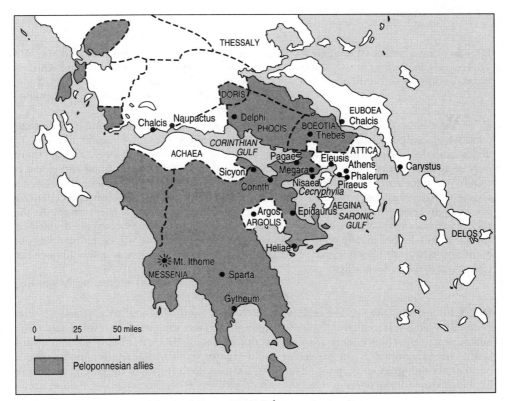

Athenian intervention in Peloponnesian territory

THE THIRTY YEAR TRUCE

The period between 460 and 445 BC, ending with the Thirty Year Truce, is often referred to by historians as the first Peloponnesian War, but Thucydides does not regard this period as part of the war at all. He sees the Peloponnesian War beginning in 431, with the breaking of the Thirty Year Truce.

Unfortunately there is no detailed account of the terms of the truce. The main references to it are scattered throughout Thucydides.

STOP AND THINK

Read the following references carefully, then use the information in them to draw up what you think are the main terms of the truce. (Note that there is a contradiction between two of the references.) Check the context of the references in Thucydides and decide for yourself which is likely to be most reliable. It is important that you reach some conclusions yourself about the terms of the truce before you check your version against a reliable secondary source.

A **S**oon after they had returned from Euboea the Athenians made a thirty years' truce with Sparta and her allies: Athens gave up Nisaea, Pagae, Troezen, and Achaea — all places which they had seized from the Peloponnesians.

1, 115

✦ ✦ ✦

B **'I**t is not a breach of your treaty with Sparta if you receive us into your alliance. We are neutrals, and it is expressly written down in your treaty that any Hellenic state which is in this condition is free to ally itself with whichever side it chooses.'

1, 35 [Corcyreans addressing Athenians]

✦ ✦ ✦

C **'W**e have shown, I think, that we have good reasons for complaint, and that the conduct of Corcyra has been both violent and grasping. Next we should like you to understand that it would not be right or just for you to receive them as allies. Though there may be a clause in the treaty stating that any city not included in the original agreement is free to join whichever side it likes, this cannot refer to cases where the object of joining an alliance is to injure other powers ... What you ought not to do is to establish a precedent by which a power may receive into its alliance the revolted subjects of another power. At the time when Samos revolted from you and when the Peloponnesian states were divided on the question whether to help them or not, we were not one of those who voted against you; on the contrary, we openly opposed the others and said that every power should have the right to control its own allies.'

1, 40 [Corinthians addressing Athenians]

✦ ✦ ✦

D **T**he Spartans also issued an invitation to their own allies and to anyone else who claimed to have suffered from Athenian aggression. They then held their usual assembly, and gave an opportunity there for delegates to express their views. Many came forward with various complaints. In particular the delegates from Megara, after mentioning a number of other grievances, pointed out that, contrary to the terms of the treaty, they were excluded from all the ports in the Athenian empire and from the market of Athens itself.

1, 67

✦ ✦ ✦

E '**A**thenians,' [Pericles] said, 'my views are the same as ever: I am against making any concessions to the Peloponnesians, even though I am aware that the enthusiastic state of mind in which people are persuaded to enter upon a war is not retained when it comes to action, and that people's minds are altered by the course of events. Nevertheless I see that on this occasion I must give you exactly the same advice as I have given in the past...

'It was evident before that Sparta was plotting against us, and now it is even more evident. It is laid down in the treaty that differences between us should be settled by arbitration, and that, pending arbitration, each side should keep what it has. The Spartans have never once asked for arbitration, nor have they accepted our offers to submit to it. They prefer to settle their complaints by war rather than by peaceful negotiations, and now they come here not even making protests, but trying to give us orders. They tell us to abandon the siege of Potidaea, to give Aegina her independence, and to revoke the Megarian decree. And finally they come to us with a proclamation that we must give the Hellenes their freedom.

'Let none of you think that we should be going to war for a trifle if we refuse to revoke the Megarian decree. It is a point they make much of, and say that war need not take place if we revoke this decree; but, if we do go to war, let there be no kind of suspicion in your hearts that the war was over a small matter. For you this trifle is both the assurance and the proof of your determination. If you give in, you will immediately be confronted with some greater demand, since they will think that you only gave way on this point through fear. But if you take a firm stand you will make it clear to them that they have to treat you properly as equals.'

1, 140 [Pericles speaking]

✦   ✦   ✦

F '**F**or the present I recommend that we send back the Spartan ambassadors with the following answer: that we will give Megara access to our market and our ports, if at the same time Sparta exempts us and our allies from the operation of her orders for the expulsion of aliens (for in the treaty there is no clause forbidding either those orders of hers or our decree against Megara)... Let us say, too, that we are willing, according to the terms of the treaty, to submit to arbitration, that we shall not start the war, but that we shall resist those who do start it.'

1, 144 [Pericles speaking]

✦   ✦   ✦

G **T**here was also the fact that the Spartans considered that Athens had been the first to break the peace treaty. In the first war they thought that the fault had been more on their side, partly because the Thebans had entered Plataea in peace time and partly because, in spite of the provision in the previous treaty that there should be no recourse to arms if arbitration were offered, they themselves had not accepted the Athenian offer of arbitration.

7, 18

✦   ✦   ✦

H **T**he people of Aegina were on her [Corinth's] side. Out of fear of Athens they had not sent a formal delegation, but behind the scenes they played a considerable part in fomenting war, saying that they had not been given the independence promised to them by the treaty.

1, 67

✦   ✦   ✦

With the declaration of the Thirty Year Truce, Athens and Sparta recognised a balance of power within the Greek world. There were now two power blocs: Sparta and the Peloponnesian League, the dominant land power; and Athens and the Delian League, which by now had been converted to the Athenian empire, the dominant naval power. Neutral states which were not part of either alliance were free to join whichever side they chose. Certain states chose to remain neutral, among them Argos and Corcyra.

It is important to remember that the truce was not made between two single powers, but between two sets of allies. Alliance systems may provide strength and security for their members, but they also carry the risk that members may be drawn in to incidents triggered by any one of the allies. In his account of the immediate events leading to the outbreak of the war, Thucydides shows that allies played a crucial role in drawing the powers into conflict.

EVENTS LEADING TO THE OUTBREAK OF WAR

Thucydides is our main source of information about the causes of the Peloponnesian War. The information he provides, however, has been interpreted in a variety of ways by modern historians. It is most important that you first familiarise yourself with the events as described by Thucydides and this is best done by reading the text itself — not a textbook. Then you should judge for yourself if the conclusions reached by Thucydides are valid on the basis of the evidence he provides. Once you have formed your own opinion about Thucydides' explanation of the causes of the war, then and only then should you consult other historians to consider their interpretations.

Thucydides states what he considers to be the reasons why the war broke out.

War began when the Athenians and the Peloponnesians broke the Thirty Years Truce which had been made after the capture of Euboea. As to the reasons why they broke the truce, I propose first to given an account of the causes of complaint which they had against each other and of the specific instances where their interests clashed: this is in order that there should be no doubt in anyone's mind about what led to this great war falling upon the Hellenes. But the real reason for the war is, in my opinion, most likely to be disguised by such an argument. What made war inevitable was the growth of Athenian power and the fear which this caused in Sparta.

Thucydides, 1, 23

✳ ✳ ✳

Five important points emerge from this statement:

1. The war began when the Athenians and the Peloponnesians broke the Thirty Year Truce.
2. The two powers had causes of complaint against each other and instances where their interests clashed and these are what broke the truce.

3. The causes of complaint and clashes of interest were openly expressed by each side.
4. These are not the real reason for the war.
5. The real reason for the war was the growth of Athenian power and the fear this caused in Sparta.

Most modern historians draw a distinction between the two types of causes mentioned by Thucydides, generally interpreting the 'causes of complaint' (in Greek, *aitia*) as immediate causes and the 'real reason' (in Greek, *alethestate prophasis*) as the underlying or truest cause. After making his general statement about the causes of the war, Thucydides goes on to describe the immediate causes of the war, the 'causes of complaint' and 'clashes of interest' between the Athenians and the Peloponnesians.

THE DISPUTE OVER EPIDAMNUS (1, 24–30)

Epidamnus was a colony of Corcyra but its original founder had been a Corinthian. When the democrats in Epidamnus drove out the aristocrats, internal strife developed which the democrats could not resolve. They appealed to Corcyra for help but Corcyra refused to intervene. After consulting the oracle at Delphi the democrats appealed to the Corinthians who came to their assistance.

There was no love lost between Corinth and Corcyra. Corcyra had been a colony of Corinth's but they had been hostile toward each other for centuries. When Corinth brought its fleet to aid the Epidamnians, Corcyra demanded that it withdraw and urged it not to start a war which would force Corcyra to 'make friends elsewhere'. The Corcyreans offered to accept arbitration of the dispute but Corinth refused and engaged the Corcyreans in battle. The Corcyreans won and destroyed fifteen Corinthian ships.

THE DISPUTE OVER CORCYRA (1, 31-55)

Corinth could not accept its defeat by Corcyra and spent the following two years building up its fleet and attracting rowers from the Peloponnese and elsewhere in Greece.

Corcyra became alarmed at these operations because it had always been an independent state and had no allies. It decided to send representatives to Athens to see if it could form an alliance with the Athenians. The Corinthians also sent representatives to Athens to prevent the Athenians accepting Corcyra as an ally.

The Corcyreans argued that it would be in Athens' interests to have the Corcyrean fleet on its side rather than have the Corinthians take it over and use it against Athens. The Corcyreans also argued that Athens would not breach the Thirty Year Truce by accepting an alliance with them because Corcyra was a neutral state and the truce allowed neutral states to join whichever side they chose. They also reminded the Athenians that in the event of a war with the Peloponnesians, Corcyra's position would be a strategic advantage, to prevent naval reinforcements coming from Italy and Sicily to the Peloponnese or going from the Peloponnese to these countries.

The representative from Corinth then addressed the Assembly and claimed it would not be right for Athens to accept an alliance with Corcyra, because to do so would injure Corinth. He warned the Athenians that an alliance with Corcyra would mean making war on Corinth.

If you join them in attacking us, we shall be forced to defend ourselves against you as well as against them.

Thucydides, 1, 40

❋ ❋ ❋

After discussion in two more meetings of the Assembly, the Athenians decided they would not enter into a full alliance with Corcyra. They compromised and offered a defensive alliance which would only operate if Athens or Corcyra or any of their allies were attacked from outside.

Athens then sent ten ships as reinforcements to Corcyra, with strict instructions to avoid battle with the Corinthians unless they sailed against the Corcyreans with the intention of landing on Corcyra or any Corcyrean territory. According to Thucydides (1, 45) these instructions were given in order to avoid breaking the treaty.

The battle between the Corinthian and Corcyrean fleets took place off Sybota. (1, 46–53) At first the Athenians took no part in the battle, but when it became apparent that the Corcyreans, who were outnumbered by the Corinthians, were facing defeat the Athenians joined in and fought against the Corinthians. A second battle was averted when twenty more Athenian ships were sighted.

The Corinthians sent a messenger to the Athenians and accused them of starting a war and not abiding by the treaty. The Athenians denied these accusations and stated that they were simply defending their allies, the Corcyreans, and would continue to do so. The Corinthians were allowed to sail home.

There was no outright winner in the battle, although both sides claimed the victory. Corcyra was not defeated and Corinth did not succeed in taking Epidamnus. According to Thucydides (1, 55), this event gave Corinth its first cause for war against Athens.

STOP AND THINK

✎ **What was Corcyra's position at the signing of the Thirty Year Truce?**

✎ **Why would Corcyra have such wealth and such a strong fleet?**

✎ **Read the full speeches from both the Corinthians and the Corcyreans (1, 32–43). Consider their arguments from the point of view of two individual Athenians, one in favour of the alliance with Corcyra and the other against it.**

DISPUTE OVER POTIDAEA (1, 56–65)

Potidaea, a city situated in Chalcidice, was originally a Corinthian colony and Corinth maintained ties by sending its own magistrates to Potidaea each year. Potidaea, however, had become a tribute-paying member of the Delian League and was an Athenian ally at the time of the Thirty Year Truce.

After the hostility Corinth had shown in the dispute over Corcyra Athens feared the presence of Corinthian magistrates in Potidaea, believing that they might induce Potidaea to revolt and so encourage other allies in the Thracian area to revolt. Athens therefore demanded that the Potidaeans pull down part of their fortifications, send hostages to Athens, banish their Corinthian magistrates and receive no more in future.

The activities of Perdiccas, king of Macedonia, also spurred Athens into taking action. He approached Corinth for support for a revolt in Potidaea and he also approached the Chalcidians in Thrace and the Bottiaeans, urging them to revolt from Athens at the same time. He hoped they would then become his allies.

The Potidaeans sent representatives to Athens to appeal against the demands. They also sent representatives to Sparta, accompanied by Corinthians, to gain its support. Athens did not withdraw its demands, but ordered its fleet to sail against Potidaea to ensure that the demands were carried out. Meanwhile, Sparta promised to invade Attica if the Athenians attacked Potideae. Strengthened by this promise, the Potidaeans decided to join with the Chalcidians and the Bottiaeans and revolted from Athens in 432 BC.

Corinth sent out a 2000-strong force of Corinthian volunteers and mercenaries from the rest of the Peloponnese to defend Potidaea. The Athenians sent a force of 2000 citizen hoplites and a fleet of forty ships to reinforce the troops who were already in Macedonia. After completing operations in Macedonia, they marched on Potidaea where they defeated the forces of Potidaeans and Peloponnesians. The Athenians then besieged Potidaea.

In his assessment of the situation, Thucydides notes that each side had grounds of complaint against the other. Corinth's grievance was that the Athenians were besieging its colony, Potidaea. Athens' grievance was that the Peloponnesians had not only supported the revolt of a city which was in alliance with Athens, but also had joined openly in fighting against it. Yet, in spite of these grievances, war between the Athenians and the Peloponnesians had not yet broken out.

Corinth was about to change all that. It sent delegates to Sparta to attack Athens for having broken the truce and committing acts of aggression against the Peloponnesians.

STOP AND THINK

Look at the map and answer the questions that follow.

↘ **Why would Potidaea have joined the Delian League?**

↘ **Why would King Perdiccas be concerned about Athenian influence in Chalcidice?**

↘ **Why was Athens so determined to quash the revolt of Potidaea?**

↘ **Discuss the following issues with reference to the Thirty Year Truce:**

- **Did Corinth have the right to defend Potidaea against Athens?**
- **What option other than armed intervention was available to Corinth? Why didn't it follow an alternative course of action?**
- **Was Corinth justified in saying Athens had broken the truce?**
- **Do you think the truce had been broken? If so, by whom?**

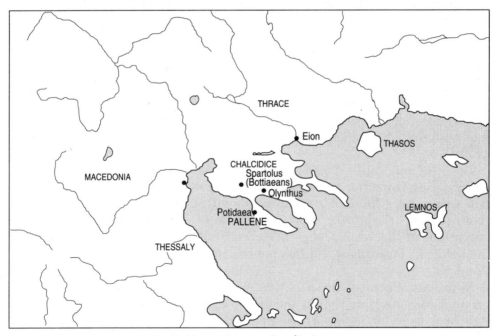

Potidaea and surrounding districts

THE MEGARIAN DECREE

After the Corinthian delegation had accused Athens of breaking the Thirty Year Truce by its actions at Potidaea, the Spartans invited their allies and anyone else who claimed to have suffered from Athenian aggression to address the Spartan Assembly. Thucydides states that many came forward with particular complaints, including a delegation from Megara which spoke of Athens excluding them from 'all the ports in the Athenian empire and from the market of Athens itself'. (1, 67)

This Megarian Decree is referred to twice more by Thucydides. In 1, 139 a Spartan embassy demands that Athens abandon the siege of Potidaea and give Aegina its independence:

But the chief point and the one that they made most clear was that war could be avoided if Athens would revoke the Megarian decree which excluded the Megarians from all ports in the Athenian Empire and from the market in Attica itself.

1, 139

* * *

The decree is next mentioned when the Athenians debate the ultimatum given by the Spartans, that peace would be possible if the Athenians would 'give the Hellenes their freedom'. Apparently there was much debate in the Assembly about revoking the Megarian Decree and finally Pericles explained why it was a matter of principle not to do so (see quoted passage E, page 143).

Later in his speech to the Athenian Assembly Pericles states that there was no clause in the Thirty Year Truce forbidding the decree against Megara, just as there was no clause forbidding the Spartan practice of expelling Athenians and their allies from Sparta as aliens. He implies by this that each state was acting well within its rights. Although some Athenians had originally been in favour of revoking the decree, nobody challenged Pericles' statement about it not being contrary to the Truce. Thucydides does not give prominence to the Megarian Decree as a cause of the Peloponnesian War. He states quite simply Athens' reasons for imposing it: that the Megarians had cultivated consecrated ground, that they had cultivated land that did not belong to them and that they had given shelter to slaves who had escaped from Athens.

Most modern historians reject these reasons given by Thucydides and many see the Megarian Decree as a significant cause of the war. They suggest more sinister political motives on Athens' part. Some see the decree as a punishment of Megara for helping Corinth in the battle of Sybota; some see it as an aspect of Athens' continuing desire to extend its economic imperialism to the west. Others see the decree as a way of forcing Megara out of the Peloponnesian alliance and into Athenian control. The decree has even been seen as an act of personal revenge on Pericles' part and as a deliberate attempt by Athens to provoke Sparta into war.

Historians not only differ on their theories about the reasons for the decree, they also differ on their interpretation of the decree, how it was applied and on its impact on Megara. One historian concludes that it was a cruel and deadly weapon which spelt economic ruin for Megara (Bury &

Meiggs, pp. 246–7), while at the opposite extreme another describes it as a humiliation and an indignity, but one which had very little effect on Megara's trade at all (de Ste Croix, p. 262).

STOP AND THINK
- **What additional information would you need to have in order to be able to judge the true intention of the decree?**
- **What evidence might indicate the effectiveness of the decree?**
- **How would you test each of the reasons given above for Athens imposing the decree?**
- **Read Pericles' speech from Thucydides, 1, 140. What evidence is there in the speech to contradict the notion that the decree was a deliberate provocation for war?**

THUCYDIDES AND THE CAUSES OF THE WAR

Thucydides goes into considerable detail about the three disputes which he cites as the immediate reasons for the outbreak of war between the Athenians and the Peloponnesians: the disputes over Epidamnus, Corcyra and Potidaea. He gives very little information about the Megarian Decree. He then presents the events which led to the final declaration of war through a series of speeches. These should be read in their entirety to appreciate fully the arguments being put forward by each side.

In the debate at Sparta the allies cried out against Athenian aggression and Corinth reprimanded Sparta for ignoring Athenian aggression and for being so slow to act when Peloponnesian allies were in danger. It warned the Spartans that if they did not act, Corinth and some of the other allies could be forced to join a different alliance. The Corinthians concluded by reminding Sparta of its leadership of the Peloponnese and urged it to 'maintain its greatness'.

Athenians who happened to be in Sparta on business at the time asked for and were given the right to address the Assembly. They reminded the Spartans of the vital role played by Athens in the Persian Wars and of how they acquired the empire when the Spartans were unwilling to carry on the war against the Persians. The Athenians claimed that their action in maintaining their empire was justified and that the Spartans would have been just as hard on their allies had they been in the same situation. The Athenians concluded by appealing to the Spartans not to be pushed into war by the complaints of their allies, not to go back on their oaths, but to settle their differences by arbitration as was laid down in the treaty.

Following this the Spartan King, Archidamus, spoke against an immediate declaration of war. He suggested Sparta take the grievances of its allies to arbitration, but at the same time carry on preparations for war.

The ephor, Sthenelaidas, opposed this appeal for caution. He argued that the Spartans had a responsibility to defend their allies quickly and with all their might. He said it was clear that the Athenians were the aggressors and that the Spartans should not allow them to grow stronger at the expense of their allies. He urged a vote for the honour of Sparta and for war.

As ephor, Sthenelaidas then put the question to the Assembly. The great majority voted that the truce had been broken by the Athenians. Thucydides suggests that the Spartans voted this way not because they were influenced by the speeches of their allies, but 'because they were afraid of the further growth of Athenian power, seeing, as they did, that already the greater part of Hellas was under the control of Athens'. (1, 88)

In order to support his claim about Spartan fear of growing Athenian power, Thucydides presents a tightly written argument describing how Athens had steadily increased its power over the preceding fifty years. (1, 89–117) He ends this section, known as the *Pentecontaetia*, with a description of Athens crushing the revolt by their fellow Greeks, the Samians.

Thucydides sees the disputes over Corcyra and Potidaea, which occurred only a few years after the revolts of Samos, in the same light: as part of Athens' growing imperialism. In his view, Athenian strength had reached a peak and when it began to encroach on Sparta's allies, Sparta could no longer tolerate the situation and finally decided to do something about it.

Although the Spartan Assembly had voted that the truce had been broken, they still had to call a meeting of their allies to officially declare a war. Once again the Corinthians urged the Peloponnesians to war, to destroy Athens and liberate the Greeks whom Athens had enslaved. The majority voted for war.

War did not begin at once however. The Spartans sent a series of embassies to Athens with various complaints 'so that there should be a good pretext for making war if the Athenians paid no attention to them'. (1, 126) Athens rejected all of these demands. Finally the Spartans sent an ultimatum. They made no references to their earlier demands but simply stated: 'Sparta wants peace. Peace is still possible if you will give the Hellenes their freedom.' (1, 139)

A debate followed in which many opinions were expressed for and against war. In his speech, Pericles argued that the Spartans were obviously plotting against the Athenians, that they had refused to settle their grievances by arbitration, which the Athenians had offered to do in accordance with the Thirty Year Truce. Pericles then outlined the strength of the Athenian empire and the weaknesses of the Peloponnesians. He was confident that Athens could win a war against the Peloponnesians as long as they did not try to expand their empire at the same time.

Pericles recommended that the Athenians should reply to the Spartans by saying:

- Athens would lift the Megarian Decree *if* Sparta would revoke her practice of expelling Athenians and allies as aliens.
- Athens would give independence to its allies (if they had been independent at the time of the Thirty Year Truce) when Sparta allowed its allies to be independent with a government of their own choice rather than one preferred by Sparta.
- Athens would willingly go to arbitration in accordance with the Thirty Year Truce.

The Athenian Assembly voted to accept Pericles' proposals and the Spartan ambassadors took this reply back to Sparta. There were no further negotiations and approximately one year later the war began when an armed force of Thebans attacked Plataea, an ally of Athens.

IS THUCYDIDES' VIEW CORRECT?

Most historians agree with Thucydides that the underlying cause of the war was the growth of Athenian power and the fear this instilled in Sparta. Historians may give a different emphasis to the more immediate causes, paying more attention to economic factors, factionalism within states and relationships between states, especially the roles of the allies, but they basically accept the idea that Sparta could no longer tolerate the growth of Athenian power, and in fact *had to go to war*.

Some historians challenge this view of the innocent and reluctant Sparta and point to evidence from Thucydides which indicates that Sparta, or at least the dominant faction in Sparta, was aggressive, opportunistic and quite prepared to break the truce and did so on several occasions. In their view Athens adhered strictly to the Truce and should bear no responsibility for the outbreak of war.

STOP AND THINK

The issue of 'war guilt' or responsibility for causing the war must be settled in your classroom. Working as a group, develop a whole campaign to support your viewpoint. After examining all the evidence carefully (including some additional research!) prepare the following:

- **the front page story of a newspaper**
- **a one-minute media release to the radio stations**
- **a speech to be delivered in the classroom.**

WAR

When war finally broke out in 431 BC the two opposing states, Athens and Sparta, had a great number of allies at their disposal. These are shown on the map opposite.

Greek alliances at the outbreak of the Peloponnesian war

STOP AND THINK: MAP STUDY

➣ **Where were most of the Spartan allies located?**

➣ **Where were most of the Athenian allies located?**

➣ **What strategies would need to be employed to protect the interests of these allies and to gain victory?**

RESOURCES OF THE OPPOSING STATES

The following extracts from Thucydides, *The Peloponnesian War*, provide an overview of the resources available to Athens and Sparta. Sources A–C present Pericles speaking to the Athenian Assembly in reply to the Spartan ultimatum that Athens stop the siege of Potidaea and revoke the Megarian Decree:

A **I** should like you to listen to a detailed account and to realize that we are not the weaker party. The Peloponnesians cultivate their own land themselves; they have no financial resources either as individuals or as states; then they have no experience of fighting overseas, nor of any fighting that lasts a long time, since the wars they fight against each other are, because of their poverty, short affairs. Such people are incapable of often manning a fleet or often sending out an army, when that means absence from their own land, expense from their own funds and, apart from this, when we have control of the sea. And wars are paid for by the possession of reserves rather than by a sudden increase in taxation. Those who farm their own land, moreover, are in warfare more anxious about their money than their lives; they have a shrewd idea that they themselves will come out safe and sound, but they are not at all sure that all their money will not have been spent before then, especially if, as is likely to happen, the war lasts longer than they expect. In a single battle the Peloponnesians and their allies could stand up to all the rest of Hellas, but they cannot fight a war against a power unlike themselves, so long as they have no central deliberative authority to produce quick decisive action, when they all have equal votes, though they all come from different nationalities and every one of these is mainly concerned with its own interests . . .

But this is the main point: they will be handicapped by lack of money and delayed by the time they will have to take in procuring it.

1, 141–142.1

※ ※ ※

B **T**hen we have nothing to fear from their navy, nor need we be alarmed at the prospect of their building fortifications in Attica.

So far as that goes, even in peace time it is not easy to build one city strong enough to be a check upon another; and this would be a much harder thing to accomplish in enemy territory and faced with our own fortifications, which are just as strong as anything that they could build. While if they merely establish some minor outpost, they could certainly do some harm to part of our land by raiding and by receiving deserters, but this could by no means prevent us from retaliating by the use of our sea-power and from sailing to their territory and building fortifications there. For we have acquired more experience of land fighting through our naval operations than they have of sea fighting through their operations on land. And as for seamanship, they will find that a difficult lesson to learn. You yourselves have been studying it ever since the end of the Persian wars, and have still not entirely mastered the subject. How, then, can it be supposed that they could ever make much progress? They are farmers, not sailors, and in addition to that they will never get a chance of practising, because we shall be blockading them with strong naval forces. Against a weak blockading force they might be prepared to take a risk . . . but if they are faced with a large fleet they will not venture out, and so lack of practice will make them even less skilful than they were, and lack of skill will make them even less venturesome.

1, 142.2

※ ※ ※

C **S**uppose they lay their hands on the money at Olympia or Delphi and try to attract the foreign sailors in our navy by offering higher rates of pay: that would be a serious thing if we were not still able to be a match for them by ourselves and with our resident aliens serving on board our ships. As it is, we can always match them in this way. Also — which is a very important point — we have among our own citizens more and better steersmen and sailors than all the rest of Hellas put together. Then, too, how many of our foreign sailors would, for the sake of a few days' extra pay, fight on the other side at the risk not only of being defeated but also of being outlawed from their own cities?

1, 143

※ ※ ※

Sources D and E are paraphrases of a speech by Pericles as the Spartans were mustering to attack.

D **P**ericles encouraged confidence, pointing out that, apart from all other sources of revenue, the average yearly contribution from the allies to Athens amounted to 600 talents, then there still remained in the Acropolis a sum of 6,000 talents of coined silver. This reserve fund, at its maximum, had been 9,700 talents. It had been drawn on to pay for the Propylaea and other public buildings, and for Potidaea. In addition to this there was the uncoined gold and silver in offerings made either by individuals or by the state; there were the sacred vessels and furniture used in the processions and in the games; there were the spoils taken from the Persians, and other resources of one kind or another, all of which would amount to no less than 500 talents. To this he added the money in the other temples which might be used and which came to a considerable sum, and said that, if they were ever really reduced to absolute extremities, they could even use the gold on the statue of Athene herself. There was, he informed them, a weight of forty talents of pure gold on this statue, all of which was removable.

*   *   *

2, 13.1

E As for their army, they had 13,000 hoplites in addition to the 16,000 others who were in various garrisons and those engaged in the actual defence of the city. This was the number originally detailed for defence in case of invasion, and the force was drawn from the eldest and the youngest of the citizens in the army together with the resident aliens who were qualified as hoplites. The wall of Phalerum ran for four miles from the sea to the city circuit; and nearly five miles of the wall surrounding the city was guarded, though part of it (the section between the Long Walls and the wall of Phalerum) was left without a guard. Then there were the four and a half miles of the Long Walls to Piraeus, the outer one of which was garrisoned. Then, too, there were seven and a half miles of fortifications surrounding Piraeus and Munychia, half of which distance was guarded. There were also 1,200 cavalry, including mounted bowmen; 1,600 unmounted bowmen, and 300 triremes ready for active service.

*   *   *

2, 13.2

STOP AND THINK
Draw up the following table and complete it to develop your own comparison of the resources of Athens and Sparta.

RESOURCES	ATHENS	SPARTA
Allies		
Land forces		
Naval forces		
Finances		
Other aspects including national characteristics		

✎ **If you were the Athenian, Pericles, what would be your major concern?**

✎ **If you were the Spartan King, Archidamus, what would be your major concern?**

**Who would you predict to be the victor?
As a totally objective historian write up the case you would
submit in support of your prediction.**

STRATEGIES PROPOSED FOR VICTORY

The strategy of the Athenians at the beginning of the war was that of
Pericles, agreed to at meetings of the Athenian Assembly. Thucydides
restates the strategy in his own words:

[**P**ericles] gave just the same advice as he had given before ... they were to prepare
for war and bring into the city their property in the country. They were not to go out and
offer battle, but were to come inside the city and guard it. Their navy, in which their
strength lay, was to be brought to the highest state of efficiency, and their allies were to be
handled firmly, since, he said, the strength of Athens came from the money paid in tribute
by her allies ...

2, 13

* * *

For Pericles had said that Athens would be victorious if she bided her time and took
care of her navy, if she avoided trying to add to the empire during the course of the war,
and if she did nothing to risk the safety of the city itself.

2, 65

* * *

The strategy adopted by the Peloponnesians is summed up by Thucydides
in two short extracts:

The Spartans on their side had found that the war had gone very differently from what
they had imagined when they believed that they could destroy the power of Athens in a few
years simply by laying waste her land.

5, 14

* * *

. . . how astonishing can be seen from the fact that at the beginning of the war some
thought that, if the Peloponnesians invaded Attica, Athens might survive for a year, and
while others put the figure at two or three years, no one imagined she could last for more
than that ...

7, 28

* * *

It is interesting to note that the words of King Archidamus, if we can
accept the speech reported to us as real and accurate, had long since been
forgotten. He said, as part of the debate over the declaration of war:

For we must not bolster ourselves up with the false hope that if we devastate their land
the war will soon be over. I fear that it is more likely that we shall be leaving it to our
children after us.

1, 81

* * *

It is important to keep these strategies in mind as we now examine the
significant events of the war.

This study divides the war into four phases:

- 431–421 BC: the Archidamian War fought primarily on the Greek mainland
- 421–415 BC: the 'cold war' or so-called inter-war period with activities largely centred in the Peloponnese
- 415–413 BC: the Sicilian expedition
- 413–404 BC: the Decelean War fought primarily in the Aegean.

TIMELINE OF SIGNIFICANT EVENTS

431	Siege of Potidaea continues Thebans attack Plataea Peloponnesians invade Attica Athenian raids on Peloponnese
430	Surrender of Potidaea Peloponnesians invade Attica Plague in Athens
429	Phormio's victory at Naupactus Athenian defeat in the Chalcidice Death of Pericles
428	Revolt of Lesbos Peloponnesian invasion of Attica
427	Plataea falls to the Peloponnesians Peloponnesian invasion of Attica Second outbreak of plague in Athens
426	Demosthenes successful in north-west Peloponnese
425	Peloponnesians invade Attica Pylos and Sphacteria incident
424	Nicias captures island of Cythera Athenian defeat at Delium Brasidas takes Amphipolis
423	Truce between Athens and Sparta Brasidas continues operations in the Thracian area
422	Battle of Amphipolis
421	Peace of Nicias Fifty-year alliance between Athens and Sparta
420	Alliance of Athens with Argos, Elis and Mantinea
418	Battle of Mantinea — Spartan victory Argos forms an alliance with Sparta
417	Nicias in the Chalcidice Ostracism of Hyperbolus Argos allied to Athens

416	Athenian conquest of Melos
415	Embassy of Segesta to Athens to seek aid against Selinus
	Athenian expedition to Sicily
	Mutilation of the Hermae, recall of Alcibiades
414	Siege of Syracuse; death of Lamachus
	Gylippus arrives in Sicily
414–13	Second Athenian expedition to Sicily
413	Spartans occupy Decelea
	Great battle in Syracuse Harbour — disaster of the Athenians
	Athenian surrender in Sicily and execution of Nicias
412	Revolt of Athenians allies
	Treaty of Miletus between Persia and Sparta
411	Revolt of Rhodes, Abydos, Lampascus, Thasos, Euboea
	Council of Four Hundred comes into office in Athens
	Four Hundred overthrown and Polity established
	Battle of Cynossema and Abydos — Athenian victory
410	Battle of Cyzicus — Athenian victory
	Spartan peace offer rejected
	Restoration of democracy at Athens
409	Athens recovers Colophon; loses Pylos and Nisaea
	Destruction of Selinus and Himera
408	Athens recovers Chalcedon and Byzantium
407	Athens recovers Thasos
	Alcibiades at Athens
406	Battle of Notion — Athenian defeat
	Alcibiades deposed
	Battle of Arginusae — Athenian victory
	Trial of the Generals in Athens
	Spartan peace offer rejected
405	Battle of Aegospotami — Athenian defeat
405–04	Blockade at Athens
	Surrender of Athens; Long Walls pulled down

The following is a very brief account of the events of the four major periods of the Peloponnesian War. You should supplement this account with careful reading of Thucydides, *The Peloponnesian War*, and by examining other source material that is available. Some of the plays of Euripides and Aristophanes, for example, might make an interesting contrast to the views presented by Thucydides.

THE ARCHIDAMIAN WAR

The war began in 431, with a Theban attack on Plataea, a Boeotian town closely allied to Athens. At this time, Athens, with its powerful navy, dominated the eastern Mediterranean. Although Sparta held the Peloponnese, its army was no match for the strength of Athens' navy. There was now widespread support for a war and Pericles planned the defence of Athens using naval strategy — Peloponnesian invasions of the countryside were to be ignored and the navy was to focus on attacking strategic points on the Peloponnesian shores, particularly to disrupt trade routes.

Headed by the Spartan king, Archidamus, 'about eighty days after the affair of Plataea', according to Thucydides (2, 19) the Peloponnesian army began invading Attica. There was no decisive victory and the Spartans, lacking supplies and anxious to return to their agricultural tasks, retreated.

In 430 Archidamus again invaded Attica and lay siege to Athens, where a serious outbreak of plague broke out. (Thucydides himself contracted the disease (2, 47-54) but survived to record it.) During this year, the Peloponnesians had moved to the shores of Attica in the east and north-east but when they heard news of the plague they departed. Meanwhile a strong Athenian fleet under the command of Pericles was inflicting severe damage on the Peloponnesian shores, but in 429 Pericles fell victim to the plague and died.

In 428 there was another blow for Athens when the island of Lesbos seceded from the Delian League. The Athenians crushed the uprising and forced the Lesbians to work as tenant farmers, like the Spartan serfs. At about the same time, Plataea fell to Spartan forces under King Archidamus.

War continued with increasing violence throughout the 420s. In 425 the Athenians captured some Spartan soldiers on the coast of Messenia, at Pylos, but this was to prove one of their few victories — they lost important battles at Boeotia and Amphipolis where the Spartan forces, led by their brilliant general, Brasidas, took the city. The loss of Amphipolis was a severe blow to Athens, depriving it of an important source of money and timber, and also a direct route to its allies in the east.

By this time, the war was taking its toll on both sides. No decisive victory had been forthcoming because the war was being fought over too great an area, and troops on both sides were becoming exhausted. The war was posing a heavy financial burden, particularly on Athens, which had had to increase direct personal tax and which was having difficulty securing tributes. The desire for peace was gaining momentum and in 423 there was a one-year truce. (Thucydides described this in Book 4, 117 ff.) However the truce did not last because Athens, under its general Cleon, who had come to great popularity in Athens, decided to try to retake Amphipolis. Athens succeeded in winning back the city but both Cleon and the Spartan general Brasidas were killed in the battle.

With two of the strongest leaders and advocates for the war slain, the ground was ripe for a peace settlement. Under the Athenian negotiator, Nicias, a peace treaty was drawn up and signed by Athens and Sparta. However Corinth, Megara and Boeotia were angered by the Peace of 421 and refused to sign it.

STOP AND THINK

✎ **Look back to the strategies outlined for the conduct of the war on page 156. How successfully did these strategies work for both sides in the period from 431–421?**

✎ **At the time of the Peace of Nicias, had any of the triggers for the outbreak of war been resolved in any permanent way? If so, how? If not, what reasons can you see for a possible resumption of hostilities?**

✎ **Look at the personalities of the leaders of both the Spartan and Athenian forces: Pericles, Cleon, Nicias, Archidamus, Brasidas. See what you can find out about these men, both by further reading of Thucydides' account of the war and other source material that you can locate.**

AFTER THE PEACE — THE 'COLD WAR'

The period after the Peace of Nicias was a time of great confusion, political trickery and inefficiency. With the agreement between Athens and Sparta, the Peloponnesian League was breaking up and new alliances began to be formed. Corinth, Mantinea and Elis allied with Argos, and when Athens allied with Argos and its other allies for a hundred years, Sparta was rendered somewhat ineffectual.

In Athens, Nicias was trying to preserve the peace to which he had given his name but Alcibiades, a brilliant and ruthlessly selfish man and a pupil of Socrates, was beginning to overshadow the more moderate and less charismatic Nicias.

Sparta and Athens resumed their hostilities with the refusal of the local commander to return Amphipolis to Athenian rule. The Athenians retaliated by retaining Pylos, which they had taken from Sparta in the battle under Demosthenes. Then Argos began a war against Epidaurus and Sparta came to Epidaurus' defence in 419–18. These attempts to assist Epidaurus were seen by Athens as a breach of the treaty.

In 418 there was a battle at Mantinea which Sparta won, thus restoring its reputation to some extent. The result for Athens was loss of its allies, and a near-restoration of the Peloponnesian League. Athens in 416 then attacked the neutral island of Melos, and its actions there caused alarm in Sparta and hatred for Athens.

Athens at this time was flourishing, culturally and economically. The Peace of Nicias had given some security back to the peasants of Attica and their agricultural enterprises were thriving. Exports of wine and oil in particular were growing, raising revenue. Alcibiades had been lulled into a false sense of security after events in Melos, when Sparta had not intervened, and had begun to dream, by 415, of Athenian control of the entire Mediterranean with himself as supreme leader.

THE SICILIAN EXPEDITION

In 415, Athens decided to intervene in Sicily. According to Thucydides, who devoted almost two entire books (6, 7) of his history of the war to this campaign, the real reason for the expedition was the widespread wish to conquer Sicily in accordance with Alcibiades' imperialist ambitions. Nicias opposed the move into Sicily but was forced to support Alcibiades. According to Thucydides: 'There was a passion for the enterprise which affected everyone alike.' (6, 24)

The fleet departed in 415. Thucydides described the magnificent spectacle as it departed (6, 31), the splendour offering little hint of the disasters that would befall the Athenians over the next two years.

Over 415–14 the Athenians gained a strong foothold in the centre of Syracuse harbour. Envoys were sent to Corinth and Sparta seeking help, and as well, Alcibiades, who had been disgraced and banished from Athens, had gone to Sparta and persuaded the Spartans to send forces to defend Syracuse against Athens.

Things had not gone badly for Athens in Syracuse until late in 414. However, when the Spartan general Gylippus and a Corinthian squadron reached Sicily and entered Syracuse, Nicias proved to be inadequate to the task. In desperation, Nicias sent a report to the Assembly in Athens and it became clear that a decision had to be made, either to withdraw from Sicily completely, or send a new force under a powerful commander. (7, 10–15) Reinforcements were despatched to Sicily but after a fierce fight the Athenians were devastated and most of the retreating Athenians under Nicias were massacred. The Sicilian expedition ended in a decisive, humiliating defeat for Athens.

STOP AND THINK: RESEARCH

✎ **Put yourself in the place of Nicias, sailing from Athens for Syracuse in Sicily. Make some diary entries about your feelings on setting sail, plans for attack when you reach Syracuse, your misgivings towards the summer of 414, and your dismay at the arrival of Gylippus. Given a chance, how would you have handled things differently?**

THE DECELEAN WAR

While the embattled Athenians were fighting it out in Sicily, war between Athens and the Peloponnesians on the mainland had broken out again.

Sparta was preparing for the occupation of Decelea, an outpost north of Athens that it established in 413. Athens was now facing war on two fronts.

Under King Agis, Archidamus' son, the Spartans moved into Attica. This invasion had serious repercussions for Athens:

- the countryside was devastated, cattle lost and the supply route from Euboea blocked.
- slaves were absconding by the thousands into Decelea.
- money became scarce as revenues were no longer reaching the city. Athens renounced the tributes in favour of a 5 per cent duty on all imports and exports.

Attica and its immediate neighbours
Consider Athens' options now with Spartan occupation of Decelea.

Athens was like a fortress under siege, and despite a lack of funds and manpower, began to build a new navy. However, within the empire anti-Athenian feelings had begun to erupt violently and people were looking to Sparta for liberation.

Sparta, however, was still weak in naval resources and short of financial reserves, and was only able to keep going with the support of two Persian provincial governors.

In 411, an oligarchy called the Four Hundred took over in Athens but democracy was restored within three months. In 410 Sparta requested peace talks but Athens refused. The war was now being mainly fought at sea where Athens was superior but by 408 war was not going well for either side.

Finally the Athenians lost a naval battle: 160 of their ships were destroyed, in 405, in the straits of the Hellespont. Persian help came to the Peloponnesians and Athens was blockaded by land and sea, finally being starved into surrender.

AFTERMATH

After the surrender in 404, a second oligarchy, the Thirty, was imposed by Sparta. Civil war ensued and Sparta helped to restore democracy in 403.

EFFECTS ON ATHENS

- In accordance with Pericles' strategy to evacuate the countryside, Attica had been occupied and devastated by the Peloponnesian armies. People had left behind their possessions, which had been plundered or destroyed. Many farms were derelict after twenty-seven years of war.
- An air of tension and fatigue prevailed in Athens, as evidenced by the hysteria that resulted after the acts of sacrilege in 415 that had resulted in Alcibiades' banishment, the imposition of the Four Hundred oligarchy, and the execution of six generals in 406.

EFFECTS ON SPARTA

- Lysander, the organiser of the Spartan victory and a ruthless politician, took control of Sparta. He planned to replace the Athenian empire with a more extensive and rigorously controlled empire. Harsh Spartan rule made them unpopular with the subject peoples and less than ten years after the end of the Peloponnesian War, Sparta found itself at war with a coalition that included Athens.
- A general weariness with war led to the 'King's Peace' of 387, which affected Greek inter-city politics and relations for a generation.
- There was a collapse of Sparta's social equality, though some historians question whether this ever, in fact, really existed (see the chapter on Sparta).

STOP AND THINK: OVERVIEW

The long duration of the Peloponnesian War shows how difficult it was for the two powers — the land might of the Peloponnesian armies and the naval strength of Athens — to come to grips with one another. Was there any way the war could have been conducted that might have led to an earlier, decisive result? You might like to form into two groups — Athens and Sparta — to go over the events of war and discuss alternative strategies.

LIST OF REFERENCES

ANCIENT SOURCES

Plutarch, *The Rise and Fall of Athens*, Penguin Books Ltd, Middlesex, 1983

Thucydides, *The Peloponnesian War*, tr. Rex Warner, Penguin Classics, Middlesex 1954 repr, 1980.

SECONDARY SOURCES

Andrewes, A., *Greek Society*, Penguin, Harmondsworth, Middlessex, repr. 1979

Bury, J.B. & Meiggs, R., *A History of Greece*, Macmillan Press Ltd., 1975

Ehrenberg, V., *From Solon to Socrates*, 2nd edition, Methuen, London, 1967, repr. 1976

Gomme, A.W., *A Historical Commentary on Thucydides*, Oxford University Press, London, 1959

Kagan, D., *The Outbreak of the Peloponnesian War*, Cornell University Press, 1969

Levi, P., *Atlas of the Greek World*, Equinox, Oxford, 1984, repr. 1989

Moore, J.M., *Aristotle and Xenephon on Democracy and Oligarchy*, Chatto & Windus, The Hogarth Press, 1983

Powell, A., *Athens and Sparta: constructing Greek political and social history from 478 BC*, Routledge, London, 1988

de Ste Croix, G.E.M., *The Origins of the Peloponnesian War*, Gerald Duckworth, London, 1972

CHAPTER EIGHT

RELIGION AND FESTIVALS

Larissa Treskin

Ancient Greek religion was a way of representing, interpreting and constructing the external world and people's experience of it. It was a systematic way by which people made sense of their human experiences, a way of dealing with any threats of disorder or chaos in those experiences.

The Greek system of religious belief pervaded every part of ancient Greek life, public and private, at every level. It was not possible to be a member of Greek society and not be affected by the beliefs through which that society viewed its world. Greek religion actually provided a system of signs which made communication about their world possible to members of that world. However this has caused difficulties for historians because our concept of the world, the assumptions on which we base our view of the world, and our experiences of that world, are very different from those of the ancient Greeks. Because the Greek system of signs often used categories and ways of looking at the world which are alien to us, we may have trouble seeing that it was a system, and not a conglomerate of rituals and beliefs.

A DIFFERENT WORLD

Life in the ancient Greek world was very precarious. Even in fifth century BC Attica, a rich and thriving community, the support of life was based on subsistence farming. Agricultural technology was minimal. There was no effective control of disease, which could attack crops, animals or people, so society was constantly vulnerable to crop failure and sickness. Life expectancy was very low. Medicine had little to offer, either in major epidemics such as the plague in Athens in the 420s or in everyday sickness. A Hippocratic doctor working for four years on the island of Thasos recorded twenty-five fatalities out of forty-two cases he attended and recorded.

Earthquakes, lost cargoes, endemic warfare with its accompanying violent deaths, and continuing political confrontations all explain why life was a constant struggle. In many ways life was seen as a competition (*agon*) between people and irrational forces over which there was no control.

STOP AND THINK
Examine the following drawings depicting various situations in ancient Greek life:

⟍ **Using these pictures to help you, make a list of all the disturbances that could affect everyday life.**

⟍ **Rank these in order of frequency of occurrence for:**
  • **rich people**
  • **poor people.**

⟍ **What do your lists show?**

ORGANISATION OF RELIGIOUS THOUGHT AND BEHAVIOUR

BASIS OF BELIEF

Greek religion had no sacred books (which claimed to be the 'word of God' or His prophets), no revelation, no creed, no Ten Commandments. Concepts such as 'grace,' 'sin' and 'faith' cannot be expressed in ancient Greek religious terms without distorting their meaning. Classical Greek religion was of *doing*, not *believing*, of behaviour rather than faith.

The Greek term *'theous nomizein'* means not 'believe in the gods' but *'acknowledge'* them, that is, pray to them, sacrifice to them, build them temples, make them the object of cult and ritual.

For the Greeks, there was no division between the sacred and the secular, between religion and the state. Individual city-states had virtually unlimited authority in religious affairs as in other matters. Thus, since there was no religious orthodoxy, there was also no heresy. Homer and Hesiod, according to Herodotus, may have first fixed the genealogy of the gods, and given them their titles, honours and functions, but these poets were only using their poetic licence to bring some measure of coherence to the religious ideas of Greek communities from the eastern end of the Black Sea almost to the Straits of Gilbraltar.

Religious ideas, therefore, were not theologically fixed and stable, and there was no distinction between false and true gods. The system was an open, not a closed one, and Greek myths, the means of explaining the world, were open-ended. Traditional stories could be retold, told with new meanings, new incidents, new versions, even with a formal reversal of old meanings. (The many stories of Helen of Troy are an example.) The ability of Greek myths to improvise is central to Greek religion, demonstrating the ability of a society to respond to changes in a world in which threats posed by disorder and chaos were always close.

STOP AND THINK: DOCUMENT STUDY

The following inscription is a fragment from one of the eleven fragments of several large marble stelai that were designed to be joined together by clamps to form at least two freestanding walls, one 120 millimetres thick, the other 92 millimetres thick.

This calendar of sacrifices (the revised Athenian law code, Athens 403/02–400/399) clearly illustrates the lack of division between the sacred (religious) and the secular (state). Firstly, it is pointing out the correct performance of ritual: the state is overseeing the correct way of acknowledging the gods, so as to prevent impiety. Secondly, the revision of the Athenian law code is on one side of the column, the sacred calendar on the other side.

Study the inscription carefully then answer the questions that follow. The sacrifices marked [–] were made every other year.

30	In Hekatombaion [the first month of the Athenian year, around midsummer]
	On the fifteenth
	From the Tribe-king's (laws) [The formula, and others like, indicates not the funds from which the monies listed in the margin were dispensed, but the legal sources from which Nicomachus and his colleagues derived their information.]
	For the tribe of the G(e)leontes, [One of the four ('Ionian') tribes of pre-Cleisthenic Athens. The others were Argadeis, Hopletes and Aigikoreis.]
35	for the Leukotainians' trittys, a
4dr	sheep without a mark
4dr 2ob	The priestly perquisite for the
40	Tribe-kings
1dr	For the back
	To the herald for the shoulder,
4ob	feet, head
	On the sixteenth [the date of the festival of Synoica (unification of Attica)]
45	From the Tribe-kings' (laws) for
	the tribe of the G(e)leontes, for
	Zeus of the brotherhood and
50dr	Athena of the brotherhood, two
50 16dr	oxen without a mark
	The priestly perquisite for the
	Tribe-kings, the leg
55 2dr 3ob	To the herald for the chest, feet,
	head
	For the rearer (of the animals),
	of barley bushels [–––]
60 12dr	To Themis [all the following gods and heroes are associated with the festival of the Eleusinia] a sheep
15dr	To Zeus of the forecourt a sheep
12dr	To Demeter a sheep
17dr	To Pherrephatta [Persephone, daughter of Demeter] a ram

Harding, *End of the Peloponnesian War to the Battle of Ipsus*, ed. and trans. by P. Harding, no. 9, 1988
Fragment C (back) columns
2 and 3

✳ ✳ ✳

> ↘ **What types of dedications were made to Greek gods?**
> ↘ **What do the dedications reveal about the dedicators?**
> ↘ **What was the purpose of a calendar of sacrifices?**
> ↘ **Quote lines from the source which prove the following:**
>
> - **the lack of division between sacred and secular**
> - **the emphasis on 'doing' in Greek religion**
> - **the open-ended nature of Greek religion**
>
> ↘ **Why are some words in round brackets? What problems does this cause?**

ROLE OF PRIESTS

The priesthood as a vocation did not exist although many men and women were involved in the administration of religion, in the cases of temples, altars and sacred sites and in the conduct of festivals and sacrifices. We may call them 'priests' today, but the great majority were public officials, whose duty, usually only in part, included responsibility for some portion of the religious activity of the community. Usually they were selected by lot and held office for only a year or even six months (as at Delphi). Some exceptional priesthoods were hereditary, and eventually many became life offices, able to be purchased openly and legally.

Greek 'priests' were not, then, holy people. They had no special training and were not necessarily expert or particularly qualified in matters relating to their duties. There were two types:

- those with ritual functions (called the '*hiereis*', meaning sacrifices) and custodians of religious tradition and customary law (such as the Athenian exegetai and the hierophants of the Eleusinian mysteries). These 'experts' settled disagreements over the rules of sacrifice or matters of pollution and purification, or of blasphemy.
- those with some closeness to divinity, the oracle-mongers and soothsayers, with a special insight into, or power to communicate with, the divine. The manteis were the dream interpreters, such as Pythia, Apollo's prophetess at Delphi. No army went into battle in fifth century BC Greece without a manteis to accompany it. Thucydides was contemptuous of these unofficial 'holy people'. He describes the way the Athenians became angry when their predictions of a successful invasion of Sicily in 415 BC were falsified by the disaster of 413. (*The Peloponnesian War*, 8, 1)

STOP AND THINK: DOCUMENT STUDY

The Establishment of a Board of Eleusinian Superintendents (after 450 or before 445 or about 432–31 BC)
This fragment from a marble stele at Eleusis describes the responsibilities of the epistatai, the board of superintendents

elected to administer the revenues associated with the Eleusian mysteries. Again, we see the lack of division between the sacred and the secular. Examine it carefully and answer the questions that follow.

[-32-] *Hieropoioi* and [-19-] and spend [-9-] [..] of the same

The Prytaneis are to bring before the Boule the [-10-] when they request (it.) Thespieus [made the motion: Let all the rest be as (resolved) by the Boule. But [men shall be elected] from the Athenians, five in number, and they [shall draw the pay of] four obols each from the Kola-kretai, and one of them shall be Secretary [according to] vote. These men shall take charge of the money of the two goddesses [Demeter and Kore (Persephone)] just as those (administering) the Akropolis works were in charge of the temple and the statue [either the temple of Athena Polias and the statue of Athena Promachos or the Parthenon and the Statue of Athena Parthenos]. Refusal of the office shall not be allowed. [Those] who are elected shall approach the Boule, if anything is owed the two goddesses, and they shall declare it and exact it. They shall hold office for a year, after taking the oath between the two altars at Eleusis, and in the future, elections shall be held in the same way every year for the men. They shall also administer the yearly revenues which accrue to the two goddesses, and if they discover that anything has been lost, they shall recover it. The Logistai shall calculate in Eleusis the money expended in Eleusis, and in the city the money expended in the city, summoning the architect Koroibos and Lysanias to the Eleusinion [in Athens] (for this purpose); and at Phaleron (they shall calculate) in the temple that (which was) spent for Phaleron. They shall spend for whatever is most necessary, consulting [this word is in the next line] with the priests and the Boule henceforth. They shall summon back (prior boards), beginning with the board [-12-] [-6-] [by which Ktesias was given] the money. A record shall be set up of this decree on a stele in Eleusis and [in the city and in Ph]al[e]ron in the Eleusinion. [-8-] [Lysanias' name is generally restored] made the motion: Let all the rest be as [Thespius (moved.) But the counting] shall be done [of the monies which the] treasurers gave over [-17-] [. . .] [by the elected five (men) and] the architect [-14-]

Fornara, *Athens to the End of the Peloponnesian War*, no. 106, 1983

✳ ✳ ✳

✎ **List all the officials mentioned in this source.**
✎ **What were the responsibilities of the epistatei (board of superintendents) at Eleusis?**
✎ **What do the numbers in brackets mean?**
✎ **What does this source prove about religion in the Attic polis?**

TEMPLES

The temple was not a place of communal worship, even though it was the most imposing building of the Greek city. The Telesterion at Eleusis and the temple of Asclepius in Epidaurus were exceptions, and very rare. Temples were houses of the gods, where their cult-images and often their treasures were stored. Public access in terms of numbers admitted and times, was very restricted: after all the treasure was valuable and could be stolen; and where there were large statues, such as in the temple of Zeus at Olympia, there was little space for anyone else.

The siting of Greek temples varied greatly.

Every sacred shrine had an altar that was outside the temple as most worship took place out of doors. The image of a divinity would be taken out of its house for the occasion, to preside over festivities, whether they be processions, games, dances or sacrifices. The sacrifice, as a central act in worship, took place outdoors. No fires were kindled on these outside altars to consume parts of slaughtered animals. Instead, certain offerings were deposited on them. Small tripod hearths were used, probably for fumigations.

Dedications illustrated another basic principle of Greek religion: reciprocity. Humans dedicated gifts to the gods to establish a relationship of obligation with them. These gifts ranged from everyday foodstuffs to implements of gold, to shells, flowers, clay images of beetles and birds, to sheep and oxen, weapons and garments.

Of course, ancient Greeks could only guess at whether or not a relationship had been established, whether or not a divine power was at work in the world of their experience. They looked for signs — strange human behaviour, plagues and epidemics, dreams, events that made no sense or events that made too much sense — and problems of interpretation were inevitable.

The two most important gods who were consulted were Apollo and Zeus. The main oracular shrine for Apollo in classical times was at Delphi. Zeus' main shrines were at Dodona and Olympia, although some Greeks also consulted, as an oracle of Zeus, the oracle of Ammon in Egyptian Thebes. The method of consultation varied: sometimes the god's will was revealed by the casting of lots or by the observation of signs; sometimes objects would be cast into a spring and the resulting water movement studied; sometimes the god's image had to be carried and its movement considered. In other cases, the rustle of the leaves in the god's sacred oak was considered significant, or perhaps the details of the entrails of an animal sacrificed on the god's altar. The Delphic oracle, of course, was inspirational; the answers were given by a woman, the Pythia, seated on a tripod.

Those wishing to consult the major oracles had to go through a preliminary process of sacrificial rites and purification. Sometimes they could approach the god directly, sometimes the questions were put in writing. The responses usually took the form of a direct command to perform some religious act such as sacrifice or the foundation of a cult, or else involved the sanction or otherwise of a constitution, law or proposed military policy or other undertaking. This kind of response was notorious for its ambiguity.

DELPHI

The oracle at Delphi was the most important, presided over by Apollo. Consultation was restricted to one day per month and not at all in winter. The site was supposed to be at the centre of the earth, marked by the sacred navel stone (*omphalos*). Questions were put to the Pythia on behalf of enquirers by a male prophet. He also interpreted the response which was often given in verse. (We do not know precisely how the Pythia's state of frenzy was induced.) Those consulting the oracle had to wash in cold water and offer a sacred cake and an animal — a costly business.

Delphi also welcomed the cult of Dionysus, his grave being shown in the inner sanctuary. In other respects the religious lore there was traditionalist, advice being given to worship 'according to ancestral custom' or 'the city's custom'. The oracle was also concerned with questions of individual morality and set great store by inner purity as well as ritual; carved on the temple were two famous precepts: 'Know thyself' and 'Nothing too much', i.e. avoid excess.

In the mid-fifth century Athenian influence at Delphi had been strong. During the early part of the Peloponnesian Wars there seems to have been an Athenian bias against Delphi because of its leaning towards Sparta. The practical effects of such stands could be serious, since the treasuries at religious sites could be the source of loans to assist states involved in costly wars. Speeches in Thucydides suggest that the Spartans and their allies considered borrowing money from the treasuries at Delphi and Olympia, and using it to improve the pay of the sailors on the Spartan ships and thus attract the best rowers. (*The Peloponnesian War*, 1, 121, 143) In any event this higher pay was given in 407 BC, but with Persian finance. Both Euripides and Aristophanes include in their plays passages attacking the Delphic oracle — Euripides notably in the *Ion* and the *Andromache*, in which the Messenger's Speech (11, 1005ff.) described the desecration of the altar by murder at which the oracle connived.

Aristophanes in the *Knights* makes much of the action turn on the production of oracles, both those which expose the weakness of Cleon, and also those featuring in the contest in oracle-mongering between him and the sausage-seller. However, although there are references to Delphi, the contest seems to be one of a general satire on oracles rather than a specific attack on Delphi. Nevertheless such passages may indicate a growing uncertainty of the Athenian relationship with Delphi (the Spartans felt similar disfavour for Olympia).

DODONA

This rather remote sanctuary of Zeus is mentioned in the *Iliad* (16, 233) when the prophets of Selloi are described as 'of unwashed feet' and sleeping on the ground. Herodotus (2, 55) however, refers in the mid-fifth century to three priestesses instead of Selloi. By this time the method of consultation was for the enquirer to write his question on a lead strip which was put in a jar, then extracted by the priestess. Fortunately, this has resulted in many questions having survived. Most are from private individuals and give us interesting information on their private or business problems, but in the late fifth and fourth centuries the oracle was sometimes consulted by Athens or Sparta on matters of state.

ATHENIAN DEDICATIONS

THE ACROPOLIS AT ATHENS

The following examples all come from the Acropolis in Athens. Many of them were carved on the bases of the female statues called *korai* [girls], in honour of Athena, the patron deity of Athens and to whose citizens the Acropolis was sacred. They show men and women of many occupations expressing their aspirations and their private devotion to Athena in this public way.

(IG I² 408, on a statue base.) Aischines the son of Chares dedicates (this) as first-fruit to Athena.

(IG I² 422, on a statue base). Kapanis dedicated (this) as a tithe to Athena.

(IG I² 436, on the handle of a vase.) Polykles the fuller dedicated (this) to Athena.

(IG I² 444, on a shield decorated with a gorgon.) Phrygia the bread seller dedicated me to Athena.

(IG I² 467, on a stele.) Chairion the son of Kleodikos dedicated (this) to Athena during his term as treasurer.

(IG I² 473, on the base of a water basin.) Smikythe the washer-woman dedicated (this) as a tithe.

(IG I² 485, on a statue base.) Nearchos the potter dedicated (this) to Athena as first-fruit of his work. Antenor the son of Eumares made the statue.

(IG I² 487, on a statue base.) Archemeros the Chian made (me.) Iphidike dedicated me to Athena Poliouchos [Guardian of the City.]

(IG I² 499, on a statue base.) Lyson dedicated (this to Pallas Athena as first-fruit of his possessions and as a delight for the goddess. Thebades the son of [--] made this statue.

(IG I² 503, on a statue base.) Timarchos dedicated me to the mighty-hearted daughter of Zeus, after he had prayed for an oracle of measured understanding. Onatas made (the statue.)

(IG I² 606, on a statue base.) Kallias the son of Didymios dedicated (this.) His victories [in the pankration]: Olympic; Pythian, twice; Isthmian, five times, Nemean, four times: Great Panathenaea.

(IG I² 643, on a votive column.) Lady Athena Poliouche [Guardian of the City,] may this city have this as a monument of Smikros and his boys and their flourishing business.

(IG I² 625, on a statue base.) Having achieved his prayer Menandros dedicated this first-fruit to thee, Mistress, re-paying thy favour; he is the son of Demetrios, from the deme Aigialeia; do thou, O daughter of Zeus, preserve this wealth which thou hast given.

(IG I² 631, on a votive pillar.) Vouchsafe great wealth to him, O daughter of Zeus, and make grateful return for these (dedications.) He who dedicated me to Hermes, Oinobios the herald, did it in thanksgiving for his skill, because of his memory.

(IG I² 650, on a votive column.) Maiden, on the Acropolis Telesinos of Kettos dedicated the statue; mayest thou delight in it and grant him to dedicate another.

(IG I² 658, on a votive column.) Philon dedicated this little tripod to Athena, having won by a surprise.

(IG I² 684, on a votive tablet.) Diophanes dedicated me to Athena Poliouchos, as a tithe of his estate, in fulfillment of his son's prayer.

(IG I² 706, on a statue base.) [-] Iochos dedicated this kore-statue as first-fruit of his catch: this one boon the Lord of the Sea with his golden trident granted.

A.E. Raubitchek, *Dedications from the Athenian Akropolos*, Cambridge, Mass, 1949, passim.

❊ ❊ ❊

A SHRINE AT PHALERON

Around 400 BC a shrine was erected at Athens' old port of Phaleron to the river-god Kephisos by a woman, apparently in thanksgiving for the education of her son Xeniades. The first inscription records the dedication; it was accompanied by a sculptured relief. The second was inscribed on an altar in the shrine and lists Hestia in her usual first place, then the god of the shrine, the three gods of Delphi, Ileithyia the goddess of birth, two other water divinities (Acheloos and Kallirhoe) and a not yet identified Rhapso, perhaps a patron of seamstresses.

(IG II² 4548.) Xenokrateia constructed and dedicated this shrine of Kephisos to him and the gods who share his altar as an offering for the blessing of children; she is the daughter of (one) Xeniades and the mother (of another), from the deme of Cholleidai. Anyone who wishes to sacrifice may do so on payment of the appropriate fees.

(IG II² 4547.) To Hestia, Kephisos, Pythian Apollo, Leto, Artemis Lochia, Ileithyia, Acheloos, Kallirhoe, the familial [*genethliai*] Nymphs of Geraistos, Rhapso.

Lois Sacrées des cités grecques, ed. and trans. F. Sokolowski, pp. 44–5

❊ ❊ ❊

THE VARI CAVE

In the foothills of Mount Hymettos southeast of Athens a cave had been considered sacred to Pan and the Nymphs ever since the sixth century. The cult was a private one, and these documents illustrate the pious activity of Archedamos, an alien from Thera who resided in Athens around 400 BC. He furnished the cave with representations of the Nymphs and, among others, the following three inscriptions.

(IG I² 784.) Archedamos of Thera planted this garden to the Nymphs.
(IG I² 785.) Archedamos of Thera also erected a dancing-floor to the dancing Nymph.
(IG I² 788.) Archedamos of Thera, the Nymph-raptured one, outfitted the cave at the admonition of the Nymphs.

C.H. Weller et al, 'The Cave at Vari', *American Journal of Archaeology*, 7: 263–349, 1903

❊ ❊ ❊

STOP AND THINK

✎ **Make a list of the various types of dedications these sources illustrate.**

✎ **What do the extracts reveal about these dedications?**

✎ **How do the dedications in the three sources vary? Why?**

✎ **What was the function of the dedication in Greek religion?**

✎ **What do these sources prove about religion in the Attic polis?**

FESTIVALS AND COMPETITION (*AGON*)

In Athens, slightly more than one-third of the days in each year were marked by some festival, though not all of them were celebrated by everyone. The number of festivals is hardly surprising given the number of private and state cults. There were private cults associated with the *oikos* (household) or wider kinship groups and with the locality or trade association. The polis too had its public cults, the most important in Athens being that of Athena.

There were also gods of the market (*agora*) the Assembly (*ecclesia*) and so on. The state cults were financed publicly and the regulation of cult activities was decided in the Assembly — the number and nature of the sacrifices, the replenishment of temple utensils, administration and maintenance of temples and shrines.

Meetings of the Assembly or boards of officials were preceded by religious rituals, usually sacrifice and prayer, and promissory oaths and curses were regarded as civic sanctions. As the orator Lycurgus put it, 'it is the oath that holds democracy together'. (against Leocrates, 79) In return for the attention given them, it was expected that the gods would act as guardians of the city. Once again, the reciprocal obligations involved in the relationships were emphasised as was the lack of a division between sacred and secular.

The way political values and religious practices were closely interwoven in the life of the polis is further demonstrated by the way stones carefully marked the boundaries of the Agora. The Agora was sacred ground and those who had been deprived of civic rights could be excluded from it.

The Olympian gods that appear on the Parthenon frieze covered most of the areas of concern to the Athenians. Humans entered into reciprocal contracts with these gods because it was seen as being the only way of preventing disorder in a fragile, life-threatening world. The twelve Olympians were:

Zeus	Cities, justice, oaths, hospitality
Hera	Women and marriage
Poseidon	Sea, earthquakes
Demeter	Corn, fertility
Apollo	Purification, music, culture, oracles, flocks and herds
Artemis	Women and children, hunting
Hermes	Messages, protection of travellers, good luck
Athena	War, Athens, learning (also associated with the olive)
Hephaistos	Fire, patron of smiths
Aphrodite	Love, beauty, procreation
Ares	War
Hestia	Hearth

(Hestia was in the process of being displaced by Dionysus, the god of wine, and it was Dionysus who took Hestia's place on the Parthenon frieze.)

The range of rituals at these festivals was extraordinary. Generally they comprised sacrifices, hymns, dances and processions. One unique feature of the festivals was the practice of competition (*agon*) in athletics, music, dance and theatre.*

OLYMPIA

The festival here was traditionally supposed to have been instituted by Zeus, but is first known to have been held in 776 BC. It took place in the summer (in the agricultural lull after the main harvest was over) and included athletic competition as well as important religious observances — sacrifices on the altar of Zeus and libations poured over the supposed tomb of Pelops. The athletic competitions were divided into sections for men and boys and consisted of running (including a race in armour), wrestling, boxing, the pancration, the pentathlon (a series of five events: discus, javelin, long jump, 200-metre sprint, and wrestling), discus, javelin, chariot racing, and mule and horse racing.

Olympia is particularly interesting because it was a sacred site only and not an inhabited centre. It lay within the territory of Eleia, and the Eleians administered the festival. It seems to have contained no domestic buildings in the usual sense, and those which have been excavated are all connected with religion or athletics. The sanctuary itself measured about 200 by 150 metres. Within this was the temple of Zeus (built about 460) which contained Pheidias' colossal seated statue of Zeus. There was also an older, smaller temple of Hera and a row of treasuries in which various states placed devotional offerings. There were also secular buildings used by the athletes and visitors, and various statues in honour of the victors, who received wreaths of olive as prizes.

DELPHI

Delphi was the scene of the Pythian games, reputedly instituted by Apollo after his victory over the serpent Python. The games here were originally musical contests, but were later modelled on the Olympic Games and included athletic and equestrian events. By the fifth century only the flute-playing among the musical events survived. The victors' crowns were of laurel. The shrine was in the cave of the Amphictyonic League and it was here in 346 that Philip of Macedonia, by taking over the place of Phocis in the Amphictyonic League, and being chosen to preside over the religious festivals, made good his claim to be a Greek. Delphi had a major theatre and was also an important oracular centre.

---

*The four major panhellenic Festivals were in politically insignificant places. Athenian efforts to elevate their own Panathenaic festival to comparable standing were unsuccessful. The rest of the Greek world did not want an already powerful state to acquire the added prestige of a major religious festival.

NEMEA

The games resembled the Olympic Games and were held at the shrine of Zeus in the territory of Argos. The victors' crowns were of celery, the symbol of grief and bereavement. This was said to refer to the origin of the games as commemoration of the death of the infant son of the king of Nemea during the expedition of the Seven against Thebes. But it is clear that the local cult was largely subservient to the ritual honours to Zeus.

ISTHMIA

The Isthmian Games took place in the Isthmus of Corinth. The victors' crowns were of pine or wild celery. One tradition claims they were reorganised by Theseus on his way to Athens after the destruction of the brigand Sciron. Appropriately the festival was dedicated to Poseidon. In any event the Athenians had right of precedence there plus a special award of one hundred drachmae for each victor. Thucydides tells us that the Athenians were represented at the Isthmian Games in 412 BC, even after the Sicilian debacle, engineered by Sparta and Corinth, and despite continued threats of naval action. (*The Peloponnesian War*, 8, 10)

STOP AND THINK: ACTIVITY
Design a travel brochure for each of the four major games, differentiating between them.

STOP AND THINK: DOCUMENT STUDY
Read the passage from Thucydides where Alcibiades gives advice to the Athenians and answer the questions that follow.

Athenians, since Nicias has made this attack on me, I must begin by saying that I have a better right than others to hold the command and that I think I am quite worthy of the position. As for all the talk there is against me, it is about things which bring honour to my ancestors and myself, and to our country profit as well. There was a time when the Hellenes imagined that our city had been ruined by the war, but they came to consider it even greater than it really is, because of the splendid show I made as its representative at the Olympic games, when I entered seven chariots for the chariot race (more than any private individual has entered before) and took the first, second, and fourth places, and saw that everything else was arranged in a style worthy of my victory. It is customary for such things to bring honour, and the fact that they are done at all must also give an impression of power. Again, though it is quite natural for my fellow citizens to envy me for the magnificence with which I have done things in Athens, such as providing choruses and so on, yet to the outside world this also is evidence of our strength. Indeed, this is a very useful kind of folly, when a man spends his own money not only to benefit himself but his city as well. And it is perfectly fair for a man who has a high opinion of himself not to be put on a level with everyone else; certainly when one is badly off one does not find people coming to share in one's misfortunes. And just as no one takes much notice of us if we are failures, so on the same principle one has to put up with it if one is looked down upon by the successful: one cannot demand equal treatment oneself unless one is prepared to treat everyone else as an equal. What I know is that people like this — all, in fact, whose brilliance in any direction has made them prominent — are unpopular in their life-times, especially with their equals and also with others with whom they come into contact; but with posterity you will find people claiming relationship with them, even where none exists, and you will find their countries boasting of them, not as though they were strangers or disreputable characters, but as fellow-countrymen and doers of great deeds. This is what I aim at myself, and because of this my private life comes in for criticism; but the point is whether you have anyone who deals with public affairs better than I do. Remember that I brought about a coalition of the greatest powers of the Peloponnese, without putting you to any considerable danger or expense, and made the Spartans risk their all on the issue of one day's fighting at Mantinea, and though they were victorious in the battle, they have not even yet quite recovered their confidence.

The Peloponnesian War, 6, 16

✳ ✳ ✳

✎ **Quote the lines where Alcibiades claims his victories bring glory to Athens and convince other states of Athenian power.**

✎ **Quote the lines where Alcibiades uses his contribution to the reputation of Athens as an argument in favour of his own leadership.**

✎ **Explain how Alcibiades has used his success at the games as a platform for political propaganda.**

✎ **The victor in the chariot race did not perform himself, merely furnished the chariots and drivers. How does this prove that the horse races at the games tended to be the preserve of the aristocrats?**

✎ **Rank the following honours a victor might expect at home in order of importance to the victor, and give reason for your ranking:**

- **free meals**
- **a commemorative statue**
- **financial reward**
- **a victory ode**

✎ **Here are the opening lines of Pindar's first 'Olympic Ode':**

[For Hieron of Syracuse, winner in the horse race]

Water is the best thing of all, and gold
Shines like flaming fire at night,
More than all a great man's wealth.
But if, my heart, you would speak
Of prizes won in the Games,
Look no more for another bright star
By day in the empty sky
More warming than the sun,
Nor shall we name any gathering
Greater than the Olympian.
The glorious song of it is clothed by the wits of the wise:
They sing aloud of Kronos' son,

When they come to the rich and happy hearth of Hieron,
Who sways the sceptre of law
In Sicily's rich sheep-pasture.
He gathers the buds of all perfections,
And his splendour shines in the festal music,
Like our own merry songs
When we gather often around that table of friends.

C. M. Bowra, *The Odes of Pindar*, Penguin, 1969

✳ ✳ ✳

Would Pindar agree/disagree with your answers to the previous question? Why?

✎ **Thucydides (5, 18) tells us that the agreement for the Peace of Nicias was to be recorded on stelai on the Athenian Acropolis, in the temple of Amyclae in Sparta, and also at the religious centres of Olympia, Delphi and the Isthmus. What does this tell you about the status of religion?**

✎ **The common word for truce was '*spondai*,' which literally meant 'libation'. *Spondai* came to mean by extension the agreement solemnised by the libation and eventually became a synonym for 'treaty'. What conclusions can be drawn from the existence of a sacred truce among those states taking part in a festival, a truce which existed for its duration?**

DRAMA

Tragedy and comedy were written for a similar annual competition in Athens, but the Greater Dionysia, at which the new plays were performed each year, made no claim to panhellenic religious status.

534 BC	Drama first incorporated into Attic festivals
490 BC	Battle of Marathon
486 BC	Comedy first allowed in the Dionysia
479 BC	Battle of Salamis
472 BC	Aeschylus' *The Persians* performed
442 BC	Sophocles' *Antigone* performed (he always won first or second prize)
431 BC	Euripides' *Medea* performed (frequently performed; not much success)
429 BC	Sophocles' *Oedipus Rex* performed
425 BC	Aristophanes' *The Peace* performed
414 BC	Aristophanes' *The Birds* performed
405 BC	Aristophanes' *The Frogs* performed
350 BC	Greek theatres of stone built
321 BC	Menander's first play produced (new comedy)

STOP AND THINK
Complete the following chart:

ANCIENT GREEK DRAMATISTS				
Aeschylus 525–456 BC	Sophocles 496–406 BC	Euripides 484–406 BC	Aristophanes 450–380 BC	Menander 342–285 BC
Titles of plays				
Structure of plays				
Main themes				
Number of plays written				
Degree of success in competitions				

A RELIGIOUS SYSTEM

Rituals were the means by which people physically related to the gods and made sense of ambiguities and inconsistencies. Through prayers, the Greeks interacted with the gods as if the gods were humans who understood Greek, liked to be respected and who accepted the principle that any action will be met by a matching and balancing reaction — good for good, evil for evil. These values ordered the relationships by which Greeks interacted with the gods as if the gods were divine, and as if they were sources of disorder, rather than order. The gods were seen to communicate with humans in a language that was not understood, in ambiguous signs, rather than words.

The ritual sequences in many festivals suggest that contact with the gods involved contact with the subversion of social normality, rather than its maintenance.

PRAYERS

Although the ancient Greeks had no 'prayer book', Greek literature is full of prayers. Three assumptions underlay these prayers:

- it was possible for a person to converse with the gods in the same language that was used to converse with other people.
- gods had to be addressed with precision and courtesy, by formal titles together with a recitation of the god's powers and attributes.
- the person uttering the prayer had to establish bonds of obligation between the god and the worshipper. The Greeks used the word '*charis*', which was both the doing of good by one person to another, but also the necessary repayment of the goods. This implied that the god would respond in kind and reciprocate human action.

The language of prayers, then, shows how relations between gods and worshippers could be construed in the same terms that make sense of relations between people.

SACRIFICES

The central ritual of Greek religion, from the pouring of libation onwards, was the offering to the god, and its most characteristic form was animal sacrifice. The animal victim — a domesticated animal, goat, sheep, or ox — was festively prepared for the ritual slaughter. Sometimes the horns were gilded and the animal groomed. It had to seem to go willingly to its death.

The place of slaughter was ritually marked out as sacred by the carrying round in procession of the sacred basket and by the sprinkling of water over the participants and the victim; the basket contained barley grain, which was thrown at the victim by all the participants, and the sacrificial knife was kept out of sight beneath the grain. The sprinkling of the water and the casting of the grain were the 'beginning' of the ritual, and these were followed by a further step in this beginning — the priest cutting a few hairs from the animal's forehead. Its head was then pulled back and raised towards the sky and its throat cut. Up to this point the participants maintained a ritual silence, but at the moment of slaughter the women present screamed the *ololyge*. The animal was then skinned and butchered. Occasionally, the heart was torn still beating from the body before all else. The entrails (heart, lungs, liver and kidneys — the *splanchna*) were removed, skewered and roasted separately, while of the remainder the tail, gall-bladder and above all the thigh-bones were wrapped in fat and burnt on the altar of the god. Lean meat was roasted and distributed among the participants so that the sacrifice ended in feasting. Before the roast meat was eaten, the *splanchna* were passed round and all tasted: the *splanchna* was seen to be the source and seat of feeling, of love, hatred, anger, anxiety.

The ritual of animal sacrifice varied in detail according to the local ancestral custom, but the fundamental structure was clear: animal sacrifice was ritualised slaughter followed by a meat meal.

WHAT DO THE SACRIFICES MEAN?

- Considered as an offering to a god, what was the meaning of this sequence of actions? Was it a shared meal, a 'communion' between humans and gods? Were humans giving food to the gods?
- Could it be considered a process of consecration whereby raw foods, through the human process of cooking, were changed and made acceptable to the gods? Did the common meal at the end renew the community of people?
- Could it be considered as simply an act of slaughter? Was the real significance the breaking of a taboo and deliberately killing a living creature, one which was domesticated, a working companion and usually a source of food or livelihood? Was it in some sense a way to control in ritual, those elements over which there was no control in the real world? By allowing death and chaos free rein, in rituals, could death and chaos thus be contained and ordered?

The answers seem to be in the series of paradoxes and contradictions which were symbolically embodied in the rituals. These ambiguities and tensions were found both in the world of the divinities and in the world of humans.

ATHENIAN FESTIVALS

PANATHENAIA

This was the annual festival in honour of Athena, celebrated on 28 Hekatombaion. Every four years it was elevated to the prestigious Great Panathenaia. It was a festival for all Athenians, with all age groups and both sexes taking part. The central feature of the festival was the presentation of the *peplos* (new dress) to Athena, which was brought via a procession. The processions were headed by the Kanephoroi (basket-bearers.) These were female virgins from the aristocratic class who carried the sacred implements and presided at sacrifices.

The *peplos* was woven by a team of maidens, the Ergastinai (workers), who were again chosen from the aristocratic families of Athens. The priestess supervised the setting of the loom and when the *peplos* was completed the Ergastinai were given a place of honour at the head of the procession. After the presentation of the peplos to the goddess Athena the slaughter of a domesticated victim occurred, according to the ritual outlined on page 181.

The festival also involved worship by drama and athletics, both of which were competitive. At the Games, the prizes took the form of olive oil (not garlands, as in the panhellenic games). The oil was provided in large, fine, marketable *amphorae*. In the boys' events each victor received thirty to fifty jars.

THE LENAIA

The Lenaia was held in the winter and although it involved a procession and dramatic presentations it was closed to both metics and foreigners. In contrast both could attend the City Dionysia.

THE DIONYSIA

This festival was held at the opening of the sailing season. Imperial tribute had to be brought and was exhibited to the audiences. There was also a parade of the sons of those killed in war and who had been raised as orphans by the polis. In the fourth century the imperial emphasis was replaced by the practice of voting a golden crown to politicians or other benefactors of the city.

THE SKIRA

The tasks involved in the cultivation of cereals were bound by seasons and succeeded each other in due order. The rites and ceremonies associated with the tasks occurred simultaneously with the tasks. The Skira — held in honour of Demeter — was celebrated at the time of threshing and was reserved for women. The women involved threw offerings into caverns in the ground, the chief object of offering being the piglet which, because of its fecundity, was the holy animal of Demeter. Models of snakes and male genital organs shaped out of dough were also thrown into the caverns. The phallic symbols, piglets and snakes which were placed deeply into the earth were obviously connected with fertility.

THE THESMOPHORIA

This festival was held exclusively by women and was connected with sowing. The central activity of the Thesmophoria (three and a half months after the Skira) was to recover the decayed remains. A group of women called the Antletriai ('balers') was chosen for this function. The Antletriai's task was to haul up the contents of the cavern in a basket and these contents were then placed on altars. Though the mixture of the contents sounds unpleasant it was considered consecrated. The women were required to maintain a state of purity three days before their ritual. To ensure that they were sexually abstinent for three days they ate garlic to discourage their husbands from making advances. The carrying of the materials to the altars was called '*thesmoi*'. The materials placed on the altar were said to have a special power that promoted fertility in crops.

Men were excluded from the Thesmophoria because of the fertility rituals involved, whereby the woman prayed not only for the fields but also for herself. Men were only involved if they were wealthy, for then they were compelled to bear the cost of the festival in the form of a tax on behalf of their wives.

THE HALOA

The Haloa festival, held at Eleusis, was another secret ritual confined to women. The chief deities worshipped were Demeter, Kora and Dionysus. The occasion for celebrating this festival was the pruning of the vines and the tasting of the wine. The only evidence we have is a muddled commentary of Lucian from which we are able to ascertain that magistrates prepared a feast for the women and then departed. The conduct of the women was similar to that attributed to them at the Thesmophoria, where they indulged in uninhibited obscenity of language and behaviour (caused by the wine) and walked around carrying models of male and female genital organs. Even the priestess went about encouraging promiscuity by whispering to wives (as a piece of secret advice) that they should take lovers. Cakes in the shape of phalli and pudenda were served on tables and much wine was consumed.

THE BRAURUNIA

This festival, held in East Attica, was organised by an Athenian commission of ten *hieropoioi* (performers of sacred rites) and was dedicated to Artemis, the Lady of the Wild Things. The myth behind the festival was based on the slaughter of a bear, which was killed by the brothers of a young girl whom the bear had attacked after the young girl teased it. The brothers' revenge killing of the bear made Artemis furious and a treaty was sought via an oracle. The oracle replied that as atonement girls must act as *arktoi* (she-bears).

The duties of the *arktoi* are mentioned in Aristophanes' *Lysistrata*. The Chorus of Women list the various religious duties they have performed. At the age of seven the women claim they 'carried the secret objects' (*arrephorein*), then each 'was a corn grinder' and 'at ten for the presiding Goddess . . . a bear shedding the saffron robe at the Braurunia'. The corn grinders are rarely mentioned in ancient sources, but their duty was to grind meal for the sacred cakes to be offered to Athena.

At night the Arrephoroi were instructed by the priestess to put on their heads what she gave them to carry and to take back (underground) something wrapped up. The girls were then released. Neither the priestess nor the Arrephoroi knew what was being carried. The procedures indicate a fertility ritual, with the secrecy of the girls' night performance creating a mystery about the ceremony.

Exploration of this underground area has revealed evidence of phallic symbols in the sanctuary. The objects borne by the Arrephoroi may have been models of male genitals and snakes.

THE KALLYNTERIA AND THE PLYNTERIA (FESTIVAL OF WASHING)

These involved the spring cleaning of Athens and her temple and were traditionally entrusted to the noble family, the Proxiergida. The cleaning, although practical, was carried out with great solemnity under the guidance of the priestess. The statue of Athena was escorted by the Epheboi to the sea where it was given a purifactory bath. It was washed by two women (bathers or washers).

THE ELEUSINIAN MYSTERIES

Eleusis was an important town of Attica and had probably been under the control of Athens since the seventh century. In the fifth century Eleusis was the centre of an elaborate mystery ritual, its two main aspects being a fertility cult and rites concerned with afterlife. The origins of the cult were probably local to Eleusis itself, and were based on Demeter, the goddess of the grain crop. The myth (recounted in the *Homeric Hymn to Demeter*) tells how her daughter Persephone was carried off to Hades by Pluto. Demeter wandered the earth in sorrow but was kindly received at Eleusis and taught the Eleusinians the secret mystery-rites of her cult. The poet ends his narrative by proclaiming: 'blessed is he among men on earth who has seen these rites; whereas whoever is uninitiated and has no share in them has no part in the same things when he has died, down in the murky gloom'. (*Homeric Hymn to Demeter*, 480–2) The hymn also states that whoever does wrong and fails to honour and propitiate Persephone as he ought to do will suffer eternal punishment. (367–9)

When Eleusis came under Athenian control the festival was taken over by Athens and elements of Athenian cult added, though the original priesthoods remained. We know little about the festival, which took place in Eleusis, and the precise detail of the initiation itself was secret then and remains so now, although we do know that initiation took place at night by torchlight. Probably there were elements of 'things said' (*dromena* — a nocturnal pageant,) 'things done' (*legomena* — in Greek) and 'things revealed'. The element of revelation (the *epopteia*) seems to have been highly emotional and to have offered spiritual support to the initiated. The secrecy was stringently maintained and charges of impiety were serious.

THE ANTHESTERIA

The three days of ritual comprising the festival called Anthesteria took place in February each year, in honour of the god Dionysus. The three days, which ran like the Jewish Sabbath from sundown to sundown, were called 'Opening the storage jars (*pithoi*)', 'Jugs' and 'Cooking pots'. The rituals of the first two days centred on the opening and first consumption of the new wine from the previous year's harvest. Their climax was the ritualised drinking of the day called 'Jugs'. The day took its name from a peculiar feature of the ritual. Participants did not merely drink from their own drinking-cup, as at any other drinking party; their wine was mixed with water also in a personal jug which they took with them to the festival, and, when it was over, this jug was dedicated to the god — there was no common mixing bowl.

The following day, 'Cooking pots', by contrast was a day of dark, ominous rituals: the door posts of all houses were smeared with pitch and men chewed buckthorn, a powerful laxative. These were apotropaic rituals, designed to keep evil at bay and to expel it. Evil, seemingly, was abroad this day and when it ended there were ritual words to say, words whose precise form, even in antiquity, was a matter of uncertainty, but of which the likeliest meaning is an injunction to alien powers to leave the community: 'Outside ... it is no longer Anthesteria.'

Its central rituals were carried out in the precinct of Dionysus 'in the Marshes'; all other sanctuaries were closed for this one day, and conversely the sanctuary in the Marshes was open only on this one day in the year. No 'normal' sacrifices or marriages took place.

THE HYACINTHIA

In the month of Hekatombaion (July-August) the Hyacinthia was celebrated in honour of Hyacinthus. He was the favourite of Apollo, but Zephyrus, the wind-god, also loved the boy; as a result, out of jealousy, when Apollo was amusing himself in a game of discus with his favourite, Zephyrus directed the heavy ring of the discus against the head of Hyacinthus, so that he died. The festival lasted three days: on the first, sacrifices were offered to the dead in solemn melancholy in memory of the beautiful youth; on the two days following, joyous processions and contests took place in honour of Apollo Carneus.

STOP AND THINK: RESEARCH
After doing some research into the various Athenian festivals, complete the following chart.

	FESTIVALS OF THE ATHENIANS				
	Time of year	**Participants**	**Divinities involved**	**Location**	**Main rituals**
Panathenaia					
Lenaia					

	Time of year	Participants	Divinities involved	Location	Main rituals
Synoikia					
Anthesteria					
Eleusian Mysteries					
Thesmophoria					
Olympieia					
Skira					
Haloa					
Braurunia					
Kallynteria					

FESTIVALS OF THE ATHENIANS					
	Time of year	Participants	Divinities involved	Location	Main rituals
Plynteria					
Hyacinthia					

Are there any other festivals you can add to the chart?

The Greek Calendar Year

Hekatombaion	July/August
Metageitnion	August/September
Boedromion	September/October
Pyanopsion	October/November
Maimakterion	November/December
Poseideon	December/January
Gamelion	January/February
Anthesterion	February/March
Elaphebolion	March/April
Mounichion	April/May
Thargelion	May/June
Skirophorion	June/July

RITUAL SEQUENCES

Evidence of the following principles can be found in the festival rituals. They reflect the idea that the gods were like humans in these respects:

a. lack of division between the sacred and secular
b. reciprocity
c. competition (*agon*)
d. multiplicity

As well, the rituals were characterised by the following features, reflecting the idea that the gods were *not* like humans — they were disordered and chaotic:

e. a juxtaposition of elements which were natural, with those that were unnatural, e.g. silent drinking followed by riotous drinking at the start of the Anthesteria

f. a juxtaposition of opposites, e.g. eating and purging; going out, then staying indoors; sexual abstinence and sexual promiscuity

g. a juxtaposition of things threatening with things alluring, e.g. fire, blood and weapons on one hand with food and sexuality on the other; gestures of submissiveness alongside imposing displays of power; sudden alterations of darkness and light

h. there was often a reversal of roles

i. suspension of order was common

j. recurring images of death and violence

k. the vulnerability of the Greek world, the importance of agriculture together with all the experiences of life — birth, initiation, death, hunting and harvest, famine and plague, war and victory — were all themes that permeated the rituals.

The last two were not openly acknowledged as being part of Greek society. The rest are the opposite of values which permeated all activities. (Can the rituals be seen as a socially acceptable safety valve for tensions in Greek society which could not be resolved?)

The ways in which Greek religion was a system, rather than beliefs that just grew, begin to emerge. The rituals were a symbolic expression of the idea that communication with the gods (whose existence was taken for granted) was ambiguous, foreign and subversive. Behaviour in communication with the gods was the reverse of what was normal. The gods, in return, seemed to communicate with humans, but their messages were ambiguous, contradictory, misunderstood. They failed to enlighten and to provide answers.

The truth was often revealed too late.

The prayers and rituals of the Greeks revealed that the gods were viewed simultaneously as being like people and not like people. Sometimes the human-divine experience was intelligible, at other times it was not. Religious rituals were a way of creating mini-chaos that was controllable, imposing some order in a threatening world.

STOP AND THINK

✎ **Under the heading 'Characteristics of Religious Festivals' make a list of examples from the various festivals.**

✎ **Rank the characteristics a–k in order of:**

  • **frequency of occurence**
  • **importance to making sense of Greek religion**

MYTHS

The Greeks had many gods, many rituals, many myths. But the multiplicity of myths did not result in chaos. The gods were imagined to be part of a family, with Zeus the father of gods and humans. Because the model of a family was used the Greeks could understand the conflict which occurred both within and outside the family. Holding the web of conflicting loyalties, interests and obligations together, however, was the fundamental unity of the family. The gods could be understood as a source of disorder, but also as the ultimate defence of order.

Because the world was not always under the control of the Olympians, older and more primitive, irresponsible powers threatened to erupt. Their duty was to terrify humanity. The dramatists expanded the range of Homer's myth to include even more of the darker side of the divinities. Again, for the most part, the gods behaved as people. Yet they could also be terrifying, alien, untamed. They were like people in their determination to defend their honour and to seek the respect which was the prerogative of their power. But the vengeful and wild way this often occurred in the myths destroyed any rapport that had been established between the gods and people. It was as if the gods had become the 'other', darker side of the world, a world where ordinary categories had lost all meaning.

STOP AND THINK

✎ **Choose a myth and show how the characteristics a–k (on page 188) are a feature of it.**

✎ **Complete the following chart outlining the darker side of Greek mythology:**

	DARK DIVINITIES		
	Gender	Who were they?	How did they threaten order in the world?
Moirai			
Furies			
Gorgons			
Graiai			
Phorkydes			
Conclusions which can be drawn:			

Lucian (born about AD 120) in his eighth *Dialogue of the Gods* deals with the story of Athena's birth from the head of Zeus, which had been split by Hephaestus with an axe.

*H*ephaestus: What must I do, Zeus? for I have come as you ordered, with the sharpest axe I have, sharp enough even if it were necessary to cut a stone with a single blow.

Zeus: Good, Hephaestus! Cleave my head and divide it into two parts with a downward blow.

Hephaestus: Are you testing me, to see whether I am mad? Come now, tell me only what you want done to you.

Zeus: Just this — divide my skull. Obey at once, or you will make me angry, and not for the first time! But mind you strike with all your might, without delay; for I am dying with the pains which distract my brain.

Hephaestus: Mind, Zeus, that we do no harm, for the axe is sharp, and will not play the midwife without bloodshed, in the gentle manner of Eilythyia.

Zeus: Come, strike down boldly; for I know what is best!

Hephaestus: I will do so, but unwillingly; for who can resist when you give an order? [Strikes] What is this? A maiden in full armour! You had a great evil in your head, O Zeus, so naturally you were ill-tempered when producing so mightily a virgin beneath the membrane of your brain, and one in full armour too; forsooth, you had a camp and not a head, without us knowing it. Already she leaps and dances the Pyrrhic dance, shakes her shield and brandishes her spear and is roused to fury; and, most wonderful of all, she is very beautiful and has attained maturity in a few moments! She is bright-eyed, somewhat like a cat, but her helmet becomes her not amiss! Now, I beg you, O Zeus, betroth her to me in lieu of my midwife's fee.

Zeus: You ask what is impossible, Hephaestus, for she will always wish to remain a virgin. Nevertheless, as far as I am concerned, I have no objection.

Hephaestus: That's what I wanted; I will attend to the rest. And now I will snatch her up and carry her off.

Zeus: If you think it easy, do so: but I know that you won't get much out of your bargain!

✳ ✳ ✳

✎ **List three comic elements in this dialogue.**

✎ **In what ways are the gods behaving as:**

- **humans**
- **non-humans**

✎ **What is the underlying serious religious meaning in this parody.**

✎ **Rewrite in the serious style which Pindar (518–438 BC) or Homer (who wrote in eight century BC) might have used.**

✎ **How does this source prove that Greek religion was open-ended and adaptable?**

✎ **Here is a list of some well-known tragedies popular with the Greeks:**

Aeschylus	***The Oresteian Trilogy* (458 BC)**
Aeschylus	***The Suppliants* (after 468 BC)**
Aeschylus	***Prometheus Bound* (after 468 BC)**
Sophocles	***Antigone* (441 BC)**

Sophocles	*Oedipus Rex* (430 BC)
Sophocles	*Electra* (415 BC)
Euripides	*Medea* (431 BC)
Euripides	*Hippolytus* (428 BC)
Euripides	*Orestes* (408 BC)
Euripides	*The Bacchae* (408 BC)

Choose one, and make four lists of the following:

- incidents where the gods behave predictably, like humans
- incidents where the gods behave unpredictably, in a non-human way
- examples of violence and destruction being accompanied by images of animal sacrifice
- conclusions which can be drawn

The story of Polycrates, tyrant of Samos, illustrates the way humans could be victims of the gods' vengeance — *nemesis*. In the Greek world wealth was attributed to good fortune, but prosperity was frequently followed by ruin and disaster. In other stories it was not wealth which made the gods act vengefully, it was human arrogance or *hubris*.

Find the story of Polycrates and read it, and from the story find examples of the following:

- ambiguous signs from the gods
- reciprocity
- death and violence
- the vulnerability of the Greek world
- expectation of irrational behaviour by the gods.

CONCLUSION

Greek religion was a system whose parts were all related to each other in a way that made sense. The Greeks saw the gods as combining contradictory aspects — the predictable and unpredictable, human and non-human. This was the essence: the gods had to be more than human if they were to offer any reassurance against the chaos which was always threatening the Greek world.

At the same time, the Greeks' view of their gods demonstrates the structural tensions which were an underlying part of their society. Their festivals re-created these situations of anxiety which in real life could not be avoided. In this way, much of the anxiety and stress could be overcome, as the festivals went through the process of controlling them in a ritualistic manner.

STOP AND THINK

Refer to your first series of answers to 'A Different World', on page 166. Complete the following chart.

Possible disturbances in Greek society	Examples of how they were controlled through ritual in various festivals

'The Greek system of religious belief pervaded every corner of Greek culture.'
Fill in the square with examples which illustrate this. Add your own squares.

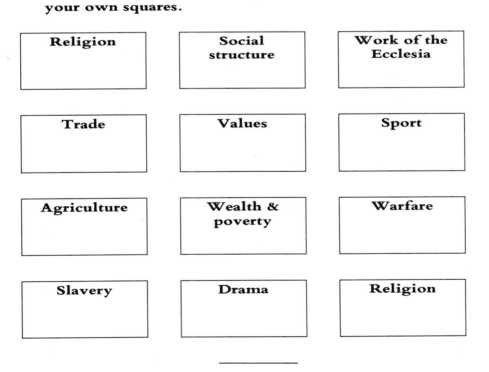

Religion	Social structure	Work of the Ecclesia
Trade	Values	Sport
Agriculture	Wealth & poverty	Warfare
Slavery	Drama	Religion

LIST OF REFERENCES

ANCIENT SOURCES

Aeschylus, *The Persians*, tr. A.J. Podlecki, Prentice-Hall, Englewood Cliffs, NJ, 1970

Aristophanes, *The Complete Plays of Aristophanes*, ed. Moses Hadas, Bantam, 1981

Euripides, *Ion*, tr. A.P. Burnett, Prentice-Hall, Englewood Cliffs, NJ, 1970

—— *Andromache*, ed. P.T. Stevens, Clarendon Press, Oxford, 1971

Thucydides, *The Peloponnesian War*, tr. Rex Warner, Penguin Classics, 1954 repr, 1980

SECONDARY SOURCES

Raubitchek, A.E., *Dedications from the Athenian Acropolis*, Cambridge, Mass, 1949

Rice, D.G. & Stambaugh, J.E., *Sources for the Study of Greek Religion*, Missoula, 1979

Welles, C.H., 'The caves at Vari', *American Journal of Archaeology*, 7: 263–349, 1903

CHAPTER NINE

PHILIP OF MACEDONIA

GARY KENWORTHY

INTRODUCTION

The role played by Philip II in creating a Macedonian hegemony over the Greek states is often overshadowed by the later achievements of his son, Alexander, and the romance that surrounds his life and career. The achievements of Philip in solving the internal problems of his state, and his ability to control the affairs of the Greek states and those neighbouring areas such as Thrace, Illyria and Paeonia, have not been given due recognition.

In order to assess Philip's rightful place in ancient history we must examine the evidence available to us and answer the following questions:

FOCUS QUESTIONS

↘ **What was Philip II really like? What was it about his personality that made him so successful?**

↘ **To what extent did he solve the internal problems of the Macedonian state?**

↘ **How did he extend Macedonian control within Greece and the Balkan peninsula?**

↘ **Was he a good military leader?**

↘ **To what extent did his achievements assist his son, Alexander, in his campaign against the Persian empire?**

THE SOURCES

Unfortunately much of our evidence regarding the career of Philip comes down to us from sources that are questionable due to bias of one sort or another or through distance in time from the actual events. However, by careful examination and analysis of even the most suspect source we may still glean much of the truth needed to answer the focus questions.

THEOPOMPUS OF CHIOS

Theopompus was a contemporary of Philip who wrote a work entitled *The Philippica* in fifty-eight books beginning with his accession and dealing with 'world history'. Unfortunately most of this has been lost and it survives only in fragmentary form via later sources who used him as their source of evidence on Philip's life.

DEMOSTHENES

Demosthenes was born in 384 BC in Athens. His political career commenced in 364 when he conducted a prosecution to preserve his own property. A writer of speeches and teacher of rhetoric in his early days, he has been acclaimed as the greatest of Greek orators. He is probably most famous for his anti-Philip sentiments and political campaign to rouse both Athens and the other Greek states to military action to suppress Macedonian expansion and power.

A contemporary of Philip, he wrote a number of political speeches aimed directly at the Macedonian king and his tactics and at the apathy of the Athenians towards this. The most useful, to our purposes, are the three *Philippics*, the three *Olynthiacs* and his speech on the Peace of Philocrates, written between the years 351 and 341 BC.

DIODORUS SICULUS

Diodorus lived during the times of Julius and Augustus Caesar (c.60–30 BC) and wrote a world history in forty books. The narrative relies heavily on earlier sources, such as Theopompus of Chios, and as such is valuable to us.

PLUTARCH

Plutarch was a Greek biographer who lived sometime between AD 46 and 120. He is best known for his *Parallel Lives* of famous Greeks and Romans. His accounts are not meant as strict works of history, as he himself stresses on occasions. His aim was to write a biography with a moral purpose and so, while he tends to follow a chronological approach, he quite often digresses to include an anecdote with which to illustrate a particular aspect of his subject's character.

A problem arises with the use of Plutarch's *Lives* as a source of evidence on Philip's life, as no separate life of Philip has survived. Hence the reliance upon three other lives, those of Demosthenes, Phoeion and Alexander, to elicit any relevant information.

Plutarch also collected, in what is referred to as the *Moralia*, a number of anecdotes and sayings of numerous famous personalities, amongst which some that relate to Philip can be found.

FLAVIUS ARRIANUS OR ARRIAN

Arrian lived during the second century AD and wrote primarily a history of the campaigns of Alexander the Great known as the *Anabasis*. Although not a contemporary of either Philip or Alexander he did make use of 'official' histories such as those of Alexander's companions, Ptolemy and Aristobulus. Evidence for Philip's reign, however, is limited.

SEXTUS JULIUS FRONTINUS, c.AD 30–104

Whilst enjoying a distinguished political career, including the governorship of Britain, Frontinus wrote a number of practical works dealing with professional subjects. His major surviving work, the *Strategemata*, is a general text of historical examples illustrating Greek and Roman military strategy. His style is straightforward and shows evidence of wide research.

ISOCRATES, 436–338 BC

An Athenian orator of importance who wrote many political speeches. His many pupils included Theopompus of Chios. In 346 BC he published his most important work, the *Philippus*, urging Philip of Macedonia to take up the cause of Greek unity and to wage war against the Persians.

THEOPHRASTUS, c.370–288/5 BC

Theophrastus was born on Lesbos and became a pupil, collaborator and successor of Aristotle. He accompanied Aristotle while Aristotle was the tutor of Philip's son, Alexander, in Macedonia. He wrote on many topics and gave many lectures on botany and other subjects, one of which was politics. He lived in Athens from 335 BC where most of his work was done.

POLYAENUS

He was a Macedonian rhetorician who lived during the reigns of the emperors Marcus and Verus. Polyaenus wrote a collection of *Stratagems* in eight books. His work, which was produced very quickly, was a compilation of earlier works.

ARCHAEOLOGICAL REMAINS

Since the work of the past thirty years of archaeologists such as Professor Manolis Andronicos, who discovered the royal graves at Vergina in Macedonia where Philip is believed to be buried, much can be learnt about the achievements of Philip.

KEY EVENTS IN PHILIP'S CAREER

c.382 BC	Born, youngest son of Amyntas III, king of Macedonia
c.368	Taken to Thebes as political hostage by Pelopidas. Spends three years there as ward of Epaminondas' father.
c.359	Becomes king of Macedonia on death of brother.
c.358	Defeats Athenian-backed usurper to Macedonian throne. Reorganises Macedonian army. First victories over Illyrians and Paeonians.
c.357	Reorganises Macedonia. Besieges and captures Amphipolis.

c.356	Captures Pydna and Potidaea. Allies Macedonia with Chalcidic Confederacy. Gives Anthemus and Potidaea to Olynthus. Phocians seize shrine at Delphi. Sacred war begins. Birth of Alexander.
c.354	Thessalians defeated by Phocians.
c.353	Philip captures Methone, the last Athenian ally in Thermaic Gulf. Port of Pagasae taken. Moves into Thessaly on request to protect them from Phocians. Defeated twice by Phocian general, Onomarchus, and retires to Macedonia to regroup.
c.352	Philip renews attack on Phocians and re-enters Thessaly. Defeats Onomarchus at the battle of Crocus Field, reorganises Thessaly and penetrates as far as Thermopylae where he is stopped by an Athenian force organised by Eubulus. Retires to Macedonia and starts organisation of Macedonian fleet to attack and harass the Athenian corn and trading fleets. Advances into Thrace. Cersobleptes of Thrace submits. Philip falls ill. War between the Greeks in the Peloponnese.
c.351	Demosthenes delivers *First Philippic*. Phocian forces, under the leadership of Phayllus, active in central Greece. Olynthus makes peace with Athens despite alliance with Philip who was at war with the Athenians.
c.349	Philip reduces the Chalcidice. Olynthus allies with Athens. Philip instigates the revolt of Euboea against Athens. Demosthenes delivers his Olynthiacs.
c.348	Philip captures Olynthus.
c.347	First Athenian embassy sent to Macedonia. Philip fights a brief campaign in Thrace.
c.346	Peace of Philocrates signed between Philip and Athens. Second Athenian embassy. Philip marches to Thermopylae and on to Phocis. Destroys Phocian forces. Phocian seats on Amphictionic Council given to Macedonia. Conflict between key politicians, Demosthenes and Eubulus, in Athens leads to inconsistency and indecision on the part of the democracy. Philip presides over the Pythian games at Delphi. Isocrates writes letter to Philip. Demosthenes delivers his speech, *On the Peace*.
c.345–44	Philip elected archon of Thessaly. Improves his small navy. Allies Macedonia with Messenia, Megalopolis, Elis and Argos. Demosthenes travels through the Peloponnese, writes and delivers the *Second Philippic*.
c.343	Campaigns in Epirus. Megara allies with Athens. Aeschines and other pro-Macedonian politicians impeached at Athens.
c.342–41	Philip in Thrace. Athenian Diopeithes sent to the Chersonese. Demosthenes writes and delivers his speeches, *On the Chersonese* and the *Third Philippic*. Journeys to Byzantium and succeeds in detaching it and

Perinthus from their alliance with Macedonia. Athenian troops sent to Euboea to overthrow pro-Macedonian tyrants.

c.340   Philip lays siege to Perinthus and Byzantium unsuccessfully. Peace of Philocrates ends. Athenian fleets active in northern Aegean.

c.339   Philip puts down Scythian rebellion in Thrace.

c.338   Philip is invited into Central Greece by the Amphictyons. Campaigns in Phocis and Locris. Demosthenes rouses Athenians against Philip and joins forces with the Thebans to oppose him in Central Greece. Battle of Chaeronea. Athenians and Thebans defeated decisively. Philip marches into the Peloponnese. Macedonian garrisons left at Ambracia, Corinth and Chalcis. First Pan-Hellenic Council (or *synhedrion*) held at Corinth. Philip elected supreme commander of the Greek forces to campaign against Persia.

c.337   Second Pan-Hellenic Council held at Corinth.

c.336   Philip sends forces into Asia Minor. Assassinated.

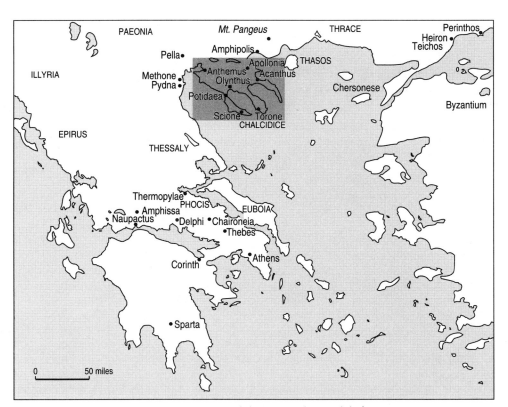

Important sites in Greece and the Aegean during Philip's career

STOP AND THINK: EXERCISE

✎ **Using the key events table and the map, assess the logic of Philip's military and political manoeuvres from 358 to 338 BC. Consider the geographic location of cities or states in relation to Macedonia and the strategic value of certain cities or states.**

✎ **List the various methods employed by Philip in the twenty years 358 to 338 BC by which he achieved success.**

✎ **Which cities or states constantly appear to be involved in battles or uprisings against Philip in this twenty-year period?**

WHAT WAS PHILIP II REALLY LIKE?

Philip was regarded by the ancient sources in a variety of ways. Demosthenes saw him as a treacherous tyrant, the panhellenists, Isocrates and Ephorus as a leader of Greeks against the Persians, and Theopompus as the greatest man Europe had ever known. Historians today, whilst divided on some aspects of his personality, are one in their appreciation of his leadership, diplomatic skills and generalship. But what should we, as historians, think of him? By studying the following selection of extracts from the ancient sources and analysing them we can draw a picture of his personality to enable us to understand his actions.

STOP AND THINK: DOCUMENT STUDY

Read the following extracts carefully and answer the questions below.

A Theophrastus has recorded that Philip, the father of Alexander, was not only great among kings, but, owing to his fortune and his conduct, proved himself still greater and more moderate.

Plutarch, *Moralia*

B . . . an unscrupulous and clever opportunist like Philip.

Demosthenes, *First Olynthiac*, 1–6, 199

C . . . a liar and deceiver

Demosthenes, *Second Philippic*, 21–7, 237

D On an occasion when he was asleep, and the Greeks who had gathered at his door were indignant and complaining, Parmenio said, 'Do not be astonished that he is asleep now, for while you were asleep he was awake'.

Plutarch, *Moralia*

E He [Philip] made you city dwellers; he brought you law; he civilized you. He rescued you from subjection and slavery . . .

From a speech by Alexander to the Macedonians at Opis as reported by Arrian, *Anabasis*
7, 9

F **T**aken all in all, Europe has never yet produced such a man as Philip, the son of Amyntas.

Theopompus, Philippica

❊   ❊   ❊

G **A**fter his victory over the Greeks, when some were advising him to hold the Greek cities in subjection by means of garrisons, he said that he preferred to be called a good man for a long time rather than a master for a short time.

Plutarch, Moralia

❊   ❊   ❊

⟍ **According to these sources what were Philip's good points?**
⟍ **What were his bad points?**
⟍ **Construct a chart using the headings shown below and for each source A–G work out what problems regarding reliability of the author you might expect to find.** (*Clue*: Reread the section, 'THE SOURCES'.)

Source	Author	Possible problem with reliability
A	**Plutarch**	

etc.

⟍ **In your opinion, what was Philip really like?**
⟍ **Why was he so successful?**

PHILIP AND THE MACEDONIAN STATE

In 359 BC upon assuming the regency for his youthful nephew Amyntas — the son of Perdiccas, the previous king — Philip was faced with what appeared to be an insurmountable set of problems. Perdiccas had been killed, along with the larger part of the Macedonian army, fighting in Illyria. Macedonia, suffering from political disunity as a result of Perdiccas' death, was also under the threat of invasion from both Illyria and Paeonia. At least two outside pretenders to the throne also existed. One, Pausanias, had gained the military and financial support of the Thracian king whilst the other, Argaeus, had gained Athenian support.

To add to this political chaos Philip was faced with the reconstruction of the Macedonian army, which had virtually been destroyed by the Illyrians. Macedonia was also a backward and underdeveloped state that had never evolved into a city-state stage of civilisation. It was primarily agricultural, feudal and fragmented. Its people were organised in tribal groups, the nobles of each tribe holding a special status with the king. From this often disunited group the king chose his 'Companions' who attended his court in peacetime and fought by his side in war.

According to a speech supposedly delivered by Alexander, Philip's son, to his troops at Opis and reported by Arrian in his *Anabasis*,

Philip found you [the Macedonians] a tribe of impoverished vagabonds, most of you dressed in skins, feeding a few sheep on the hills and fighting, feebly enough, to keep them from your neighbours... He gave you cloaks to wear instead of skins; he brought you down from the hills into the plains; he taught you to fight on equal terms with the enemy on your borders, till you knew that your safety lay not, as once, in your mountain strongholds, but in your own valour. He made you city dwellers; he brought you law; he civilized you. He rescued you from subjection and slavery, and made you masters of the wild tribes who harried and plundered you; he annexed the greater part of Thrace, and by seizing the best places on the coast opened your country to trade, and enabled you to work your mines without fear of attack. Thessaly, so long your bugbear and your dread, he subjugated to your rule, and by humbling the Phocians he made the narrow and difficult path into Greece a broad and easy road. The men of Athens and Thebes, who for years had kept watching for their moment to strike us down, he brought so low... Passing into the Peloponnese, he settled everything there to his satisfaction, and when he was made supreme commander of all the rest of Greece for the war against Persia, he claimed the glory of it not for himself alone, but for the Macedonian people.

Arrian, *Anabasis*, 7, 9

✽   ✽   ✽

STOP AND THINK: DOCUMENT STUDY

➘ **What does Alexander tell us about the Macedonia that existed when Philip became king?**

➘ **What changes were brought about by Philip?**

➘ **Why might Alexander have made such a speech?**

➘ **Where might Arrian have got his information about this speech?** (*Clue*: See the section on sources.)

➘ **What problems might exist with the authenticity of this speech?**

Philip quickly rid himself of all political opponents to the Macedonian throne, and in 358 BC he acted to rid himself of all neighbouring enemies. His initial response was to buy off the Paeonians with gifts in order to gain time to complete the retraining and reformation of the Macedonian army.

MILITARY REFORMS

Philip set about his reorganisation based upon what he had learnt while a political hostage in Thebes. By early 358 BC he could field 10 000 infantry and 600 cavalry. At Chaeronea in 338 BC this had risen to 30 000 infantry and 2000 cavalry. He financed his army by seizing the rich goldmines of Mt Pangaeus.

... and having reformed the military formations to give greater strength and equipping them with the weapons suitable for these formations, he was constantly parading and training them for combat. He devised both the close array of the phalanx and its equipment, in imitation of the close shield formation of the heroes before Troy, and he was the first to put together the Macedonian phalanx...

Diodorus Siculus, 16.3

✽   ✽   ✽

The army contained three distinct elements: the infantry, the cavalry and a corps of siege engineers.

THE INFANTRY

THE PHALANX OR PEZETAIROI (FOOT COMPANIONS)

The main troop type of the Macedonian army as organised by Philip was the *pezetairoi* or phalangite. By 334 BC these troops were organised into twelve or fifteen taxeis of about 1500 men. Each of these was raised from one of the Macedonian 'provinces'. These were further grouped into files called *dekades* (tens).

STOP AND THINK: LIBRARY RESEARCH TASK

✎ **Using your school library find out what formations of Greek hoplites and Macedonian phalanx looked like. Now answer these questions.**

  • **What advantages did this type of formation offer the individual hoplite or phalangite?**
  • **Why was this type of military formation adopted by the Greeks?**

The equipment used by Philip's phalangites was based on the pattern of the light-armed peltasts used by the Athenian general Iphicrates. They were armed with the sarissa, a pike some 5.5 metres in length and held in both hands, as their principal weapon and a sword for closer fighting. For protection they wore a leather tunic or in some cases cuirass, bronze greaves on their shins and a bronze helmet most commonly of the 'Phrygian' type. They also carried a small shield suspended around their necks by leather straps whilst fighting. This shield, called a peltas or aspis, was approximately 60 centimetres in diameter and once again was made of bronze. Excellent examples of all of these have been found at various sites, the most notable at the Great Tomb of Vergina believed to be that of Philip himself.

Diodorus places the reorganisation of the Macedonian infantry plus the introduction of the sarissa in the early part of Philip's reign but modern historians, based on the available archaeological evidence, are in dispute over this. Javelins are described as being used against the Phocian forces of Onomarchus in 353 BC and no sarissa heads have been found at Olynthus (349 BC) but several came from the battlefield of Chaeronea (338 BC).

STOP AND THINK

✎ **Can you suggest a reason for the lack of archaeological evidence, e.g. sarissa heads, to support Diodorus' claims at Olynthus?**

✎ **With this in mind, can we dismiss his claims?**

The importance of the introduction of the sarissa to the battlefield lies in its length, which allowed a greater striking reach not only to the front rank of the Macedonian phalanx but also to those in the next four or five rows. The shaft of the sarissa was made from two pieces of cornelwood joined in the centre by an iron tubular sleeve approximately 17 centimetres long. The spear head was about 50 centimetres long with the tail butt being 45 centimetres long and weighted to counterbalance the weight of the pike whilst being held in the fighting position. (These dimensions are based upon the sarissa found in the Great Tomb of Vergina.)

The sarissa, once held in a fighting position, was then jabbed at the oncoming enemy as the phalangite moved forward. If one bears in mind that the average Greek hoplite's primary fighting weapon — the long thrusting spear — was only 2-3 metres in length, one can gauge the effectiveness of the sarissa in the hands of a well-drilled phalangite.

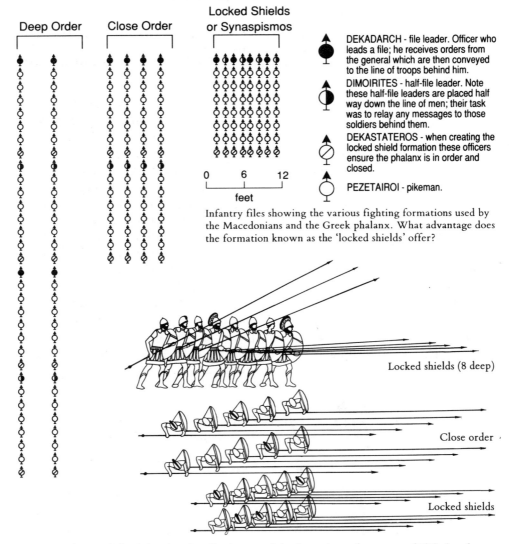

Deep Order **Close Order** **Locked Shields or Synaspismos**

DEKADARCH - file leader. Officer who leads a file; he receives orders from the general which are then conveyed to the line of troops behind him.

DIMOIRITES - half-file leader. Note these half-file leaders are placed half way down the line of men; their task was to relay any messages to those soldiers behind them.

DEKASTATEROS - when creating the locked shield formation these officers ensure the phalanx is in order and closed.

PEZETAIROI - pikeman.

0   6   12
feet

Infantry files showing the various fighting formations used by the Macedonians and the Greek phalanx. What advantage does the formation known as the 'locked shields' offer?

Locked shields (8 deep)

Close order

Locked shields

The Macedonian phalanx showing the effectiveness of the formation and weapons of Philip's reforms

The effective use of this weapon required skill and discipline as the phalangite had not only to hold it and fight with it but also to contend with those weapons of the other members of the phalanx in front, behind and to the sides of him. Diodorus mentions that Philip trained and disciplined his troops to what was, by contemporary Greek military standards, an exceptionally high degree of proficiency.

Training for the phalangites included 50-kilometre marches, even during peacetime, in full kit and carrying rations for thirty days. Women were banned from the armies' camp as were baggage wagons and such weakening customs (according to the Macedonians) as hot baths. Servants were limited to one groom per cavalryman, and one per ten infantry. These servants apparently also fought as light javelin or sling armed troops.

THE HYPASPISTS (SHIELD BEARERS)

These troops were an elite force trained as the king's own. There is some dispute as to whether they were royal bodyguards. There were three units of 1000 men trained in the use of the sarissa as well as in the shorter thrusting spears of the Greek hoplite and the javelin, thus allowing a flexibility in their use as the occasion demanded. References in Arrian to Alexander's use of them in various situations, such as when capturing the rock Aornos in India attest this. (Arrian, *Anabasis*, 4, 29–30) This unit was probably distinguished by its shield blazon — a five-pointed white or silver star, the royal Macedonian symbol. These units were also the only ones not raised and organised by province. This was possibly to foster loyalty to Philip and to counterbalance any ideas of provincial separation.

The Hypaspist or 'shield bearer' and a typical Macedonian shield design
How did the Hypaspists' armour differ from that of the pezetairoi?
Why would a soldier have a design like this on his shield?

THE AGRIANIANS

These troops were light-armed specialists from the lands north of Macedonia and allied to Philip. Their primary weapon was the javelin, a throwing weapon, and they relied solely on a small shield for protection. Their main function was to harass the enemy forces, particularly in rough or wooded terrain, and to provide a screen as protection from the arrows of opposing archers from the phalangites.

An Agrianian javelin man

MERCENARIES

These were primarily hoplites or peltasts (Arrian, *Anabasis*, 4, 29–30) although archers could be obtained. Philip relied upon these 'bought' professionals to fill his army when necessary. Demosthenes said in his *Third Philippic* '... that it is no close formation whose leadership enables Philip to go where he will, but light troops, cavalry, archers and mercenaries, and this is the kind of army he puts together'. (46–52)

A slinger and archer from the light armed troops (psiloi) employed by Philip

A hoplite, a Greek peltast and a Thracian peltast
How do these troop types differ from the basic Macedonian infantrymen, the pezetairoi?

STOP AND THINK

- **What was a peltast?**
- **Look at Demosthenes' statement. What does he mean by the term 'close formation'?**
- **Demosthenes seems, in this quote, to be criticising Philip's army. Why do you think he is doing this? (*Clue*: Who is his audience?)**
- **Why couldn't citizen soldiers be used all throughout the year?**

Mercenaries were much more flexible than citizen soldiers, such as those available to most of the Greek city states like Athens, and could be put into the field at any time of the year. As Demosthenes again stated, '. . . summer and winter are alike to him . . . he has no particular season for rest'. (*Third Philippic*, 46–52) This was essential to Philip's methods of warfare which relied on speed and professionalism, something relatively unknown at the time in the rest of Greece.

THE CAVALRY

THE COMPANIONS (*HETAIROI*)

The mounted troops that Philip found were organised by him as regular cavalry and divided into squadrons called ilae. These were about two hundred strong and were commanded by an ilarch. Traditionally these troops were drawn from the old Macedonian aristocracy but Philip threw open membership to new men of his choice who were given lands and titles in conquered territories. The Companions were equipped with a shorter spear than their infantry counterparts, the doru or xyston, which was approximately 3.6 metres long, and a sword called a kopis. For protection they wore a bronze helmet of the Boeotian type, examples of which can be found in the Ashmolean Museum in Oxford; linen or metal cuirasses, with the addition of leather *pteruges* (strips) to protect their thighs and upper legs; and metal greaves. No shields were carried as both hands were used in either controlling their horse or the lance whilst in battle. Archaeological evi-

A Hetairoi or 'Companion cavalryman'
Note the lack of stirrups. How would a cavalryman
be able to fight effectively without them?

A bronze 'Boeotian' helmet worn by the Hetairoi.
Why might a cavalryman wear a helmet like this and
not like the ones worn by the foot companions?
What advantages do they offer over others?

dence for the equipment of the Companion comes from several sources, the most important of which are the so-called Alexander sarcophagus, which was commissioned for Alexander's vassal, King Abdalonymus of Sidon (see page 231); the Issus or Alexander mosaic from Pompeii, which is a Roman copy of a contemporary Greek painting showing Alexander fighting the Persians; a monument to a soldier named Alcetas killed in Pisidia in 320; and a late fourth century grave painting from Egypt.

STOP AND THINK
- **Which of these sources might you expect to be the most reliable?**
- **Which might you expect to be the least reliable? Provide reasons for your decisions.**

The Companions were heavily armed forces who were used as shock troops designed to break up enemy formations, such as at Chaeronea in 383 BC, by charging through them, thus creating confusion and allowing the Macedonian infantry to take advantage of the situation. The Companions used their spears to stab at the enemy as they charged, rather than as lances, as they rode without the aid of stirrups and so could be easily dislodged from their mounts. Nonetheless Philip's use of them in this manner gave him the advantage over his Greek opponents who rarely used cavalry at all.

As with the phalangites the Companions were highly trained and disciplined and could use several different formations, e.g. the wedge or rhomboid, depending on the situation.

THE PRODROMOI
These were light armed cavalry who were used as scouts for reconnaissance.

A Prodromoi or 'Scout'
Notice the lack of any body armour apart from the helmet. What advantage does this offer this troop type?

THE THESSALIANS AND THRACIANS

Philip enlisted a number of cavalry from areas such as Thessaly and Thrace. He used these troops primarily to ward off any enemy cavalry or to outflank enemy forces. They were also used to pursue fleeing enemy troops. Their armour and weapons varied depending upon regional preferences but most relied on javelins and so were used as were the Agrianian infantry.

A Thessalian cavalry man, a Paeonian light cavalry man and a Thracian cavalry man
What are the main differences in weaponry and armour between the Macedonian cavalry and these types also used in Philip's army?

THE SIEGE ENGINEERS

Philip was the first in Greece to employ siege engines to capture opponents' cities. Previously the preferred Greek tactic had been to starve the inhabitants out of their walled strongholds. This was not only time-consuming but it also did not guarantee any great degree of success. Philip, by creating a highly trained corps of engineers and sappers, was able to revolutionise siege warfare and speed up campaigns that required the capture of such strong points.

Philip's forces were thus better equipped and trained than their predecessors. The fear of foreign invasion, Philip's ability to gain the respect of his men by sharing their hardships, the promise of loot from successful campaigning — all helped to mould the Macedonians into a successful and enthusiastic fighting force and to accept the harsh training and discipline forced upon them. However Philip took this one step further by developing a professional pay structure which not only gave extra pay for promotion but also for distinguished service. Philip also quite often gave troops land grants as rewards in conquered territories.

The creation of this new professional army was also important in providing a focus of national sentiment and unity, as well as giving Philip the military might to impose it.

Philip's final accomplishment in the reorganisation of the army was his introduction of various formations to the different troop types. The phalangites were able not only to close ranks by 'locking their shields' but also were able to march into battle obliquely (see diagram below), thus refusing the enemy the chance to engage the whole Macedonian force at once. This tactic was extremely successful against much larger forces as was evidenced by Alexander's success at Gaugamela against the Persians in 331 BC.

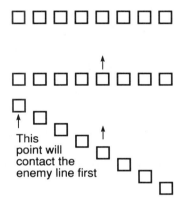

A normal deployment, a straight line
The oblique line formation practiced by Philip at Chaeronea and used brilliantly by his son, Alexander, at Gaugamela

STOP AND THINK

✎ **Why would this tactic help a smaller force against a larger one? Draw a diagram to illustrate your answer.**

The infantry were also able to retire — go backwards — whilst still fighting, thereby giving the impression of running away and thus drawing the enemy troops on one part of the battlefield on and so destroying their battle order by creating gaps in it. The classic example of this in use was at Chaeronea in 338 BC.

The Companion cavalry was likewise trained in special formations such as the wedge (see diagram on the next page). This provided a point with which to drive the cavalry into the ranks of the enemy infantry and so cause maximum confusion.

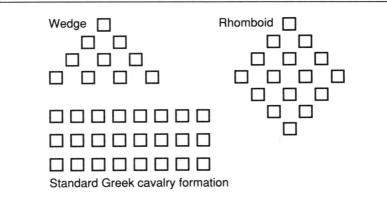

Two cavalry formations used by the Macedonian cavalry and introduced by Philip
What advantages do these formations have over a standard cavalry formation?
(*Clue*: how fast could cavalrymen change direction in each formation? Which formations could fit through gaps in the line of the infantry easiest?)

Philip had by 356 BC, therefore, largely solved the internal problems of his nation. He had assumed the kingship and rid himself of any potential rivals. His reconstruction of the army allowed him to assert Macedonian dominance in the northern Balkan region and to encourage Macedonian unity. His seizure of rich gold mines and trading ports such as those at Mt Pangaeus and Pydna allowed the Macedonian economy to change from its primarily agricultural and pastoral nature to one of industry and commerce, as well as to finance his military reforms and foreign policy. It was also apparent that his ambitions were, however, greater than the mere protection of his nation, much to the disgust of Demosthenes who stated: 'He [Philip] is not content to rest on his laurels, but is continually adding to the haul he collects in the net in which he ensnares our hesitant, inactive country.' (*First Philippic*, 5–10)

THE UNIFICATION OF PHILIP'S KINGDOM

Philip has been credited with making one kingdom and people out of many tribes and nations. Besides his military reforms, perhaps Philip's greatest achievement lay in his creation of a unified Macedonian nation that allowed him the luxury of military expansion and glory.

The creation of a strong national army and Philip's military successes against troublesome neighbours was the main bonding force of his kingdom. However he also bridged the cultural gaps inherent within the kingdom by the founding of new cities and towns of mixed racial groups. (We know of six in Thrace alone.)

Many of the 'new' aristocracy that he created and drew to his court were the outstanding men of the various races who owed not only their wealth but also their position directly to Philip. They became his companions who fought beside him whenever necessary.

Philip's encouragement and development of agriculture and trade, for which settled conditions were essential, made the kingdom prosperous and his people content under his rule. He developed the productivity of Upper Macedonia by enforcing a conversion from pastoralism to agriculture and stock raising. East of Axios he planned new towns, improved the working of the mines and again encouraged agriculture. He undertook flood control, drainage and irrigation works near Philippi and at Pella, which became a part of an artificial waterway to the Thermaic Gulf. He was the first Macedonian king to build a fleet which travelled as far as the Black Sea. The economic strength of Philip's kingdom enabled the minting of magnificent gold and silver coinage.

EXTENSION OF MACEDONIAN CONTROL

Ulrich Wilcken in his book *Alexander the Great* wrote: 'In the first year of his reign Philip has already reached the height of his powers. His extraordinary capabilities as general, statesman and diplomat, which made possible this

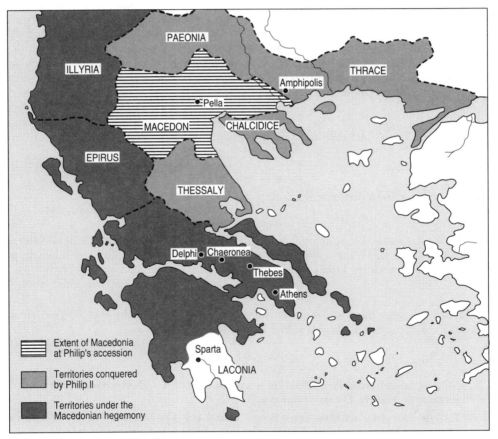

The extent of the Macedonian hegemony by the time of Philip's assassination

rapid and thorough salvation of the state, explain to us also the extraordinary success of his career.' Demosthenes, on the other hand, describes him as '... an unscrupulous and clever opportunist'. (*First Olynthiac*, 1–6) Whatever the opinion, the facts remain that by the year of his death, 336 BC, Philip had extended Macedonian control throughout Greece and the Balkan peninsula, and was recognised as hegemon.

STOP AND THINK: DOCUMENT STUDY

Philip's methods varied, depending upon the situation, and reflected the adaptability and genius of the man. Demosthenes, although the leading anti-Macedonian advocate in Greece at the time, still provides us in his speeches with an insight into Philip's methods. Read the following extracts carefully, then answer the questions that follow.

A **A**s it was he observed with insight that these strategic points were the prizes of war, that they were open to the contestants, and it is a natural law that ownership passes from the absentee to the first comer, from the negligent to the energetic and enterprising. This is the spirit which has won him control of what he holds, in some cases by the methods of military conquest, in others by those of friendship and alliance.

First Philippic, 351: 5–10

B **H**is personal control of all activities, open or secret, his combined position in command of the army, state and exchequer, his invariable presence with his forces, give him a real superiority in military speed and efficiency.

First Olynthiac, 349: 5–6

C **T**here is not a state that has tried to make use of him without falling victim to his duplicity.

Second Olynthiac, 349: 5–10

D . . . a liar and a deceiver.

Second Philippic, 344: 21–31

E **W**hy did Philip choose one treatment for the others and a different one for ourselves? [Athens] Because this is the only state in which licence is given to speak on his behalf, in which it is safe to accept bribes from him and still address you . . .

On the Chersonese, 342–1: 61–6

F . . . Yet again there was the case of Pherae the other day. Philip entered Thessaly in the guise of a friend and ally and seized Pherae which he now holds.

Third Philippic, 342–1: 8–10

> **What methods for Philip's success are highlighted in the extracts from Demosthenes?**

> **Look closely at the language used by Demosthenes. What is Demosthenes' attitude to Philip? Does he admire him? Despise him? Fear him?**

匚

STOP AND THINK: LIBRARY RESEARCH TASK

↘ **Go to the library and using some of the texts there on Philip's life list under the following headings one or two examples of where and when he used each of these methods to achieve his goals: force and threats; bribery; diplomacy; promises later broken; pro-Macedonian political factions; opportunism. What did Philip hope to achieve by each of these actions in the examples you have selected?**

PHILIP AS MILITARY LEADER

The easiest criterion by which to judge the ability of a military leader is the degree of his success. As Machiavelli wrote in his *Art of War*, 'If a general wins a battle, it cancels all other errors and miscarriages'. (p 275) This, in itself, is too simplistic a means by which to assess the ability of generals of the calibre of Philip as luck sometimes plays a major role in battlefield results. Other criteria need to be assessed: ability as a logistics expert and strategist; ability to win the respect of the men and tactical ability on the actual day of the battle. Philip's generalship offers lessons in all of these areas — his major contribution to the Greek world was revolutionising the art of warfare.

THE REORGANISATION OF THE MACEDONIAN ARMY

Much has already been said about Philip's reorganisation of the Macedonian army despite the grave situation at hand in 359 BC. His ability and genius as a military leader are indicated by his introduction, whether they be borrowed or original, of new and superior weapons such as the sarissa; of new fighting formations, the wedge and locked shields; manoeuvres such as the oblique line; and of new training drills, all within a very short period of time. His ability to rebuild and reorganise a defeated force and create a new national standing army that was also the model of professionalism for the time gave rise to Macedonia's dominance of the Balkans and eventually to Alexander's success against the Persians.

LOGISTICAL EXPERTISE AND ABILITY AS A STRATEGIST

The logistic organisation of the Macedonian army, developed by Philip, was fundamentally different from that of contemporary Greek and Persian armies. In these armies the number of camp followers often was equal to the number of soldiers within the force. Rations, weapons and body armour were carried in carts or by servants. Philip changed this practice, making, as Frontinus (4.1.6) tells us, his soldiers carry their equipment and rations, thus doing away with the need for carts or as many servants. The result of these reforms was a dramatic reduction in the size of the baggage train. It made the army the fastest, lightest and most mobile force in existence, capable of making lightning strikes on strategic points.

Demosthenes summed up the success of Philip's reforms and organisation in his speech *On the Chersonese* written in 342–41: 'With his standing army on the spot and his anticipation of his aims, he can attack where he likes in a moment'. (12)

Strategically too Philip was brilliant. He chose his targets to suit his immediate needs, as in the case of the rich gold mines and ports of the north, and with a view to the future. This is evidenced by his methodical approach to Macedonian expansion within the Balkans and his ability to use the disunity of the Greek states to his advantage.

He also marks a turning point in the development of strategy; for he was the first in Greece with a view to the total destruction of the enemy, the first who consciously carried out what is known as the 'strategy of defeat'. Whereas earlier battles were usually regarded as competitions by the Greeks, the victor being the one who kept the battlefield and erected some form of trophy to commemorate the event while the defeated side retired, Philip after winning a victory pursued the fleeing enemy to the last to maximise the enemy's losses. This meant that battles such as Chaeronea in 338 BC were decisive, unlike earlier ones.

STOP AND THINK

  ＼ **What do the terms 'logistics', 'strategy' and 'tactic' mean?**
  ＼ **Explain in your own words the differences between them.**
  ＼ **List the tactics employed by Philip and rank them in the order of their effectiveness. Explain the reasons for your ranking.**

ABILITY TO GAIN THE RESPECT OF HIS MEN

Diodorus states: 'Despite the presence of such great terrors and dangers [in 359 BC] Philip was not dismayed at the gravity of the impending trials, but he made the Macedonians confident by convening them in assembly after assembly and exorting them by his eloquence to be brave'. (16.3)

The ability of a general to gain the respect of his men and inspire confidence in them is a rare quality. Philip, like Hannibal a hundred years later, is reported to have shared the hardships of his troops and to have led his forces from the front line. His preparedness to share the dangers of the battlefield with his troops often resulted in his being wounded, as in the case of his lameness apparently gained whilst pursuing the fleeing Triballi in 339 BC at the head of his men. His bravery, confidence and presence on the battlefield lifted morale and won him the loyalty and respect of his men.

TACTICAL ABILITY

Tactically Philip is responsible for realising the special function of each arm of his forces and co-ordinating these on the battlefield to devastating effect. His phalanx required support from other units. Hence the development of the hypaspists' and peltasts' role during the battle. The days of individual combat, as in the past, were now dead and buried.

Cawkwell in his book, *Philip of Macedonia*, sums up Philip's achievement when he states:

> . . . the equestrian skill of the Macedonian troopers combined with the highly trained, relentless phalanx allowed the use of the latter as a base or pivot for all out attack by the former, the striking arm. The Greek armies, with their heavy, cumbersome line of hoplites, were no match for the variety of tactics open to Philip and his successors, although these are seen only in glimpses during Philip's reign itself, for the sources allow no more, but are clearly evident during that of Alexander.

SUCCESS ON THE BATTLEFIELD

In the early years of his career Philip was successful in Paeonia, Illyria and Thrace. His success over the Illyrian king, Bardylis, in 359–58 BC is a credit to his ability and reorganisation of the army. The Illyrians had been the greatest military power in northern Greece. They had overrun Macedonia in 393–92 BC and killed Perdiccas and 4000 of his 10 000-strong army in battle in 359 BC. They then occupied the upper areas of the Macedonian kingdom and as Diodorus tells us (16.2.6) were preparing to march on Lower Macedonia. Yet in a single battle, only a few months later, Philip overthrew Bardylis once and for all.

Philip met Bardylis on an open plain in western Macedonia with some 10 000 infantry and 600 horse. Bardylis, with a force of 10 000 picked infantry and 500 horse and worried about the threat of being outflanked, formed a square. Philip led his infantry forward, delaying the advance of his centre and left wing, and ordered his cavalry on the right to charge in, on the flank and rear of the Illyrians, as soon as an opening appeared. The spearhead of the infantry hit the left corner of the Illyrian square, smashed it in, and spread confusion into the flank and rear, into which the cavalry galloped and attacked. This concentrated onslaught shattered the left half of the Illyrian square. The Illyrians fled leaving 7000 men dead. Philip had adopted the oblique line in imitation of the tactics of Epaminondas at Leuctra but he added a new dimension with the use of his cavalry to capitalise on the confusion created and to deliver the decisive blow. Frontinus (*Strategems* 2.3.2.) tells us that Philip had observed in advance that the elite Illyrian infantry had been positioned on the front of the square. He therefore struck at the point of junction with the weaker troops of the flank, ensuring victory.

Philip's adaptability and ability to learn are perhaps best illustrated by his battles against Onomarchus, the Phocian general, during the Sacred War. In 353 BC, tricked by a feigned retreat, Philip was defeated by a much larger force and forced to retire to Macedonia to regroup. In 352, however, at the Battle of Crocus Field, he made up for his previous defeat by soundly beating a Phocian force of some 20 000 foot soldiers and 500 horse. This time he destroyed the enemy army — 6000 dead and 3000 captured — and its leader Onomarchus was killed.

STUDIES IN ANCIENT GREECE

During the next fourteen years he was successful in campaigns in Thrace and to the areas north of Macedonia and captured many cities, Olynthus being one. He reduced Epirus and the Chalcidice and incorporated Thessaly into his Macedonian empire. His greatest victory though came in 338 BC at Chaeronea against a combined Greek force led by Athens and Thebes.

STOP AND THINK: DOCUMENT STUDY
THE BATTLE OF CHAERONEA: PHILIP'S GREATEST VICTORY?

The fullest account that survives of the Battle of Chaeronea is by Diodorus Siculus. Read the following extract carefully, then answer the questions that follow.

At dawn the forces drew up in their lines. The king stationed his son Alexander (who was little more than a child in age but was noted for his bravery and for the swiftness of his action) on one wing and stationed at Alexander's side the most outstanding of his generals. The king himself held the command of the other wing, accompanied by a select group. He arranged as the circumstances required the ranks that could be disposed at will. The Athenians made the division of their line according to nationality. They assigned one wing to the Boeotians but kept command of the remaining one for themselves. When the battle began, it was hotly contested for a long time and many men fell on both sides, to the point that neither side could be certain of the hope of victory that was held out by the struggle. Alexander was eager to display his prowess to his father and exceeded all the rest in ambition; likewise many of the men who fought alongside him were able. At this point he made the first break in the solid line of the enemy. He killed many and kept wearing down the troops drawn up opposite him. His companions did the same, and kept making breaks in the solid line. The pile of corpses grew. Alexander and his men were the first to overpower their opponents and put them to flight. After this the king himself bore the brunt of the battle and did not yield the credit for the victory even to Alexander. He first forced back the troops that were stationed opposite him and then, after compelling them to take flight, he became responsible for the victory. Of the Athenians more than a thousand fell in the battle, and no less than two thousand were captured. Similarly many of the Boeotians were killed, and a considerable number were taken prisoner. After the battle Philip set up a trophy, yielded the dead for burial, performed victory sacrifices for the gods, and rewarded his men who distinguished themselves according to their worth.

Diodorus Siculus, 8, 86 (translated by Graham Joyner, Macquarie University)

✳ ✳ ✳

✎ **Using this account reconstruct the various stages of the battle in diagramatic form. You may choose how many stages are necessary to reconstruct the effectiveness of Philip's tactics and the events of the day.**

✎ **How useful is Diodorus' account to us, as historians, in search of details on this battle?**

Apart from Diodorus' account we have some information from Polyaenus, a Macedonian rhetorician of the second century AD, who collected from various sources bits and pieces of information about various generals' tricks and devices. Some are totally unreliable; some because we have their source are known to be reliable. So although no one can be sure of Polyaenus' reliability on the subject of Chaeronea, neither can we dismiss his evidence lightly.

Polyaenus says,

When Philip was in position at Chaeronea, he yielded to pressure by the Athenians and began to give ground. The Athenian general Stratocles cried out, 'We've got to keep on attacking until we shut the enemy into Macedonia', and did not give up pursuit. Philip, remarking 'the Athenians don't know how to win', kept retiring as he contracted the Phalanx and stayed on guard. Shortly, on attaining higher ground, he encouraged the ranks, stopped retiring and stoutly attacked the Athenians. After a glorious contest, he gained the victory.

＊ ＊ ＊

Did Philip give ground to the Athenians? Was this a preconceived tactic or not? Is Polyaenus' account accurate?

It has already been noted that the Greeks held a defensive position advantageous to themselves because it denied Philip any chance of attack using his oblique line tactic against their superior numbers and of his cavalry to outflank the Greeks. How then did he break the Greek line, or even give his cavalry the chance to outflank the Greek forces?

The obvious answer is that Polyaenus' account refers to a tactical withdrawal on the part of Philip which induced the Greek line to stretch and break itself. As the Macedonian left went forward, the right under Philip's command retired whilst the cavalry under Alexander waited for the gap to appear in the Greek line. Proof that the withdrawal was controlled and not the result of Athenian pressure is that there can have been no break in the Macedonian line, for if there had, the outcome of the battle would have been different. Philip must have had his forces execute a wheeling manoeuvre, pivoting on the centre, and as the well-trained Macedonians retired on the right, the Athenians followed, eagerly stretching the Greek line which broke under Alexander's attack on the left. (Alexander was said to be the first man to break into the ranks of the Sacred Band, which was apparently simultaneously engaged with the Macedonian phalanx.)

Philip's victory came then as a result of a cleverly preconceived plan of action designed to defeat a larger force fighting in a strong defensive position.

Philip's statesmanship is undoubted. He united his people, built up the economic prosperity of his country and won its dominion over Greece. His settlement of the Greek states after Chaeronea was masterly and he is said to have prided himself more on his diplomacy than his military victories. Alexander inherited a well-organised and united kingdom and army. In fact Philip's achievements were the basis of Alexander's success in Persia.

Without them, he might not have even set foot on Persian soil. Philip had vision and was inspired by what was best in Greek learning. He was an enlightened conqueror, was tolerant in outlook and brought peace, good organisation and economic prosperity to the lands he conquered.

STOP AND THINK: EXERCISES

↘ **Design a series of six commemorative stamps that could have been issued at the death of Philip II of Macedonia. Give the reasons for your selection of each design.**

↘ **Write two newspaper accounts of the Battle of Chaeronea. One should be suitable for an Athenian reader, and the other for a Macedonian reader.**

↘ **Write the speech Alexander might have delivered at the burial of his father in 336 BC.**

LIST OF REFERENCES

ANCIENT SOURCES

Arrian, *The Campaigns of Alexander*, Penguin Classics, Harmondsworth, 1971

Asclepidotus, *Tactics*, Loeb Classical Library, Heinemann, London, 1962

Demosthenes and Aeschines, *Political Speeches*, tr. A.N.W. Saunders, Penguin, 1975

Diodorus Siculus, *Universal History*, Loeb Classical Library, Heinemann, London, 1933–67

Frontinus, *Stratagems*, Loeb Classical Library, Heinemann, London, 1969

Greek Political Oratory (Demosthenes, Isocrates), Penguin Classics, Harmondsworth, 1986

Plutarch, *The Age of Alexander* (Alexander, Demosthenes) trans. Ian Scott-Kilvert, Penguin Classics, Harmondsworth, 1973

———— , *Moralia* (sayings of Kings and Commanders), Vol. III, Loeb Classical Library, Heinemann, London, 1968

SECONDARY SOURCES

Adcock, F.E., *The Greek and Macedonian Art of War*, University of California Press, 1957

Cawkwell, G., *Philip of Macedonia*, Faber & Faber, London, 1978

Engels, D.W., *Alexander the Great and the Logistics of the Macedonian Army*, University of California Press, Berkeley, 1978

Hammond, N.G.L., *A History of Greece to 322 BC*, Clarendon Press, Oxford, 1967

Laistner, M.W.L., *A History of the Greek World, 479–323 BC*, 3rd ed, Methuen, London, 1962

Sekunda, N., *The Army of Alexander the Great*, Osprey Publications, London, 1984

Wilcken, U., *Alexander the Great*, Chatto & Windus, London, 1932

CHAPTER TEN

ALEXANDER THE GREAT

Gary Kenworthy

No other historical personality of the ancient world has managed to capture the imagination of people throughout history as Alexander III of Macedonia has. Alexander's achievements, his military genius and his personal magnetism have earned him the title 'the Great'. His exploits became legendary even within his own lifetime. Such towering figures as Julius Caesar and Augustus, who left an imperial standard as tribute, are reported to have visited Alexander's tomb in Alexandria, Egypt.

A silver tetradrachm showing Alexander wearing the ram's horn of the god Zeus Ammon
This was not minted during his life but by one of his successors, Lysimachus, who became king of Thrace. Why would he use an image of Alexander on his coins?
How might this image distort our view of Alexander the Great and his character?
(*Clue*: why would a king, such as Alexander, wear the crown of a god?)
How might this coin contribute to the Alexander myth?

Perhaps much of the reason for our fascination with his life lies in the contradictory nature of the existing sources of evidence upon which we are forced to draw in order to create our picture of the man. C.B. Welles interprets the problem: 'There have been many Alexanders. No account of him is completely accurate.'

What, then, can you make of Alexander's life and career? What will your opinion of him be?

FOCUS QUESTIONS
- **What influences shaped Alexander's early life?**
- **Why did he invade Persia?**
- **Was Alexander a military genius?**
- **Why was he able to defeat the numerically superior Persians and conquer their empire?**
- **How did Alexander administer his empire?**
- **Does Alexander deserve to be called 'the Great'?**

THE SOURCES

Unlike his father, Philip, Alexander was well supplied with contemporary or near-contemporary historians. Unfortunately the works of these primary sources remain only in fragmentary form as reported by later secondary sources. To add to this problem we have the bias of various philosophical schools of thought, notably the Aristotelian or Peripatetic, which became hostile towards Alexander after his execution of Callisthenes, Aristotle's nephew, and of Alexander's own official histories.

Finally we need to be aware of what is known as the Alexander 'romance'. Alexander's exploits and personality very quickly became legendary and larger than life. This romantic or heroic view of Alexander has also tended to corrupt our sources. We must therefore carefully scrutinise all of our available evidence as to its reliability.

THE CONTEMPORARY HISTORIANS

EUMENES OF CARDIA (c.362–316 BC)
A Greek and Alexander's secretary, he later became satrap of Cappadocia. Eumenes was responsible for the recording of events in the official journals, the *Ephemerides*. These were later published. Essentially factual, some of this information has found its way into the works of Plutarch and Arrian.

ARISTOBULUS OF CASSANDREIA
He was one of the Greek technicians serving with the Macedonian army who wrote a history of Alexander. He wrote before Ptolemy and was used by Arrian to supplement Ptolemy's account. Strabo used his account for Alexander's journey through India. More of a geographer and natural historian than a military expert, he knew a lot about the personality of Alexander and must have had his confidence.

PTOLEMY LAGUS (c.367/6–282)
A Macedonian who was one of Alexander's companions and generals, Ptolemy, who became king of Egypt, wrote whilst king the best of the

eyewitness histories of Alexander. He used the official journal of the army along with other official documents to supplement his own knowledge of events. Arrian makes use of his account and but for this, practically all knowledge of his work would have disappeared.

NEARCHUS OF CRETE

Alexander's admiral and friend who circumnavigated the coast from the Indus to the Tigris river, his honest and reliable work written before 312 BC was not a history of Alexander. It did give an account of India, which Strabo and Arrian used and referred to, and of his voyage, which is reproduced in Arrian's *Indika*.

CALLISTHENES OF OLYNTHUS

He was a nephew of Aristotle and official historian during the campaign. His report covered only the first four years of the expedition and was grossly flattering to Alexander. It portrayed him as the champion of Panhellenism, possibly to overcome Greek opposition, and of divine birth. He opposed Alexander's introduction of Persian court ceremonies, such as *proskynesis*, and was executed after being implicated in the 'Conspiracy of the Pages'.

LATER HISTORIANS

DIODORUS SICULUS

Diodorus Siculus lived during the times of Julius and Augustus Caesar (c.60–30 BC) and wrote a world history in forty books. The whole of Book 17 is devoted to the history of Alexander's campaigns and the affairs of Greece in Alexander's absence. The history has survived incomplete as a large gap in the narrative occurs at the end of Chapter 83 with a jump from the capture and death of Bessus to the capture of Massada. A summary of the missing sections can be found in his table of contents at the beginning of the book.

CURTIUS RUFUS

A teacher of rhetoric in Rome during the first half century AD, he wrote a text — the *Historiae Alexandri Magni*. His history was the first full-scale work on Alexander in Latin, in ten books, of which 1 and 2 are missing and books 5, 6 and 10 have large gaps. The portrait of Alexander reflects the Aristotelian school of thought and is one of a tyrant favoured by luck. It tends to be dramatic, romantic and rhetorical.

PLUTARCH

A Greek biographer who lived sometime between AD 46 and 120, he is best known for his *Parallel Lives* of Greeks and Romans, of which Alexander and Julius Caesar form a pair. His accounts are not meant as strict works of history, as he states himself. His aim is to write biography with a moral purpose and so whilst following a chronological approach, he often digresses to include an anecdote with which to illustrate a particular aspect of his subject's character.

Plutarch also collected, in what is referred to as the *Moralia*, a number of anecdotes and sayings of Alexander. He also wrote two essays on the 'Fortune or Virtue of Alexander' in which he sets out to prove that Alexander's success was due to his virtue, not fortune.

FLAVIUS ARRIANUS OR ARRIAN

Arrian lived during the second century AD and wrote a history of Alexander's campaigns known as the *Anabasis*, or journey up country. He also wrote a history of the Indian campaign, (the *Indika*) based on the writings of Nearchus, and a history of events following Alexander's death. Of these two only the former remains intact and is often appended to the *Anabasis*. The *Anabasis* is in seven books and is based upon the histories of Ptolemy and Aristobulos. He also mentions the use of a great many other primary sources such as the royal diaries. This history is admittedly the best on military matters and administration but due to its reliance on Ptolemy is suspect on 'controversial matters'.

JUSTIN

Written in Latin about the middle of the third century AD an epitome of the Philippic history in forty-four books of Pompeuis Trogus who wrote under the Emperor Augustus. Books 11 and 12 deal with Alexander's career but there is little not already found in Plutarch or Arrian.

KEY EVENTS IN ALEXANDER'S LIFE

356 BC	Born, son of Philip II of Macedonia and Olympias of Epirus.
341-40	Aged sixteen appointed regent of Macedonia whilst Philip was campaigning in Thrace. Reduces a Thracian tribe, the Maedi, who had rebelled and established a city, Alexandropolis, in the area.
340-39	As a Macedonian general subdues some rebel cities in southern Thrace. Accompanies Philip on several campaigns. Helps prevent an Illyrian invasion of Macedonia.
338	Leads the Companion cavalry at the Battle of Chaeronea. Said by some ancient sources to have been the first to break the enemy line.
336	Philip assassinated. Alexander succeeds to the Macedonian throne. After his first descent into Greece elected general of the League of Corinth.
335	Campaigns in Thrace and Illyria. Marches on Thebes and destroys the city in order to reassert his control of the Greeks. Darius II becomes the Persian king.
334	Persian campaign begins in the spring. Alexander leads a combined Macedonian and Greek force across the Hellespont. Defeats the Persian

	forces at the Battle of Granikos. Conquers Lydia. Besieges Miletus and Halicarnassus.
334–33	Conquers Lycia, Pamphylia, Pisidia and Cilicia. Unravels the Gordian knot.* November fights the Battle of Issus and defeats Darius' forces. Founds Alexandria and Issum.
332	Between January and July, besieges Tyre. Receives submission of Syria and Judaea. October, besieges Gaza. Welcomed as a liberator in Egypt. Becomes pharaoh.
331	Founds Alexandria. Visits the oracle of Zeus Ammon at Siwah. Receives submission of Cyrene. 1 October, defeats vastly numerically superior Persian forces at Gaugamela (Arbela). Travels to Babylon and Susa. Antipater defeats Agis, the Spartan king, at Megalopolis and crushes revolt. Alexander assumes title of King of Asia.
330	From January to April marches through Persia. Persepolis burnt supposedly in revenge for Xerxes' destruction of the Acropolis in Athens in 480 BC. The Persian cities of Pasargadae and Ecbatana are occupied. The allied Greek forces are sent home symbolising the end of the Panhellenic campaign. July, Bessus kills Darius III and assumes title of Great King.
	Alexander conquers Hyrcania, Areia and Drangiana. Founds Alexandria Areion (Herat) and Alexandria Prophthasia. Proclaims himself Great King. Adopts Persian dress. Macedonian resentment and disaffection commences. Philotas implicated in conspiracy, tried and executed. Parmenio murdered. Macedonian forces winter in Drangiana.
329	Conquest of Arachosia. Arachosian Alexandria (Kandahar?) founded. Bessus captured and executed. Advance across the Jaxartes River. Macedonians winter in Afghanistan near Kabul.
329–28	Alexandria under Caucasus founded.
328	Alexander reaches Hindu Kush. Conquers Bactria and Sogdiana. Founds Alexandria Eschate, 'the furthest'. (Khodjend?) Marries Roxane, the daughter of the Sogdian prince. Attempts to introduce Persian court ceremonial procedures, e.g. *proskynesis* to his court. Macedonian and Greek resentment stiffens.
327	Murder of Cleitus in a fit of anger. Conquest of eastern Sogdiana. Conspiracy of the Pages uncovered. Callisthenes, one of the official historians, executed. Plans for Indian campaign made.
327/6	Winter campaigns in the Kunar, Chitral and Sarat regions.

---

* Gordias, an ancient king in Asia Minor, tied a knot which was to be undone by the one who should rule Asia. Alexander was said to have cut the knot with his sword.

326	Alexander crosses the Indus river. Defeats Porus, the local Indian ruler, at the Battle of the Hydaspes River. Conquers the Punjab region. Founds Alexandria Buclephala.
325	A mutiny of the Macedonian army forces Alexander to return westward. Defeats the Malli. Founds several towns on the Lower Indus. Constructs fleet, journeys down the Indus. Sends Nearchus as admiral along the coasts to the Persian Gulf and Babylon. Alexander and Craterus journey through Gedrosian desert and Carmania to Persepolis. Founds Alexandria Carmania.
324	Alexander tries to 'fuse' Macedonians and Persians into a new ruling class. Marriage ceremony at Susa of Macedonians and Iranian women. Alexander marries a Persian princess. Punishes satraps guilty of misgovernment. Macedonian troops mutiny at Opis. Persian troops introduced into the army. Veterans sent home. Death of Hephaestion. Harpalus, the empire's treasurer at Babylon, flees to Athens after expropriating funds. During the Olympic Games in Greece (July to August) Alexander requests the restoration of all Greek exiles and supposedly divine honours.
324–23	Alexander subjugates the Cossaeans.
323	Funeral of Hephaestion (May). Alexander dies — inconclusive suspicions of poisoning. Greece revolts against Macedonian control and the empire begins to fragment.

STOP AND THINK: LIBRARY RESEARCH

Go back over the information in the table of key events in Alexander's life.

✎ **On a map trace the route Alexander took to reach India.**

✎ **Complete the table to highlight the information on the key battles fought by Alexander.**

Battle	Date	Opponent	Result
Battle of Granikos			
Battle of Issus			
Battle of Gaugamela			
Battle of Hydaspes River			

✎ **Using additional information found in the library, find out more about each of the following people mentioned in the key events:**

- **Hephaestion**
- **Harpalus**
- **Bessus**
- **Agis of Sparta**
- **Antipater**

- **Porus**
- **Cleitus the Black**
- **Callisthenes**
- **Parmenio**
- **Philotas**

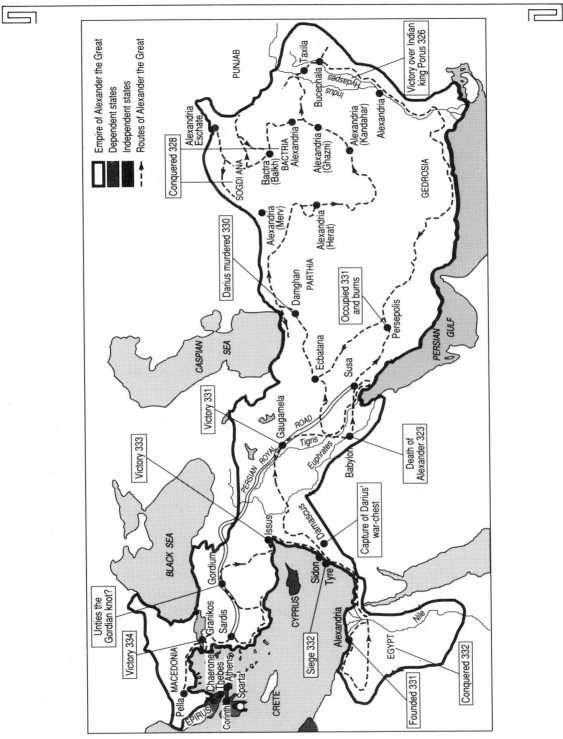

The campaigns of Alexander

EARLY LIFE

Alexander was born to Olympias, a princess of Epirus, and Philip II of Macedonia in 356 BC, on the same day according to the biographer, Plutarch, as the destruction by fire of one of the wonders of the ancient world, the temple of Artemis at Ephesus.

Other portents and dreams had accompanied the pregnancy. Olympias reportedly dreamt of being struck on the womb by a bolt of lightning. This was followed by a blinding flash from which a great sheet of fire blazed up, spreading far and wide before it finally died away. Philip reported that he had himself dreamt that he had sealed up his new bride's womb using a seal bearing the figure of a lion.

Alexander's mother, Olympias, was a proud, intelligent and ambitious woman. Plutarch describes her as '. . . a woman of a jealous and vindictive temper, who incited Alexander to oppose his father.' (Plutarch, *Life of Alexander*, 9) Olympias' main preoccupation became her son and his eventual ascension to the Macedonian throne. The plethora of stories regarding Alexander's supposed divine birth can probably be attributed to her influence. Whether Alexander believed these stories is uncertain as the reliability of some sources on this question is suspect but nevertheless there is sufficient evidence that he at least greatly admired the heroes of Greece's past such as Achilles, from whom he was reportedly a descendant on his mother's side. It is said that he kept a copy of the *Iliad* near him at all times. (Plutarch, *Life of Alexander*, 9)

On his father's side Alexander was supposedly descended from Hercules and Perseus. These semi-divine personalities figure strongly throughout his career as influences on his actions. Philip, on the other hand, was king of Macedonia and had recently (see Chapter Nine) rebuilt the Macedonian state and promoted it to a leading position within the Balkan peninsula, both politically and militarily. It would have been only natural then for such a person to see in his son the continuation of his own ambitions and to want to foster similar ambitions in his child.

Philip is reported to have said to Alexander later in his life when the boy complained about Philip fathering other children by other women, 'Well then, if you have many competitors for the kingdom, prove yourself honourable and good, so that you might obtain the kingdom not because of me, but because of yourself.' (Plutarch, *Sayings of Kings and Commanders*)

He bade Alexander also to give heed to Aristotle, and study philosophy, 'so that you may not do a great many things of the sort that I am sorry to have done'.

Alexander's early childhood experiences, influenced by his parents and their positions, were further developed by a number of teachers whom Philip especially imported to Macedonia. At the age of seven Olympias' uncle Leonidas, a severe disciplinarian, was selected to tutor him. Leonidas introduced Alexander to the rigours of military life with a spare diet, thin clothing and hard exercise.

At the age of thirteen (343 BC) Alexander received a new teacher, the philosopher Aristotle. Aristotle instilled within the young prince a scientific curiosity in a number of subjects such as botany, zoology and medicine. He was taught rhetoric and studied philosophy, which dealt with topics such as law, statecraft and personal ethics. Alexander's personal rivalry with the achievements of Achilles, Hercules and Dionysus may also have been encouraged. Alexander diverged from Aristotle's teachings in only one respect. Aristotle taught that non-Greeks should be regarded as subhuman; Alexander upon conquering a multiracial empire could hardly adhere to this belief and survive.

At the age of sixteen (340) Alexander was appointed regent whilst his father campaigned in Thrace. This was his first real taste of political and military power. He immediately showed his aptitude by subduing a rebellious tribe, the Maedi, and founding a town, which he named Alexandropolis, to secure the region thus protecting the supply routes into eastern Thrace. He was later given the task of subduing some southern Thracian cities and is reported to have saved Philip's life (probably at Perinthus) although Philip apparently refused to acknowledge this.

In 339, under Philip's orders, he mobilised the Macedonian army and repelled an attempted invasion by the Illyrians. In the following year he commanded the Companion cavalry at Chaeronea and was said to have been the first to break the enemy line. Philip chose him to head the embassy to Athens where he showed his diplomatic skill as well.

To date Alexander and Philip, despite growing pressure from Olympias, had remained close. This was to change with Philip's decision to marry a new wife, the niece of his general, Attalus, in 337. At the wedding feast an argument erupted over a comment made by Attalus which was a thinly veiled insult questioning Alexander's right to the Macedonian throne as his mother was an Epirot. Father and son quarrelled and Alexander left Macedonia with his mother to live at Dodona, the Epirot capital. Some months later the two were reconciled. However, Philip still exiled many of Alexander's friends.

In the following year Philip was assassinated by Pausanias, a Macedonian who had been humiliated by Attalus and could get no redress from Philip who, according to Diodorus, had been his lover some eight years before. (Plutarch, *Life of Alexander*, 10) Alexander, who had already displayed his military competence and had the support of Antipater and Parmenio, Philip's two most experienced and trusted generals, was proclaimed king by the Macedonian army. Alexander quickly punished those found guilty of the conspiracy against his father and removed any rivals to the throne. To quell unrest in Greece he marched his army southward. Attalus was convicted and executed for treason and Alexander accepted the positions of archon of Thessaly and commander in chief of the forces of the League of Corinth. Meanwhile the Thracians were uneasy. Alexander marched north in 335 and conducted his first independent campaign. He defeated the Triballi and Getae who accepted his overlordship. In Macedonia trouble arose with an invasion by the Illyrians, but Alexander and his army reached Pelium and inflicted a decisive defeat on Cleitus, the Illyrian king.

Whilst on these campaigns a rumour reached Athens and Thebes of Alexander's supposed death. The Macedonian garrison was blockaded in the Cadmea at Thebes and Athens, Aetolia and several Peloponnesian states prepared to join the rebellion. Alexander, however, cut short the rising by force marching to Thebes. An engagement was fought against the Thebans who lost. Their city was razed and its inhabitants sold into slavery. The other Greek states, led by Athens, quickly reaccepted Alexander's position at the head of the League of Corinth. With peace and Macedonian hegemony restored Alexander began his plans for an expedition against Persia.

STOP AND THINK: DOCUMENT STUDY: ALEXANDER'S CHARACTER
Carefully read the following extracts and answer the questions below.

A Being nimble and swift of foot, he was urged by his father [Philip] to run in the foot race at the Olympic Games. 'Yes, I would run', said Alexander, 'if I were to have kings as competitors'.

Plutarch, Sayings of Kings and Commanders

✳ ✳ ✳

B As for his hot temper and his love of wine, just as these were intensified by youth, greater age may have moderated them.

Quintus Curtius, History of Alexander, X.V.33

✳ ✳ ✳

C While Alexander was still a boy and Philip was winning many successes, he was not glad, but said to his playmates, 'My father will leave me nothing to do'. 'But,' said the boys, 'he is acquiring all this for you.' 'But what good is it,' said Alexander, 'if I possess much and accomplish nothing?'

Plutarch Sayings of Kings and Commanders, 1

✳ ✳ ✳

D After the capture of a seemingly impregnable rock [Aornos] Alexander's friends were saying that he had surpassed Hercules in his deeds, but he remarked, 'No, I do not feel that my deeds, with my position as commander, are to be weighted against one word of Hercules.'

Plutarch, Sayings of Kings and Commanders, 27

✳ ✳ ✳

E Even while he was still a boy, he gave plenty of evidence of his powers of self-control. In spite of his vehement and impulsive nature, he showed little interest in the pleasures of the senses and indulged in them only with great moderation, but his passionate desire for fame implanted in him a pride and a grandeur of vision which went far beyond his years.

Plutarch, Life of Alexander, 4

✳ ✳ ✳

F **A**s for his reputed heavy drinking, Aristobulus declares that his drinking bouts were prolonged not for their own sake — for he was never, in fact, a heavy drinker — but simply because he enjoyed the companionship of his friends.

Arrian, *Anabasis*, 7, 30

✳ ✳ ✳

➘ **List Alexander's *good* qualities.**

➘ **List his *bad* qualities.**

➘ **How might these qualities have helped him during his life?**

➘ **How reliable are each of the different sources used here? What problems might you expect with their respective authors?**

➘ **Do any of the extracts contradict each other? How? Why might this be so? Which do you believe and why?**

(*Clue*: These extracts do not all come from Alexander's youth. Some come from the end of his life.)

THE INVASION OF PERSIA

Upon Philip's death in 336 Alexander inherited not only the Macedonian throne but also the position of commander in chief of the combined forces of

Alexander the Great from the Alexander sarcophagus from Sidon
What is a sarcophagus?
What image of Alexander is portrayed by this source?
What is the significance of the lion helmet being worn by Alexander?
This sarcophagus was commissioned by Alexander's vassal King Abdalonymus of Sidon. Why might he have placed a scene with Alexander on his sarcophagus?
Could this source be biased?

the League of Corinth and their respective responsibilities. With this position, he also inherited, despite the initial Greek uprisings which culminated in the complete destruction of Thebes, the war against Persia that Philip had declared in 337 when the League had met in Corinth. Early in 336 an advance party of 10 000 troops under the command of Parmenio and Attalus had been despatched and had already liberated the coastal Greek city-states as far south as Ephesus. The islands of Tenedos, Lesbos and Cheos had likewise been freed of Persian control. Ostensibly initiated as an act of Greek revenge on the barbarians in retaliation for their acts of sacrilege and destruction during Xerxes' invasion of Greece in 480–79, Philip no doubt had ulterior motives. The idea was not new, as the formation of the Delian League by Athens in 478 testifies, and recently philosophers and orators, such as Isocrates, had called for the unification of the Greek states and the invasion of Persian territory as an honourable act. Isocrates wrote his first letter to Philip in 346; in it the philosopher refers to the idea of the war as a reconciliation of the various Greek states and 'an end to the insanity which now afflicts them'. (Isocrates, *Philip*, 88-90)

Philip, no doubt, saw the war as a way to unify the Greeks and to harness their military energies, thereby pacifying them and protecting Macedonia whilst he invaded Asia Minor. The invasion was primarily, therefore, to benefit the Macedonians. It would not only assert their domination over the area but would also protect the Macedonian empire against both Greeks and Persians at the same time. The sacking of the royal Persian treasury at Sardis would greatly enrich Philip's own treasury and the freeing of the Greek city-states of Ionia and the islands would encourage trading links away from the Persians and towards the Balkan states. The intrigues of the various Persian satraps, provincial governors, would also be stopped. Philip may well have harboured thoughts of extending his empire into the interior of Asia Minor also.

The Greek states, despite having granted Philip the title of 'Strategos Autokrater', i.e. commander in chief with dictatorial powers over the combined Greek and Macedonian forces, were reluctant to undertake the expedition. It had not risen out of any general Greek feeling and so in many cases was not voluntarily accepted, although smaller states accepted it as Philip's position offered them some security against domination by the larger states. Philip, however, in his usual style used both bribery and propaganda to ensure its eventual acceptance by all except Sparta which had refused to join in any actions of the League.

Upon Philip's death and with the consequent actions of Alexander at Thebes in 335, however, the possible main reason for Philip's expedition against Persia no longer really existed. Alexander had asserted his complete domination over the Greek states who, after the destruction of Thebes, were cowed by the experience. Arrian's account is testimony to this. (*Anabasis*, 1, 10) Athens, the leading Greek state, sent an embassy of pro-

Macedonian politicans to congratulate Alexander on his success and to tell him that 'the Athenian people rejoiced to see him safely returned from Illyria and the Triballians, and thoroughly approved his punishment of the Thebans for their revolt.' The hypocrisy of this action indicates the fear generated by the event.

Why then did Alexander wish to undertake the expedition?

STOP AND THINK: DOCUMENT STUDY
Read the following extracts from various sources which may throw some light on this question and answer the questions below.

A Whenever he heard that Philip had captured some famous city or won an overwhelming victory, Alexander would take no pleasure at the news, but would declare to his companions, 'Boys, my father will leave nothing for me to do. There will be nothing great or spectacular for you and me to accomplish to show the world.' He cared nothing for pleasure or wealth but only for deeds of valour and glory.

Plutarch, *Life of Alexander*, 5

* * *

B He burnt the palace of the Persian kings [Persepolis], though this was against the advice of Parmenio... Alexander's answer was that he wished to punish the Persians for their invasion of Greece; his present act was retribution for the destruction of Athens, the burning of Greek temples, and all the other crimes they had committed against the Greeks.

Arrian, *Anabasis*, 3, 19

* * *

C When Darius offered him ten thousand talents, and also to share Asia equally with him, Parmenio said, 'I would take it if I were Alexander.' 'And so would I,' said Alexander, 'if I were Parmenio.' But he made answer to Darius that the earth could not tolerate two suns, nor Asia two kings.

Plutarch, *Sayings of Kings and Commanders*, 11

* * *

D Your ancestors invaded Macedonia and Greece... You sent aid to the people of Perinthus in their rebellion against my father; Ochus sent an army into Thrace, which was part of our dominions; my father was killed by assassins whom, as you openly boasted in your letters, you yourself hired to commit the crime... you unjustly and illegally seized the throne... you sent the Greeks false information about me in the hope of making them my enemies; you attempted to supply the Greeks with money... your agents corrupted my friends... it was you [Darius] who began the quarrel.

Arrian, *Anabasis*, 2, 14, a supposed letter from Alexander to Darius

* * *

E He had great personal beauty, invincible power of endurance, and a keen intellect; he was brave and adventurous, strict in the observance of his religious duties, and hungry for fame.

Arrian, *Anabasis*, 7, 28

* * *

F On one occasion some Persian ambassadors arrived in Macedonia whilst Philip was away. Alexander received them. He talked with them and questioned them on matters such as the distances they had travelled by road, the nature of the country, the character of the Persian king, his experience in war, and the military strength and prowess of the Persians.

The ambassadors came away convinced that Philip's celebrated astuteness was as nothing compared to the adventurous spirit and lofty ambitions of his son.'

Plutarch, *Life of Alexander*, 5

✹ ✹ ✹

G **A**t Ecbatana Alexander dismissed his Thessalian cavalry and the other Allied contingents and ordered them back to the Aegean . . . Alexander himself also proposed to make for Parthia.

Arrian, *Anabasis*, 3, 19–20

✹ ✹ ✹

✎ **Draw up the following chart and complete it.**

Extract:	Author:	Alexander's Reason for Invading Persia:	Problem with Reliability of Source
A			
B			
C			
D			
E			
F			
G			

✎ **What is the significance of the event mentioned in extract G to the question of why Alexander wished to undertake the expedition?**

✎ **If the letter referred to by Arrian (extract D) is genuine where might he have obtained it?**

✎ **What was the 'official' reason for the expedition? Which extracts give this as Alexander's reason?**

✎ **After assessing the reliability of these extracts, why do you think Alexander invaded Persia?**

WAS ALEXANDER A MILITARY GENIUS?

In arming and equipping troops and in his military dispositions he was always masterly. Noble indeed was his power of inspiring his men . . . and . . . of sweeping away their fear by the spectacle of his own fearlessness . . . his ability to seize the moment for a swift blow, before his enemy had any suspicion of what was coming, was beyond praise.

Arrian, *Anabasis*, 7, 29

✹ ✹ ✹

Alexander's expedition lasted eleven years from the crossing of the Hellespont into Asia in 334 to his death in Babylon in June 323. He was only twenty-two years old when he started and thirty-three when he died. His army crossed some 20 000 kilometres of difficult terrain mainly by foot, fought in four major battles, countless minor ones and conducted a number of extremely difficult sieges, all successfully. His military genius is beyond doubt:

Granted he started out with the initial advantage of inheriting from his father the most scientifically trained and equipped army that the world had yet seen, but his own military genius is apparent in every undertaking from the Granikos to the Hydaspes. If the basic plan of attack in each of his pitched battles was that which he had learnt from Philip, he on each occasion modified or changed his dispositions to meet the special circumstances of the day.

M.L.W. Laistner, *A History of the Greek World 479-323*, 3rd ed, Methuen, London, 1962, p 318

Alexander the great as Hercules from a silver coin, a tetradrachm, struck at Amphipolis.
Who was Hercules?
Why might a person like Alexander want to portray himself as Hercules on a coin?

A detail from the Alexander mosaic showing what is thought to be Alexander in battle at Issus.
What does this tell us about the character of Alexander?

There are four aspects to consider in acknowledging Alexander's military genius:

- his logistical skill and planning
- his strategic skill
- his tactical skill
- his ability as a leader.

LOGISTICAL SKILL AND PLANNING

The sheer distances needed to be covered by his army across extremely harsh terrain; severe climatic extremes; and often, vast distances between cultivated inhabited regions were immense obstacles to be overcome. Alexander took his army of some forty to sixty thousand men across this land and, apart from one setback in Gedrosia, managed to supply and provision them. His army, it has been calculated, using US Army statistics, needed some 338 600 litres of water alone each day. Grain and forage was likewise needed in great quantities. According to W. Engels, Alexander managed to accomplish the task of provisioning his forces because of 'his superior abilities in gathering intelligence, planning, preparation and organisation'. He was aided too by his highly experienced lieutenants, to whom the actual tasks of supply were delegated.

Arrian makes mention on many occasions of Alexander's practice of splitting his forces for marches through the country. This helped to increase the army's chances of provisioning its men and animals with water and forage whilst on the way to a strategically significant point.

STRATEGIC SKILL

The vast size of the Persian empire and its military and naval resources dictated the need for careful strategic planning by Alexander and his general staff. His initial consideration was the protection of his home base, Greece and Macedonia, against a possible Persian counterattack, and so the defeat of the Persian forces in Asia Minor was a priority. This he managed at the Battle of Granikos in 334 and by securing the Ionian coastline.

His next consideration was the elimination of the Persian naval threat by the capture of the Persian naval bases in Phoenicia, hence his need to capture Tyre, Egypt and Cyrene before he advanced into the Persian heartland.

Despite these obviously careful strategic moves Alexander has sometimes been criticised as a military strategist. His decision to disband his fleet (334), his failure to cover Darius' movements at Issus (333) and his decision to march across the Gedrosian desert (325), which proved disastrous, have been cited by many modern historians as examples of poor strategy. Historians such as G.L. Cawkwell and P. Green are but two (see Reading List for details).

STOP AND THINK: DOCUMENT STUDY: DO YOU AGREE?

Read the extracts from Arrian on these three incidents and answer the questions that follow.

A **A**lexander now decided to disband his fleet. He had not, at the moment, the money for maintaining it; he knew that it was no match for the Persian navy, and he had no wish to subject any part of his strength, in ships or men, to the risk of disaster. Moreover, now that his army was master of the continent, he was well aware that a fleet was no longer of any use to him: by seizing the coastal towns he could reduce the Persian navy to impotence, for they would then have no port on the Asian coast which they could use, and no source of replacement for their crews.

Arrian, *Anabasis*, 1, 20

✳ ✳ ✳

B **D**arius now moved; he crossed the high ground by what are called the Amanian Gates — the pass across Mount Amanus — and, making for Issus, established himself without being perceived in Alexander's rear. Once in possession of Issus he mutilated and put to death every Macedonian he found left there unfit for service ... Alexander, not trusting the report that Darius was in his rear dispatched a party of his Companions in a galley ... to find out for themselves whether or not it was true.

Arrian, *Anabasis*, 2, 7

✳ ✳ ✳

C **F**rom there Alexander marched through Gedrosian territory. The route was a difficult one, and no supplies were to be had; worst of all, in many places there was not even water for the men. They were forced to cover great distances at night, going some way inland, in spite of the fact that Alexander was anxious to work along the coast in order to see what possible anchorages there were and, so far as he could in the brief time at his disposal, to assist the fleet by digging wells, and doing what could be done to provide markets and shelter for the ships.

Arrian, *Anabasis*, 6, 23

✳ ✳ ✳

✎ **After reading Arrian's accounts what is your opinion of Alexander's actions in each of these three circumstances? Were his decisions strategic mistakes?**

✎ **Arrian makes mention on several occasions of his use of 'official' documentation as sources of evidence for his work. If this were so, how might his accounts of these three incidents be unreliable?**

✎ **Can you suggest any ways in which we might be able to check on Arrian's accounts and their reliability?**

✎ **Compare extract C with the following account by Plutarch of Alexander's march through the Gedrosian desert:**

Here he endured terrible privations and lost great numbers of men, with the result that he did not bring back from India so much as a quarter of his fighting force ... Some of his men died from disease, some of the wretched food, some of the scorching heat, but most from sheer hunger, for they had to march through an uncultivated region whose inhabitants only eked out a wretched existence.

Plutarch, *Life of Alexander*, 66

✳ ✳ ✳

Can you explain why Plutarch has omitted any mention of Alexander's motives for marching his army through this region?

TACTICAL SKILL

In order to assess Alexander's tactical skill we must examine the four major engagements that were fought during the expedition.

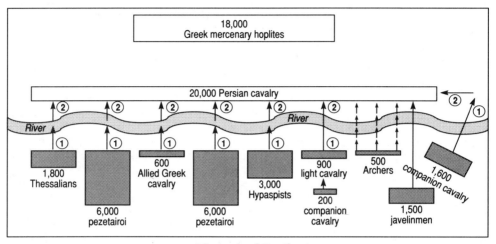

The battle of Granikos

GRANIKOS   334 BC

Alexander invaded Asia with approximately 43 000 infantry and 5000 cavalry and was met at the river Granikos by 20 000 Persian cavalry and nearly as many Greek mercenary infantry. It was early summer and the river would have been fairly narrow, running in the centre of a broader flood channel; this had steep banks, and beyond it, on the Persian side, the ground was at first flat, then rising to low hills.

The Persian cavalry deployed on the banks massed strongest on the left opposite Alexander himself. The infantry were well to the rear. Alexander had cavalry on both wings, supported on the right by archers and Agrianians, with the phalanx and hypaspists in the centre. His Greek and Thracian infantry were not engaged. The reason for this may well be the same as for the Persian attempt to hold a riverbank with cavalry, leaving the more appropriate infantry to the rear; namely that this was an encounter battle, with both sides racing for the river. The Persians sent their cavalry ahead of their infantry and reached the bank first, while Alexander in turn attacked before all his infantry arrived, a bold move motivated by the fact that Alexander saw the necessity of securing the riverbank before the more suited Persian infantry could reach and hold it. He sent a force of light cavalry and some Companions across first and whilst they diverted the Persians' attention he and the remaining Companions outflanked the

Persian cavalry and charged in gaining the upper hand. The Macedonian phalanx and hypaspists meanwhile, taking advantage of the chaos, crossed the river and engaged the cavalry in its centre, which promptly turned and fled. The mercenary infantry, unable to reach the battle, halted on a hill and asked for terms. Alexander refused and attacked them, killing all but 2000. The Persian cavalry lost 1000–2500, with the Macedonian losses said to be as low as 85 cavalry and 30 infantry. Quick thinking and resolute action obviously won the day and ensured the fall of Asia into Alexander's hands.

ISSUS   333 BC

Alexander's next major engagement came at Issus in Syria in 333. With between 25 000 and 42 000 foot and 5000 horse he discovered that Darius with some 250 000–600 000 men was behind his force. Alexander retraced his steps and forced a battle in a narrow plain between the mountains and the sea, where Darius' superior numbers would be restricted. The deployment is shown in the map, with Alexander commanding the Companions personally. Alexander extended his troops to stop an outflanking move and then gave orders for a rapid advance to minimise the effect of Persian archery.

He realised that he was outnumbered and that having to cross the Pinarus would disadvantage his phalangites so once again a bold move was needed. By charging through the Persian left wing with his Companions he headed for the Persian centre and the Greek mercenaries. This also gave him access to Darius who stood behind them. Darius, upon seeing Alexander, lost his nerve and ran, causing morale problems throughout the reserve troops behind him. Alexander and the Companions then swung into the Persian

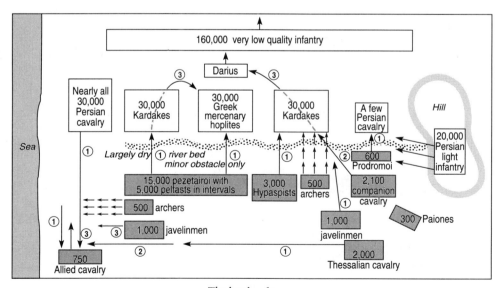

The battle of Issus

centre and cut the Greek mercenaries to pieces allowing the phalangites to cross the river bed and gain the upper hand. The Persians ran when they saw the mercenaries defeated and in the end lost some 100 000 men compared to 450 Macedonians killed and 4500 wounded. Again quick and resolute action won the day, despite there having been a numerically stronger force in opposition in a better position on the battlefield, i.e. holding the upper ground on a riverbank. The western half of the Persian empire was now controlled by Alexander.

GAUGAMELA   331 BC

Darius raised another army with allegedly 40 000–200 000 cavalry and 200 000–1 000 000 infantry, 200 scythed chariots (see diagram) and 15 elephants. He even cleared a plain to give a completely flat arena for the chariots.

He proposed to surround Alexander with his superior cavalry. To meet this threat Alexander once again showed his genius by taking elaborate precautions. His force of 7000 cavalry and 43 000 infantry advanced obliquely to the right, to edge out of the cleared ground. Darius at first followed suit, but then committed Bessus' cavalry to ride around the Macedonian right and stop them. Bessus did so but found the need to commit more and more of his troops, thus creating a problem in the Persian centre. The Macedonian left likewise caused problems for the Persians'

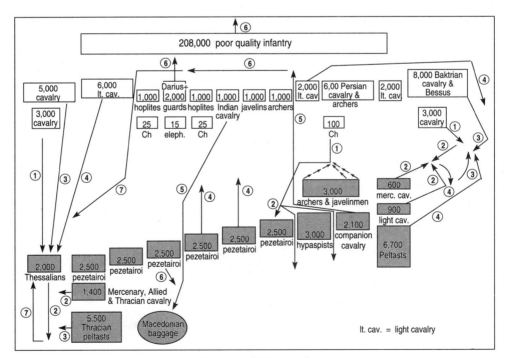

The battle of Gaugamela

cavalry on Darius' right. Darius then launched his chariots to break up the Macedonian line. Macedonian discipline and Alexander's careful planning countered this by providing lanes for the chariots to charge down and light troops to shoot them down.

Amidst this confusion, with the Persian centre weakened, Alexander charged the Companions through a gap and at Darius. The phalangites and hypaspists too engaged the line, holding it and stopping anyone from reaching the Companions. After the defeat of his cavalry bodyguard Darius believed all was lost and once again ran, taking with him half of his force.

During the engagement a Persian and Indian cavalry force had managed to attack the Macedonian baggage camp but was driven off. Alexander and the Companions proceeded to deal with the remaining Persian forces and had virtually taken control of the Persian Empire. Persian losses were reckoned at 40 000–300 000 killed and even more captured with only 100–500 Macedonian dead. Alexander and his army had defeated a vastly superior force due largely to his tactics.

HYDASPES   326 BC

The final major encounter was at the river Hydaspes against a much different force from that of the Persian one (see diagrams). This battle is perhaps the best example of Alexander's brilliance due to the circumstances under which it was fought.

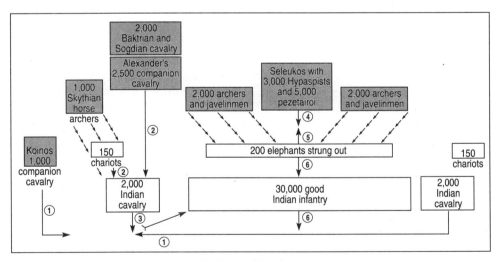

The battle of Hydaspes

Alexander, with approximately 7000 cavalry, 40 000 infantry and 5000 Indian allies, met Porus, the Parvataka king, with an army of 30 000–50 000 good infantry, 85–200 elephants and 400–1000 chariots. The river was swollen and Alexander realised he could not force a crossing in the face of the elephants; he proclaimed his intention to wait till the river went down and collected supplies for a long stay, all the time looking for opportunities for an unexpected crossing. He kept Porus alert by regular noisy night-time feints; at first these were met by calling out troops and elephants but eventually the Indians relaxed and did not respond. Alexander found a crossing place and split his force into three. Craterus stayed with the Indian allies and a force of Macedonians, with orders to attack across the river if it were left unguarded. Meleager with some phalangites and mercenaries went up river and was told to cross once the main Indian force was diverted. Alexander took the cavalry, the hypaspists and some other troops to cross at an island 17 miles downstream.

Alexander crossed at dawn but was spotted. Porus sent a force under the command of his son which arrived too late to stop Alexander who promptly defeated the force.

Porus then advanced with his best troops against Alexander. With his elephants in front of him and the cavalry and chariots on the wings he attacked (see diagram on the previous page). Alexander kept his infantry back and by massing his cavalry on his right with Coenus, attacked their flank. Porus sent his remaining cavalry to support his left wing who soon found themselves surrounded.

The Indian cavalry now fell back on the elephants and infantry to regroup but only caused chaos as the Macedonian infantry attacked. Eventually successive Macedonian charges compressed the Indian army into a confused mass. The elephants, harassed by light troops with axes and with many of their drivers dead, turned on their own men, trampling many. The exhausted elephants finally retreated, leaving the rest of the Indian force surrounded.

Indian losses were said to be 12 000–23 000 killed, all chariots destroyed, and all the elephants killed or taken. Macedonian losses were 230–280 cavalry and between 80 and 700 infantry. Alexander once again, with a force of some 18 500 troops, had defeated a much larger force, some 34 000 with 200 elephants and 300 chariots, by his tactical brilliance and the discipline of his forces.

STOP AND THINK: LIBRARY RESEARCH: CHECK THE SOURCE

These were not the only times that Alexander showed his tactical brilliance. Go to your library and find a copy of Arrian's *Anabasis* (The Penguin Classic's translation is titled Arrian: *the Campaigns of Alexander*). Look up these references and summarise the events referred to.

Book 1 : 1–2	**Alexander vs the Triballians**
Book 1 : 27–28	**Alexander vs the Telmissianas**
Book 2 : 17–26	**Alexander vs Tyre**
Book 3 : 17–18	**Alexander vs the Uxians**
Book 4 : 18–19	**Alexander vs Rock of Sogdiana**
Book 4 : 24–25	**Alexander vs the Indians**

Soldiers from Porus: 1. a heavy chariot; 2. basic troop type; 3. Indian cavalry; 4. archer

LEADERSHIP

As well as logistics, morale was another problem to be faced. Alexander's ability to lead his men through the hardships of an eleven-year campaign can be attributed to his personal magnetism. Apart from two incidents, in India (325) and at Opis (324), where his troops refused to do as he ordered, they followed him everywhere.

Incidents such as the murder of Cleitus (327), the execution of Parmenio (330) and the Conspiracy of the Pages (327) were indications of discontent amongst the officer class with Alexander's decisions rather than threats to loyalty to his leadership.

STOP AND THINK: DOCUMENT STUDY

The ancient sources are full of references to incidents where Alexander inspired his men and displayed his leadership qualities. Read the following extracts and answer the questions below.

A Just before he fought the battle at Granikos he urged the Macedonians to eat without stint, and to bring out all they had, since on the morrow they should dine from the enemy's stores.

Plutarch, *Sayings of Kings and Commanders*, 5

＊ ＊ ＊

B Parmenio entered Alexander's tent, stood by his couch and called him several times; when Alexander woke, Parmenio asked how he could possibly sleep as if he were already victorious, instead of being out to fight the greatest battle of his life. Alexander smiled and said, 'Why not? Do you not see that we have already won the battle, now that we are delivered from roving around these endless devastated plains, and chasing Darius, who will never stand and fight?' And indeed, not only beforehand, but at the very height of the battle Alexander displayed the supremacy and steadfastness of a man who is confident of the soundness of his judgement.

Plutarch, *Life of Alexander*, 32

＊ ＊ ＊

C He had tables set up in the army quarters with money on them, and instructed the clerks in charge to pay off the debts of every man who produced an I.O.U. . . . This gift to his men is said to have been worth 20,000 talents.

Arrian, *Anabasis*, 7, 5

＊ ＊ ＊

D He also made a number of other money awards for distinguished conduct in the field, or in recognition of a man's reputation for good service generally.

Arrian, *Anabasis*, 7, 5

＊ ＊ ＊

✎ **Read each of the extracts. List the methods mentioned by each source that Alexander used to gain the respect of his troops.**

✎ **Where might the information in extract B have come from regarding this conversation? Would it have been common knowledge to his troops? Knowing that Parmenio was murdered (in 330), how reliable do you think this extract is?**

Arrian sums up the nature of Alexander's leadership when he states:

Noble indeed was his power of inspiring his men, of filling them with confidence, and, in the moment of danger, of sweeping away their fear by the spectacle of his own fearlessness. When risks had to be taken, he took them with the utmost boldness... No cheat or liar caught him off guard, and both his word and his bond were inviolable. Spending but little on his own pleasures, he poured out his money without stint for the benefit of his friends.

Anabasis, 7, 29

REASONS FOR ALEXANDER'S SUCCESS

HIS MILITARY GENIUS AND CHARACTER

Alexander's genius as a military leader has already been discussed in detail and so further discussion is not really necessary here. It is sufficient to say that his flexibility of thought enabled him to overcome whatever obstacle came his way militarily, whether it was a pitched battle or a siege operation. He was adaptable and intelligent and no doubt could draw upon

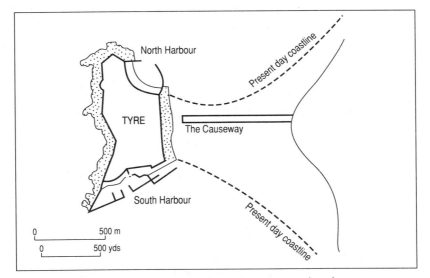

The siege of Tyre was an example of Alexander's ability to overcome obstacles.

The sea ports all gave in without a fight except for Tyre. Tyre was built on an island 800 metres off the coast so the Tyrians were not frightened of the Macedonian army. Alexander set his men to build a causeway to the island but when it was half built the Tyrians crashed a fireship into it and it went up in smoke. The Macedonians started all over again. This time they had warships to protect them for the Cypriot and Phoenician captains in the Persian fleet were beginning to desert to the Greek side. Eventually catapults were battering at the city wall from three sides - from the completed causeway, from a Cypriot fleet to the north and a Sidonian fleet to the south. Seven months after the siege began the south wall crumbled and Alexander and the Longshields fought their way in. The causeway is the only one of Alexander's works to survive today. Silt has collected on either side of it and Tyre now lies at the end of a peninsula, the spine of which is Alexander's siegework.

the years of experience of some of his subordinate officers such as Parmenio. He also owed much of his skill to the training and experience gained from his father Philip.

HIS ARMY

Alexander also inherited from Philip a highly experienced and efficient army (see Chapter Nine for a full description). This army, which under Philip had dominated the Balkans, was now, in the hands of Alexander, to conquer the armies of the East with its superior weaponry, flexibility and discipline. Alexander's army differed slightly from that of Philip in its composition. It contained far more allied troops as could be expected on a joint league mission. Nonetheless it maintained its essentially Macedonian nature and was, in fact, to set the pattern of armed forces in the eastern Mediterranean until the advent of the Roman legion of Marius at the end of the second century BC.

THE PERSIANS

If we look at the illustrations on pages 247–248 we can see some of the different troop types used within the Persian army. The Persians relied heavily upon cavalry, usually armed with a bow and or some sort of short spear or javelin designed to be used as a throwing weapon or to thrust at an opponent from a close range. These would have been no more than 1.8 metres long.

The infantry, like the cavalry, also relied upon the bow or sling as a major weapon. They also carried spears of about 1.8 metres long. The Royal Guard carried shields, similar to the Greek hoplon, for protection and wore leather cuirasses similar to those worn by the Macedonians. The regular Persian troop type was the kardakes, who carried a wicker shield and wore lighter armour.

As well as the Persian troops the Persians quite often relied heavily on subject troops of questionable reliability and upon mercenaries, many of whom were Greeks and fought as hoplites.

THE MACEDONIANS

The Macedonians, on the other hand, relied heavily on two major troop types, the Companion cavalry (*heteroi*) and the phalangites (*pezetairoi*), both of which used the sarissa or pike as their main weapons.

Thus when a pike phalanx engaged a spear phalanx, the spearman was at a great disadvantage; he could not reach his opponent at all until he had himself passed through some three or four pike points, and even then he could not put as much strength into this thrust as his opponent was able to do. The Companions, likewise, outreached their opponents.

As well as a superior weapon the Macedonians also possessed superior discipline and organisation. The cavalry, unlike conventional cavalry, were able to fight in wedge in close proximity to the phalanx. The hypaspists, the

Darius' Persian infantry: 1. Kardakes; 2. Persian archer; 3. an 'apple bearer' or Royal foot guard; 4. Scythian infantryman; 5. Persian officer; 6. peltast; 7. hoplite

Darius' Persian cavalry: 1. Persian cavalry types; 2. Bactrian cavalryman; 3. Arachosian; 4. A Scythian horse archer

elite infantry, were also specialists who could be used in difficult situations such as at Aornos.

Alexander's army also made use of various other nationalities and troop types such as the Thracian or Greek peltasts or Paeonian light cavalry. Usually, however, he relied on quality rather than quantity — another sign of a good leader.

STOP AND THINK: EXERCISE
In your own words compile a series of points to explain why the Macedonian army was able to dominate the Persian forces.

STOP AND THINK: DOCUMENT STUDY
Diodorus Siculus gives us an army list for the Persian expedition. Read this extract and answer the questions that follow.

[**A**fter visiting Troy] Alexander made an accurate count of the forces he commanded. He found their numbers to be as follows. Of infantry, there were 12,000 Macedonians, 7,000 allies, 5,000 mercenaries, all under Parmenio's command. 7,000 Odrysians, Triballians, and Illyrians accompanied him, together with 1,000 Agrianians and archers, so that the total of infantry was 32,000. Of cavalry, there were 1,800 Macedonians commanded by Philotas, son of Parmenio, 1,800 Thessalians, commanded by Callas, son of Harpalus, 600 from the Greek allies led by Erigyius, and 900 Thracians, Scouts and Paeonians under Cassander, making a total of 4,500 cavalry [actually 5,100].

This was the number of men who crossed to Asia with Alexander. The soldiers left behind in Europe, under the command of Antipater, totalled 12,000 infantry, and 1,500 cavalry.

Diodorus, 17, 17

❊　❊　❊

✎ **List the various army numbers according to Diodorus.**

✎ **Using the information presented above, and that in Chapter Nine on Philip, work out what weaponry each of these various nationalities used.**

✎ **What nationality, do you think, would the troops left with Antipater have been? Why?**

✎ **Where might Diodorus have obtained this information?**

✎ **What problems might exist with this information (apart from the maths!)? Can we trust it?**

THE MILITARY INEPTITUDE OF DARIUS
Despite the vast resources available to him, both in number of men and monetary terms, Darius' constant poor judgement (or advice) put him at a disadvantage. Darius was certainly no match militarily for the boldness and genius of his opponent as can be discovered by a close look at several extracts from Arrian's *Anabasis*.

STOP AND THINK: DOCUMENT STUDY
Read the following extracts and answer the questions below.

A [At Issus] First one, then another of them [his advisors] blew up the bladder of his conceit by saying that the Persian cavalry would ride over the Macedonian army and trample it to pieces... [this] led Darius to take up a position where he could get little advantage either from his cavalry or his superiority in numbers of men and weight of missiles — a position where he had no chance of dazzling the enemy [the Macedonians] with the splendour of his great host, but was doomed to make a present of easy victory to Alexander and the Macedonians.

Arrian, *Anabasis*, 3, 6–7

B [At Gaugamela] ... Darius, who had been on edge since the battle began and now saw nothing but terrors around him, was the first to turn tail and ride for safety.

Arrian, *Anabasis*, 3, 14

C Such was the end of Darius... In military matters he was the feeblest and most incompetent of men... The loss of Phoenicia and Egypt was followed by the *débâcle* at Arbela, his own shameful flight from the field, and the destruction of the mightiest army of the whole East...

Arrian, *Anabasis*, 3, 22

- **What picture do we get of Darius' character from these extracts?**
- **Can Darius be seen as the person solely responsible for the loss of the Persian army?**
- **In extract C, what is probably meant by the word 'mightiest'?**
- **How might the information contained in extract A have been obtained by Arrian?**
- **How reliable are these accounts as sources of evidence on Darius?**

ALEXANDER'S ADMINISTRATION OF HIS EMPIRE

The problem of administering an empire as large and as politically, racially, economically and geographically diverse as that conquered by Alexander is a difficult one. The solutions found by him, at least in the short term, show Alexander at his best — empirical, adaptable and diplomatic.

As historians we are faced with several problems in examining the results of these actions. Many have seen in them signs of poor administrative ability. These historians point to Harpalus' misappropriation of funds in 324 and to the number of satraps who had to be replaced for misconduct and corruption upon Alexander's return from India.

Whatever your opinion, in examining this section two things must be kept in mind:

- Alexander planned the administrative organisation of the empire whilst on campaign, varying his organisation depending upon the area, its people and his needs.
- He died young and had little real time, free from campaigning, to reform it, if in fact he ever intended to.

What then were his plans? How did he administer his empire? Arrian is possibly our best source on these questions and his text gives evidence of the adaptability of Alexander's approach to administration.

MACEDONIA AND GREECE

In the Balkans Alexander was the king of Macedonia and strategos of the League of Corinth's forces. He was also unofficially hegemon. His power and control was maintained by Antipater who acted as regent in Alexander's absence with rather ill-defined powers over the Macedonians, their possessions in Thessaly and Thrace, and over the 'free' Greek allies who were members of the League of Corinth. With a strong Macedonian army and the loyalty of several of the smaller Greek states, he was able to control the area until after Alexander's death. His only real problem came with the revolt led by King Agis of Sparta in 331, which was quickly quelled. Members of the League contributed money, men, supplies and ships to the expedition but largely, if one ignores the reality of the Macedonian military dominance as a threat, maintained control of their own affairs. As such they had to be asked or consulted on key issues within Greece.

ASIA MINOR

With the original intention of the 'liberation' of the Greeks in Asia Minor Alexander was forced to treat these peoples differently from the 'barbarians'. The Greek city-states of the Asian coastline usually had democracies established in them by Alexander. This occurred for political reasons, because democracies tended to be anti-Persian. (The Persians had preferred the use of small oligarchies.) The cities paid no tribute to Alexander, largely ran their own affairs and were not strictly under any governor's control, although they did have to subordinate themselves to Alexander and accept a Macedonian garrison. Most also paid a levy for the expedition, the *syntaxis*. Important matters, such as foreign affairs, had to be discussed with Alexander.

Just how far this freedom extended in reality can be best illustrated by the experience of Aspendus. (Arrian, *Anabasis*, 26–27) This city had submitted freely but Alexander, short of money and supplies, ordered the people to pay 50 talents in cash and to supply horses to the army just as they had done for Darius. They eventually refused. Alexander besieged the town, captured it and not only doubled the *syntaxis* but subjected the city to paying an annual tribute to Macedonia and to the satrap. Hostages were taken and some disputed land was possibly given to neighbouring cities. Whether or not these Greek cities gained membership of the League of Corinth is uncertain.

Finance officers, such as Coeranus of Beroea (Phoenicia) and Philoxenus (Asia, this side of the Taurus), were appointed but how long they maintained their positions is again uncertain. (Arrian, *Anabasis*, 3, 6) Their jurisdictions extended over several satrapies and they were responsible for the collection and transfer of funds raised to the royal treasury in Babylon. These appointments were a departure from previous arrangements as the satraps normally fulfilled this function under the Persians. The reason for this change may lie in the fact that Phoenicia had previously no satrap and the newly 'liberated' Greek states now had the same degree of independence. With Alexander about to travel east, it was necessary to co-ordinate the collection of the funds paid by these cities and their dispatch to the royal treasury controlled by Harpalus.

After the capture of Ecbatana (330) and the end of the joint League action, contributions of the Greeks in Asia Minor may have been remitted as Philoxenus is now seen performing other tasks. Alexander had now also captured all of the Persian treasuries — Babylon, Susa and Persepolis — and so possibly no longer needed these contributions.

THE BARBARIANS

Alexander's treatment of the 'barbarians' he conquered varied from people to people. After the capture of Sardis (334) he virtually followed a policy of appeasement in his relations with local people by posing as a liberator from the sometimes intolerant rule of the Persians.

He achieved this in a number of ways:

- by using established forms of government where possible, as well as local and respected leaders.
- by showing respect for the religious and political institutions of the various peoples. A good example of this is his visit to the Oracle of Ammon at Siwah (331) whilst in Egypt. His recognition there as the son of the god would have ensured his acceptance as the new pharaoh.
- by granting religious freedom and encouraging racial tolerance. His adoption of Persian dress (331) and court customs, the rebuilding of the temple of Bel Marduk in Babylon, his marriage to Roxane (328) and the marriage ceremony at Susa (324) are good examples of this.
- by including other nationals within the governing class, either as satraps or as members of the army. (Arrian, *Anabasis*, 7, 6)
- by planting over seventy strategically placed colonies throughout the empire.
- by the introduction of a uniform currency to foster trade within the empire.

These actions tended to make him popular and so helped him maintain control of his empire.

LYDIA

Alexander 'freed' the Lydians and allowed them to use their traditional laws. A Macedonian, Assander, was made satrap and was given a Macedonian force to garrison the area. A Greek, Nicias, was left as a financial official.

CARIA

Again Alexander was welcomed as a liberator (according to the sources). The rightful queen, Ada, was restored to the throne and a Macedonian garrison was left. With characteristic political tact, Alexander adapted the existing Persian organisation and anti-Persian sentiments to attach the area to him. After Ada's death Alexander inherited the kingdom — she had officially adopted him — and sent out a governor to take her place. (Arrian, *Anabasis*, 1, 24)

STOP AND THINK

> Why might our sources be suspect on the subject of Alexander's 'liberation' of these states? (*Clue*: Where did Arrian and Plutarch get their information from?)

In other areas of the west Alexander substituted his own satraps, who were usually Macedonian. Judaea was given some freedom with the high priests there allowed to govern according to their laws.

EGYPT

The administration of Egypt was to be special. The Egyptians had once rebelled and thrown out the Persians, maintaining their independence for some time. They had a strong hatred of the Persians and surrendered to Alexander without a fight. The consequent enthusiasm with which he conformed to Egyptian traditions — unlike the Persians — by acts such as his visit to Siwah to be recognised as the Son of Ammon and legitimate claimant to the position of pharaoh may be explained by this. His political tact and opportunism once again showed through. Arrian (*Anabasis*, 3, 5–6) gives us an account of his settlement of Egypt. Two natives, Doloaspis and Petisis, were appointed as 'nomarchs' to control the civil administration of Upper and Lower Egypt. Native customs and laws were to be maintained. Alexander's portrait even appears in the Temples of Luxor as pharaoh in traditional style. His obvious aim was to placate the native people and to win their affection.

The military control of the area was separated. Two Macedonians, Peucestas and Balacrus, were given command of the army in Egypt. Under these two, others controlled the garrisons at Memphis and Pelusium whilst a third commanded any mercenary forces. A separate officer controlled the Nile fleet.

The areas east and west of Egypt were placed under separate control again. Libya was under the command of an Apollonius, whilst an Egyptian

Greek, Cleomenes of Naucratis, controlled Arabia by Heröpolis. Cleomenes was also in charge of the collection of the tribute from Egypt. Native tax collectors were used.

Thus Egypt was securely held, without the nucleus for rebellion that had existed under Persian rule. The task of the immediate tax collection also fell to Egyptians not to the Macedonians, Egypt's new rulers.

BABYLON

Like Egypt, Babylon had resented Persian rule. Local religion, the worship of Bel Marduk, had been suppressed and the temple destroyed. This may have enticed the Persian satrap, Mazaeus, to surrender the city without a fight. Alexander, again showing his diplomacy, honoured the local priesthoods and ordered the rebuilding of the temple. (Arrian, *Anabasis*, 3, 16) This ensured his popularity. Mazaeus was reappointed satrap and allowed to continue minting coinage. (Mazaeus also apparently had two sons with Babylonian names. He may well have had a local wife and been well respected by the local people.) Mazaeus was the first Persian appointed to a satrap's position under Alexander. A tax official was appointed, as was a commander of the Macedonian garrison, Apollodorus, a Greek.

This arrangement — a Persian or local satrap combined with a Macedonian or Greek military commander and a financial official — was to become a common feature of Alexander's administrative organisation. On a few occasions, however, no mention is made of an independent military commander, e.g. Oxydates and Artabazus.

STOP AND THINK

✎ **Who were these two satraps? Why were their positions special? Most satraps would still have probably commanded provincial levies and may even have been able to hire mercenaries when necessary.**

INDIA

India proved itself, as with Egypt, a special case. The Persians had not really controlled the area for some generations and so Alexander was forced again to adapt local systems of government. Native princes, if friendly, were left in control of their lands with the lands of hostile neighbours added to their own. Satraps were appointed with the princes subordinate to him. An example of this is Taxiles who ruled the land between the Indus and Hydaspes rivers. A satrap named Philip, who later proved a problem, was appointed.

Alexander saw the Hydaspes river as the eastern most extent of his empire for the moment and so instigated a new form of administrative control over the region past it. He had defeated Porus, its king, but saw in him a good leader. Porus was proclaimed king of all the land conquered in India so far and became both satrap and king. No Macedonian troops were left there and in fact the area became a 'buffer' zone that was subject to Alexander, yet friendly.

THE CITIES

One means of controlling and administering the vast empire was by the planting of cities that were in effect Greek and Macedonian colonies. Alexander reportedly built seventy of these, of which only a few have been accurately identified today. Cities such as Alexandria in Egypt, Alexandria Areion (Herat) and Alexandria of the Caucasus (Kabul) are but a few.

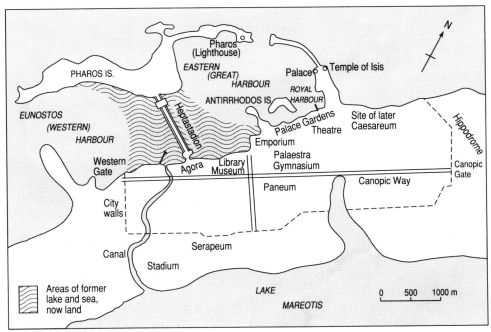

Alexandria in Ptolemaic times
What architectural and other features made Alexandria a distinctive city in antiquity?
What does this tell us about Alexander's ability to organise his empire?

The site of Alexandria was most conveniently set near to the harbour of Pharos, and by judicious town-planning he [Alexander] made the city breathe with the etesian winds [north-west summer breezes]. As these blow across the open sea they cool the city's atmosphere and furnish the inhabitants with a moderate and healthy climate. The circuit wall that he set up was of vast size and marvellously strong. Situated between a great lake and the sea it has only two approaches from the landward side, and they are narrow and eminently defensible. In shape rather like a cloak, it has an avenue that almost cuts the city in half, and is remarkable for its size and beauty. It runs a distance of forty stades from gate to gate, and is a plethron wide, the whole decorated with varied facades of houses and sacred buildings. Alexander ordered a palace to be built, outstanding for its size and massiveness, and not only he, but successive rulers of Egypt up to my time have almost all improved the palace with elaborate additions.

Diodorus, 17.52.2–4

STOP AND THINK: LIBRARY RESEARCH
See if you can find a list of any of the other cities known to have been founded by Alexander.

All these cities were formed by mixing elements of Macedonian veterans, Greek mercenaries and local people. Some historians have seen in this an attempt to hellenise the empire by fusing the races. They certainly later brought Greek culture to these areas but whether this was the intended outcome is open to debate. More to the point would be the fact that each city was sited primarily for strategic reasons. Most were east of the Tigris river, in areas that lacked existing administrative centres and that would encourage trade, communication and the control of that key area. Places to leave behind sick and injured troops and to ensure supply routes for the army were also needed. These cities were subject to the satraps and were instrumental in holding the empire together by fulfilling their various functions.

COINAGE
Alexander introduced a uniform silver currency based on the Attic standard. This was designed to encourage trade throughout the empire. Older currencies still circulated and areas such as Babylon and Phoenicia were allowed to maintain their trading links and monetary systems.

PROBLEMS IN ADMINISTERING THE EMPIRE
RELIABLE OFFICIALS
The use of Persians as satraps did not work well in most instances. The eastern satraps proved rebellious and incompetent. In 330 Satibarzanes revolted in Artacoana (Arrian, *Anabasis*, 3, 25) resulting in his replacement. In 329 Arsaces, the satrap of Aria, was replaced by Stasanor, a Greek. Proexes, who had been appointed satrap of Parapamisadae in northwestern India, was dismissed for incompetence (Arrian, *Anabasis*, 4, 22) and was replaced by Tyriaspes, who in turn was replaced by Oxyartes, a Bactrian and father of Roxane, for provincial management.

Alexander had originally used Persians as civil administrators as they had the best local knowledge. This practice also assured the conquered that they were part of the new regime, thus decreasing their potential for conspiracy and rebellion.

Men of the calibre of Mazaeus, the satrap of Babylon, and Artabazus, the satrap of Bactria, were hard to find. By 324 key eastern satrapies such as Bactria, Sogdiana, Aria and Arachotia were all in the hands of Macedonians or Greeks.

The problem was not strictly a Persian one. High-ranking Macedonians like Cleander and Sitalces were also tried and executed on charges of misgovernment and plunder. (Arrian, *Anabasis* 6, 27) Harpalus, a long-time companion of Alexander, was even found guilty of expropriation of funds from the royal treasury at Babylon.

THE MACEDONIANS AND GREEKS

At first Alexander maintained the loyalty of his troops and the Macedonian nobles. During the campaign this changed. The troops mutinied at the Hydaspes river in India in 325 and again at Opis in 324. Alexander, with little danger to himself, rallied the army. The reason for their disagreement with his plans was not disloyalty but rather the fact that they were tired and a long way from home; some had not seen Macedonia in nearly ten years.

STOP AND THINK: LIBRARY RESEARCH

Read Plutarch's *Life of Alexander* and Arrian's *Anabasis* and then answer the questions below.

➢ **Using both sources, describe the events of 325 at the river Hydaspes in India.**

➢ **Using both sources again describe the events of 324 at Opis.**

➢ **What reasons are given as the causes of each of these events?**

➢ **How did Alexander deal with them?**

Alexander's problems with the Macedonian nobility were more severe. Various incidents had affected his relationship with this group. Alexander had, after 330, started to adopt Persian dress and customs (Plutarch, *Life of Alexander*, 45) in an attempt to appease the Persians whose empire had been captured. He saw the value of his acceptance as the Great King by its people and tried to encourage it. This move was seen by some Macedonians and Greeks as a sign of Alexander's growing arrogance and orientalisation. These same people were insulted to think that they, as conquerors, were now being asked to adopt barbarian customs.

Around the same time Alexander started to introduce Persian youths (30 000 of them) into the army, training them in the use of the Macedonian arms and tactics. Attempts were also made to encourage other leading Macedonians and Greeks to adopt the changes. Hephaestion joined Alexander whilst others like Craterus grew more unhappy.

In 327 matters came to a head with the murder of Cleitus by Alexander in Sogdiana. Cleitus had saved Alexander's life at Granikos but had grown unhappy with the changes being made. According to the sources, both Cleitus and Alexander were drunk, they argued and eventually, after Cleitus gave vent to Macedonian resentment to the changes, he was killed. Alexander apparently was distraught and took to his tent for three days without food to repent his actions.

STOP AND THINK: CHECK THE SOURCE

Read Arrian's *Anabasis*, 4, 8–9 and Plutarch's *Life of Alexander*, 50–52 on this event. Answer the following questions.

➢ **Describe the event as told by other historians.**

➢ **According to these sources what effects did this event have on Alexander?**

Possibly the most misunderstood custom that Alexander tried to introduce to his court was that of *proskynesis* or prostration. To the Persians this was a gesture of respect performed by all to the Great King, whom they did not regard as a god and hence it was not a sign of worship. Unfortunately both Greeks and Macedonians saw it this way and many resented it bitterly. Alexander's motives for the attempted introduction of this custom are not clear. Perhaps it was to show that Persians and Macedonians held equal positions within his government. Perhaps it was, as some sources suggest, to appease his vanity and arrogance by encouraging the idea of his divinity. Whatever the reason it failed and one of its chief critics was Callisthenes, the official historian of the expedition and up till that time advocate of Alexander's success.

STOP AND THINK: CHECK THE SOURCE
Read Arrian's *Anabasis*, 4, 9 and Plutarch's *Life of Alexander*, 54–55 and answer these questions.

✎ **According to Arrian why did Alexander want to introduce this custom?**

✎ **According to Plutarch why did Alexander want to introduce this custom?**

✎ **What problems might exist with these sources on this question?**

✎ **Why, do you think, did Alexander want to introduce this custom?**

Macedonian resentment came to a head in 327 with the discovery of what is known as the Conspiracy of the Pages. A group of adolescent Macedonia-ians, led by one Hermolaus, plotted to kill Alexander. The plot failed and Alexander informed. Callisthenes, who was implicated in the plot on very thin evidence, was arrested and either executed or died in custody. This event was significant in that it showed the lengths to which the Macedonia-ians were prepared to go and how their loyalty to Alexander was slipping seriously. It also led to greater Greek resentment at home.

ALEXANDER 'THE GREAT'?

Any attempt to assess the strengths and weaknesses of an historical personality is by nature subjective. The criteria used depend upon the person undertaking the task. Perhaps the best assessment of Alexander's right to claim the title 'the Great' was undertaken by Arrian at the end of his work.

STOP AND THINK: DOCUMENT STUDY
Read these extracts from Arrian, *Anabasis*, 7, 28–30.

A He had great personal beauty, invincible power of endurance, and a keen intellect; he was brave and adventurous, strict in the observance of his religious duties, and hungry for fame.

❉ ❉ ❉

B In arming and equipping troops and in his military dispositions he was always masterly. Noble indeed was his power of inspiring his men, of filling them with confidence, and, in the moment of danger, of sweeping away their fear by the spectacle of his own fearlessness. When risks had to be taken, he took them with the utmost boldness, and his ability to seize the moment for a swift blow, before his enemy had any suspicion of what was coming, was beyond praise.

❉ ❉ ❉

C Doubtless, in the passion of the moment Alexander sometimes erred; it is true he took some steps towards the pomp and arrogance of the Asiatic kings: but I, at least, cannot feel that such errors were very heinous, if the circumstances are taken fairly into consideration. For, after all, he was young; the chain of his successes was unbroken, and, like all kings, past, present, and to come, he was surrounded by courtiers who spoke to please, regardless of what evil their words might do. On the other hand, I do indeed know that Alexander, of all the monarchs of old, was the only one who had the nobility of heart to be sorry for his mistakes.

❉ ❉ ❉

D Surely, too, his adoption of Persian dress was, like his claim to divine birth, a matter of policy: by it he hoped to bring the Eastern nations to feel that they had a king who was not wholly a foreigner, and to indicate to his own countrymen his desire to move away from the harsh traditional arrogance of Macedonia. That was also, no doubt, the reason why he included a proportion of Persian troops (the so-called 'Golden Apples', for instance) in Macedonian units, and made Persian noblemen officers in his crack native regiments.

❉ ❉ ❉

E 'It is my belief that there was in those days no nation, no city, no single individual beyond the reach of Alexander's name; never in all the world was there another like him . . .

❉ ❉ ❉

F . . . and there is the further evidence of the extraordinary way in which he is held, as no mere man could be, in honour and remembrance. Even today, when so many years have passed, there have been oracles, all tending to his glory, delivered to the people of Macedonia.

❉ ❉ ❉

G In the course of this book I have, admittedly, found fault with some of the things which Alexander did, but of the man himself I am not ashamed to express ungrudging admiration. Where I have criticized unfavourably, I have done so because I wished to tell the truth as I saw it, and to enable my readers to profit thereby.

✎ **Using the sources A–G and any evidence presented throughout this chapter, assess Alexander's worthiness to the title 'the Great'. Consider the following questions:**

- What factors make someone great?
- What aspects of Alexander's personality made him great?
- What were his achievements?
- What were his setbacks and mistakes?
- How much of his 'greatness' has been the result of the opinions of our ancient sources, or the Alexander romance that arose during the Middle Ages?

Now choose one of the following ways to present your findings:

- an essay
- a class debate
- a class forum
- a presentation of 'Alexander: This is your Life!'
- a eulogy
- a radio show script interviewing various historical personalities and Alexander on the question.

LIST OF REFERENCES

ANCIENT SOURCES

Arrian, *The Campaigns of Alexander [Anabasis]*, Penguin Classics, 1971

Diodorus Siculus, *Universal History*, Loeb Classical Library, Heinemann, London, 1933–67

Plutarch, *The Age of Alexander: nine Greek lives*, tr. Ian Scott-Kilvert, Penguin Classics, 1973

——, *Moralia: Sayings of Kings and Commanders*, Vol. III, Loeb Classical Library, Heinemann, London, 1968

SECONDARY SOURCES

Adcock, F.E., *The Greek and Macedonian Art of War*, University of California Press, 1957

Cawkwell, G.L., *Philip of Macedonia*, Faber, London, 1978

Ellis, J.R. & Milns, R.D., *The Spectre of Philip: Demosthenes' first 'Philippic', 'Olynthiacs' and 'Speech on the Peace' : a study in historical evidence*, Sydney University Press, 1970

Engels, D.W., *Alexander the Great and the Logistics of the Macedonian Army*, University of California Press, 1978

Green, P., *Alexander of Macedonia*, Penguin, 1974

Hamilton, J.R., *Alexander the Great*, Hutchinson University Library, London, 1973

Hammond, N.G.L., *A History of Greece to 322 BC*, Clarendon Press, Oxford, 1967

Hogarth, D.G., *Philip and Alexander of Macedonia*, Murray, London, 1897

Laistener, M.W.L., *A History of the Greek World, 479–323 BC*, 3rd ed, Methuen, London, 1962

Lanefox, R., *Alexander the Great*, London, 1973

Milns, Robert David, *Alexander the Great*, Hale, London, 1968

Sekunda, N., *The Army of Alexander the Great*, Osprey, London, 1984

Tarn, W.W., *Alexander the Great*, Cambridge University Press, 1948 repr. 1979

Wilcken, U., *Alexander the Great*, Chatto & Windus, London, 1932

Welles, C.B., 'Alexander's Historical Achievement', *Greece and Rome*, 12 February 1965

ACKNOWLEDGMENTS

The author and publisher would like to acknowledge the following for their permission to reprint copyright material: A.M. Hakkert Ltd, Toronto, for Xenophon's 'Constitution of the Spartans', in Naphtali Lewis' *Greek Historical Documents*; American Journal of Archaeology, for 'The Cave at Vari', by C.H. Weller et al; Harcourt Brace Jovanovich, for Aristophanes' *The Complete Plays of Aristophanes*, ed. Moses Hadas; Basil Blackwell, Oxford, for A.H.M. Jones' *Sparta*; Cambridge, Mass., for A.E. Raubitchek's *Dedication from the Athenian Acropolis*; David Campbell Publishers, London, for Aristotle's *The Politics and Athenian Constitution*, ed. and trans. John Warrington from the Everyman's Library; J.M. Dent for J.T. Hooker's *The Ancient Spartans*; Faber, for G. Cawkwell's *Philip of Macedon*; Loeb Classical Library, and Harvard University Press, for Diodorus Siculus' *Universal History*, and Plutarch's *Moralia (sayings of Kings and Commanders)*, vol. III; Methuen, London, for M.L.W. Laistner's *A History of the Greek World 479–323*; Penguin, for C.M. Bowra's *The Odes of Pindar*, and Demosthenes and Aeschenes' *Political Speeches*, trans. A.N.W. Saunders, and Herodotus' *The Histories*, trans. Aubrey de Selincourt, and Thucydides' *The Peloponnesian War*, trans. Rex Warner, and Xenophon's *A History of My Times (Hellenica)*, trans. Rex Warner; Penguin Classics, Harmondsworth, for Arrian's *The Campaigns of Alexander*, and Plutarch's *The Rise and Fall of Athens: nine Greek lives* and *Themistocles*, trans. Ian Scott-Kilvert; and Prentice-Hall, Englewood Cliffs, for Aeschylus' *The Persians*, trans. A.J. Podlecki.

For permission to reproduce photographs and illustrations the following are thanked: Ashmolean Museum, Oxford, p. 208 (helmet); DAI (Deutsches Archaologisches Institut-Athen) Athens, p. 76 (terracotta mask, bone relief and mourning youth); Ian Heath from Duncan Head's book *Armies of the Macedonian and Punic wars 359 BC to 146 BC*, Wargames Research Group Publication, pp. 206–10, 243, 247, 248; Dianne Hennessy pp. 12, 13, 14 (Prince with the lilies), 15, 26, 121; The Mansell Collection pp. 7, 9, 10, 14 (Ladies in blue), 20, 21, 76 (peasant boy riding horse), 77, 81 (Greek hoplite), 107, 122, 123, 231; Salamander Books for permission to redraw the Macedonian phalanx from *Warfare in the Classical World*, p. 204.

Every effort has been made to trace and contact copyright holders. Where the attempt has been unsuccessful the publisher would be pleased to hear from the author or publisher concerned.

GLOSSARY

AMPHORA Tall pottery jar

ARCHON Nine in number, (eponymous, basileus, polemarch and six thesmothetai) they were the most powerful officials in the Athenian state until 487/6 BC when they ceased to be elected directly by the people and became chosen by lot from an initially elected group.

AREOPAGUS Name given to an ancient Athenian council after the hill upon which they met. Made up of ex-archons it had wide-ranging powers including a supervisory role of the laws and the magistrates. It came under attack, specifically in 462-1 BC, by Ephialtes who shared its powers between other institutions.

BOULE Council of 500 created by Cleisthenes to work in groups of 50 for one-tenth of the year. It largely managed the day to day running of the Athenian state.

CHOREGOS One of the terms used to describe an Athenian citizen undertaking the public burden (liturgy) of putting together a chorus, required at dramatic arts competitions held at festivals. The choregos paid all the expenses involved with the chorus, including its training, as a form of public taxation.

CLERUCHY Under Pericles, these settlements abroad were developed to check on subject allies; acted as a garrison.

DEMOS Used to describe the people as a whole or the people from a country district (a *demo*).

ECCLESIA Athenian general assembly made up of all male citizens which met on the Pnyx.

FIBULA A brooch; a dress pin

HELIAEA In Athens, the popular jury courts in the mid-fifth century.

HELOTS The subject population in Sparta

HIPPEIS Originally the social group who could supply cavalry at Athens; one of the upper classes.

HOPLITE Name given to Greek soldiers from their shield, the hoplon.

MOTHER CITY The city responsible for sending out and founding a particular colony.

OECIST The individual charged with the responsibility of leading a colonial group.

OLOLYGE In Bacchus religion this was a loud cry which invoked the gods; the chant repeats the sound made by the sound of the word or letters.

OSTRACISM A vote of the people carried out at a special meeting of the assembly to rid the state of a dangerous person.

PANCRATION An athletic competition combining boxing and wrestling.

PANTHEISTIC Having many gods.

PENTECOSIOMEDIMNOI Literally 'five hundred bushel men', members of the richest four Athenian census classes devised by Solon.

PERIOECI Literally 'dwellers around about', Dorian settlers of Sparta who were not Spartan citizens.

PITHOI Large storage jars, often standing taller than people.

POLIS The term used for the Greek city-state. Its territory included the town and the countryside surrounding it.

POTSHERD Broken pieces of pottery, sometimes used for writing names on for electoral proceedings.

PROSKYNESIS Persian custom of prostration, where they placed themselves at the feet of the ruler.

PRYTANEIS The name given to the men who were the presiding officers of the boule during their tenth of the year.

SATRAP Name given to the governor of a Persian province.

SPARTIATE Full blooded Spartan citizen with both parents Spartans; membership to the mess hall maintained by continued payment of food supplies.

STRATEGOS Generals, a college of ten, one from each tribe. After 487-486BC the most important magistrate in Athens.

THALASSOCRACY Rule or empire of the sea.

THETES Wage labourers, the lowest of the four census classes in Athens. Could not hold public office, but under Solon they were allowed entry in ecclesia and heliaea.

THOLOS A round building with a conical roof.

TYRANNY A form of illegal monarchy which arose when usurpers took control of oligarchic cities in the seventh and sixth centuries BC.

ZEUGITAE Owners of a pair of oxen, the third Athenian census class who became eligible for the archonship in 457-456 BC.